D1824817

Learning at the Practice Interface

Reconstructing dialogue for
progressive educational change

Neil Hooley

Routledge
Taylor & Francis Group

LONDON AND NEW YORK

First published 2015
by Routledge
2 Park Square, Milton Park, Abingdon, Oxon OX14 4RN

and by Routledge
711 Third Avenue, New York, NY 10017

Routledge is an imprint of the Taylor & Francis Group, an informa business

© 2015 N. Hooley

The right of N. Hooley to be identified as author of this work has been asserted by him in accordance with sections 77 and 78 of the Copyright, Designs and Patents Act 1988.

All rights reserved. No part of this book may be reprinted or reproduced or utilised in any form or by any electronic, mechanical, or other means, now known or hereafter invented, including photocopying and recording, or in any information storage or retrieval system, without permission in writing from the publishers.

Trademark notice: Product or corporate names may be trademarks or registered trademarks, and are used only for identification and explanation without intent to infringe.

British Library Cataloguing in Publication Data
A catalogue record for this book is available from the British Library

Library of Congress Cataloging in Publication Data
Learning at the practice interface : reconstructing dialogue for progressive educational change / Neil Hooley.
pages cm
Includes bibliographical references and index.
1. Educational sociology. 2. Education–Philosophy. 3. Education and state.
4. Educational change. I. Title.
LC189.H665 2015
379–dc23
2014043218

ISBN: 978-1-138-85129-0 (hbk)
ISBN: 978-1-315-72423-2 (ebk)

Typeset in Bembo
by Swales & Willis Ltd, Exeter, Devon, UK

Printed and bound in Great Britain by
TJ International Ltd, Padstow, Cornwall

Contents

PART III
Critical theorising and research   **129**

Figures

Tables

About the author

Dr Neil Hooley is a lecturer in the College of Education, Victoria University, Melbourne, Australia. He has interests in critical theory, critical pedagogy, participatory action research and pragmatic inquiry learning as they apply across all areas of knowledge and the curriculum in schools and universities. He has been involved in projects that investigate professional practice, community partnership and praxis learning for pre-service teacher education to pursue social justice and educational equity for all students. In addition, he has participated in projects concerning narrative inquiry as research methodology and curriculum construct in primary and secondary schools. Dr Hooley is committed to reconciliation between the Indigenous and non-Indigenous peoples of Australia and sees progressive educational reform as a step towards this end. He strongly supports partnerships between schools, communities and universities as democratic means of improving dignified social life and of learning from and theorising social and educational practice to challenge organisational structures and personal understandings.

Preface

Formal education in the twenty-first century has lost direction and purpose. It needs to re-evaluate its ambiguous relationship with knowledge and how it is conceptualised, organised and taught in schools. This is particularly so for the vast majority of students in the dominant economies of the world whose families have modest or low incomes and for whom schooling has become a strategic process of potential mobility, socialisation and opportunity. In contrast, encounters of daily life and schooling differ markedly at either end of the income spectrum for families and children who live in abject poverty, or who endure the predicaments of substantial wealth and influence. Public systems of primary education were not established until the end of the nineteenth century and it was not until after the end of World War II that the expansion of public secondary education occurred in the major economies. For many countries, mass secondary schooling still remains too large a cost for national budgets and many families to bear, or for some ideologies to embrace. For others, as retention rates have increased to the end of secondary schooling over the past 30 years, there has been increasing national and international emphasis on systemic outcomes through examination procedures. Positioning of the People's Republic of China and of India as emerging economic heavy weights over recent years has contributed to vigorous educational competition worldwide. Given that schooling regimes are inherently conservative and reflect the values and practices of dominant groups and their respective ideologies in society, the approach of schools towards the internal structures and correlations of knowledge is similarly conformist and often alienating for large numbers of students.

Learning at the Practice Interface investigates practice at the interface of sociology and epistemology for progressive educational change. It suggests that orthodox sociology and sociology of education have not sufficiently analysed contemporary educational situations due primarily to the strength of the economic and educational influence of neoliberalism. In addition, late modernity has seen ongoing criticisms offered by postmodernism and poststructuralism, gender politics and a subsequent weakening of epistemological insight based on social class. Theoretical deformation and frailty of this type within sociology of schooling have combined to create a highly incorrect and prejudicial view that many low-income families are deficient or, worse still, dysfunctional, that

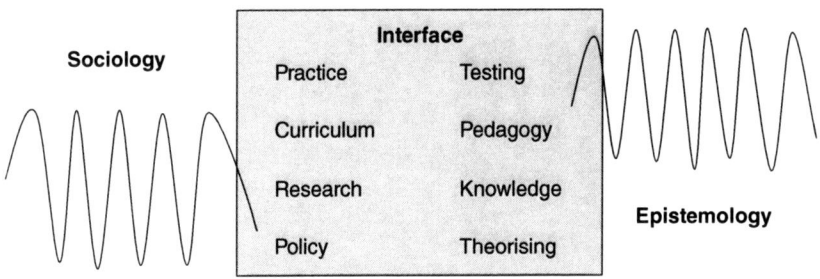

Figure 0.1 Interface between sociology and epistemology

children of low-income families are defective in terms of learning and capability and that private schooling is by definition superior. A new more meticulous and nuanced analysis is required, one that begins with a linkage of sociology and epistemology (Figure 0.1), reflection on the structures and organisation of knowledge within the curriculum, approaches to pedagogy and arrangements for schooling and an innovative epistemological concept of social justice and equity that is based on the socio-economic background of the majority of citizens.

After considering how this perspective might be implemented across the public school curriculum, the book then turns to the production and research of knowledge and the concept of reflexivity as the central means of theorising knowledge and learning. Praxis inquiry structures are described for establishing democratic partnership investigations involving teams of teachers, pre-service teachers and university staff working on projects that challenge conservative educational practices and understanding. Critical theorising of such teaching and learning practice for ongoing change and improvement of practice requires open arrangements of collaborative discourses, planning and implementation that seek to construct new impulses of learning. In drawing upon key aspects of the work of Dewey, Freire, Bernstein and Bourdieu, *Learning at the Practice Interface* heralds a new reflexive sociology of knowledge that revolutionises public schooling and emancipates learning for all students. It is now possible (Figure 0.2) to give greater detail to the sociology–epistemology interface through the identification of a series of major epistemological practices that embrace all children and are ubiquitous at school, home and community.

While remaining a significant concept of sociology, social class is often seen now as only one of a number of constructs that strongly influence social events. In some respects, this is understandable. Following the horror of World War II, both philosophy and sociology sought new ways of analysing and understanding society which could guide more harmonious and egalitarian futures. Marxism's class nature of society inevitably led to class antagonism and mass violence and, for the idealist scholar, these had to be avoided. A conventional Marxist

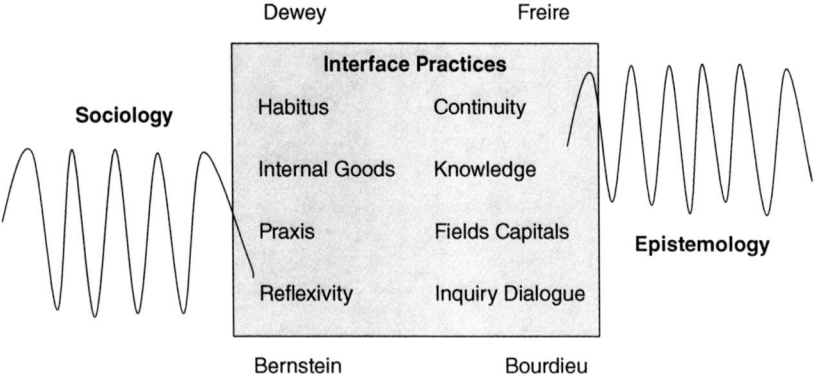

Figure 0.2 Interface practices of sociology and epistemology

view of schooling usually involved a singular emphasis on ideology with little emphasis on epistemology and how capitalist schools actually worked. Nor was there acceptance that the decontextualised knowledge arranged by schools in the 'academic' curriculum could be of benefit to marginalised children. The attack on 'grand narratives' by postmodernism and poststructuralism also saw events in isolated spaces rather than connected and formed by the threads and themes of history. Under this premise, 'local' narratives could be tolerated, but generalised narratives (as narratives rather than actualities) such as science, poverty, war, exploitation, racism and the like were oppressive and must be denied. It became fashionable to speak of undermining theory, of destabilising ideas, of making the reader uncomfortable, of standing outside and providing unnerving accounts. Presumably there was no contradiction to be found in speaking and writing for maximum discomfort while accepting that the qualified and experienced airline pilot could safely manage humanity's latest scientific achievement en route to the next academic conference.

Social class was subsequently narrowed and demeaned through definitions that concentrated on income and manual labour. Important factors no doubt, but social class is a broad ideology that also involves the relationship that working people have with the means of production, their capacity to sell their intellectual, managerial and physical labour for a living wage, the surplus value they produce over and above their cost to production and their understanding of production due to their closeness to productive processes. These factors generate a distinctive history and way of life, a way of viewing the world, a national and international unity amongst people in similar positions around the world, a unity of respect that prevails regardless of cultural background. Public schooling for the working population needs to take these social factors into account when it comes to consider the origins of knowledge, how learning occurs, how teaching should proceed and how children from all backgrounds can best engage formal knowledge in classrooms.

Converting a worldview of knowledge that reflects the history, language, community and aspiration for the majority of a national population into a public curriculum of schooling is not an easy task. This does not reject privileged knowledge, but begins with the storehouse of community knowledge and connects with privileged knowledge for understanding. It is possible that both privileged and community knowledge will change in the process, or at least different interpretations will be acknowledged and coexist. Funding of education is not really a problem for the major economies as many billions of dollars are allocated to education at all levels each year. What is at stake is respecting and recognising a paradigm of knowledge and of learning that constitutes the basis of learning in schools and that when connected with the privileged knowledge of schools opens up new avenues of learning for children. Children are wonderful learners and it makes no sense at all to suppose that they are alienated from knowledge, except if the procedures and frameworks imposed by adults are alienating and confusing. Much of the learning achieved by children is in fact 'invisible' and misrecognised or overlooked by adults because the epistemologies, knowledge structures and systems assumed by adults may not apply for that child at that time, subsequently distorting the adult's view of children's learning. This is the weakness in orthodox sociology and sociology of education.

There has been an emphasis on describing the conditions that surround schooling, those of the home, the child and education itself, rather than the conditions that enhance learning, those that support a working view of life and learning and which enable learning to occur through social practice. It could be argued that it is not the role of sociology to do more than describe the conditions that exist, but to not indicate the next steps of linking to the varied epistemologies of working people means that frustrations with schooling are magnified and reach a dead end. Worse, we become enmeshed in an unresolvable argument that test results and indeed intelligence are determined by family income. From this, it follows that more funding is required to somehow compensate for a deficient family background, or more funding is required to somehow improve teaching and learning in schools from deprived neighbourhoods. Both of these options miss the knowledge and epistemological questions entirely.

Some explanation as to why sociology has not taken up the issue of epistemology has been mentioned above. Neoliberalism has seeped into every nook and cranny of daily life for over three decades, while a number of other competing political viewpoints have been successful in founding their own place and influence. Few noted theorists have become associated with epistemology during this time and words like epistemology, learning, knowledge and pedagogy can all be defined in both progressive and conservative terms, distracting and alienating new readers to the field. In attempting to navigate these issues, the following chapters begin by revisiting key concepts including that of social justice, outline some detail of how these concepts can be applied at the school level, including for marginalised groups such as Indigenous children and, finally, move to the broad issue of knowledge production via research, framed within a new reflexive sociology of knowledge.

Central to this discussion is the problem of student assessment in schools and the assumptions made regarding the connections between family income and intellect. There is a vicious ideological pincer movement at work here. While neoliberals insist on international evaluations of teaching and learning through high-stakes testing across countries, active conservatives at home seek to control and reproduce curriculum content and pedagogy in their own image. This insidious manoeuvre must be broken so that children from all family backgrounds can find learning satisfaction across the curriculum in formal schooling and can pursue their interests to the fullest extent. The critical and radical reconceptualisation of curriculum and teaching and the democratic inclusion of all children into structures of privileged and community knowledge as theorised and described in *Learning at the Practice Interface* open up a new epistemological stage in the sociology of education undermining the constrictions of neoliberal society that dominate classrooms and mask the delight of knowing worldwide.

Neil Hooley
Melbourne, July 2014

Acknowledgements

I acknowledge the Elders, families and forebears of the Indigenous peoples of Australia. I recognise that the land on which we live, meet and learn is the place of age-old ceremonies of celebration, initiation and renewal and that the Indigenous people's living culture has a unique role in the history and life of Australia. We live and learn together in the interests of peace and justice.

I express my warm appreciation to Aunty Lois Peeler, Aunty Melva Johnson and Mat Jakobi for their continuing friendship and collegiality in providing advice on Indigenous matters and for discussions regarding Indigenous knowledge, learning and education generally. I am most grateful for the intensity of discussions with colleagues Julie Arnold, Jo Williams and Tony Edwards regarding educational equity and the theorising of professional practice, community partnership and praxis learning. I also express my gratitude to colleagues Marie Brennan, Martyn Brogan, Peter Burridge, David Jones, Tony Kruger, Greg Neal, Maureen Ryan, Tony Watt and Mary Weaven for their principled advice and discussions regarding Indigenous education, the problematic nature of educational research and the continuing tribulations and uncertainties of higher education.

I am constantly challenged and astounded by the scope and complexity of the writing, ideas and theorising of John Dewey, Paulo Freire, Basil Bernstein and Pierre Bourdieu. They all encourage learning through personal and social action and respect the culture and experience that all humans bring to learning. It is this question that has proven too difficult for many schools around the world, especially in the face of highly conservative ideologies that exclude and discriminate. We continue the struggle for democratic and critical public education as a basic human right for all citizens.

Dedication

To John Dewey and to all those who have and will continue to act courageously, think critically and engage collaboratively with the social and natural worlds for collective human satisfaction and fulfilment.

> Finally, the notion that knowledge is contemplation is likewise accounted for. To contemplate is consciously to possess meanings; to behold them with relish; to view them so absorbingly as to revel in them. It is a name for the perception of significant characters, plus an emphatic allusion to an accompanying esthetic emotion. Hypotheses which, like the one advanced in this book and chapter, hold that no knowing takes place without an overt act of taking and employing things on the basis of their meanings, have been attacked as over-devoted as keeping busy; as ignoring the place and charm of contemplation. Well, contemplation assuredly has a place. But when it is ultimate and is a fruition, knowing has stepped out of the picture; the vision is esthetic. This may be better than knowing; but its being better is no reason for mixing different things and attributing to knowledge characters belonging to an esthetic object. Omit the esthetic phase, the absorbing charm of contemplation and what remains for a theory of knowledge is that meanings must be had before they can be used as a means of bringing to apparition meanings now obscure and hidden.
>
> (Dewey, 1958, p. 331)

Continuity

Finally, the great experiment observed from afar for the first time,
a tiny blue orb, dangling in dark space, no bigger than a human hand,
by our best reckoning the journey already a few million years in duration
with many more to come before action and reason achieve closer alignment;
a tiny blue orb, dangling in dark space, the interactions of matter and energy
transforming landscapes, creating scenarios, consciousness and morality.
Life as a function of complexity itself provides the grand explanation.

Note: All poems, including *Continuity,* above, and those at the head of chapters, are the work of the author. They are intended to connect with one of the main themes of each chapter and to illustrate the integrated nature of knowledge and creative human thinking. Like all art, the poems exist in the eye of the beholder and are designed to challenge interpretation and meaning.

Part I

Concepts and commentaries

For over three decades, the ideology of neoliberalism has been very successful in determining not only the direction of economic advancement around the world, but in dictating the nature of social discourse as well. Neoliberal economic impressions of social life that focus on marketisation, privatisation, individualism, prosperity, efficiencies, accountabilities and narrow empirical measurement have shown themselves difficult to combat. The chapters of Part I highlight qualities still held dear by ordinary people worldwide but which are more often ascribed to the period of post World War II reconstruction. These values include democracy, equity, collaboration, community, peace and justice for all and deference towards knowledge and culture not dependent on wealth and status. Such a democratic ethos is described within the context of social and educational activity involving schooling, pedagogy and culture, providing avenues for progressive practice and resistance to conservative principles and beliefs.

1 Re-evaluating knowledge

Searching for the incomplete known
curious and confused by patterns of light
scattered through the dust at sunset
streaking amongst the avenues of mind
tentative ideas in ceaseless formation
desperate to make sense of impulses.

It is most regrettable, to say the least, that war, aggression, poverty, hunger and disease remain basic attributes of human society around the world. This must mean that the powerful and privileged, although small in number, see it in their mutual interests to continue in this way rather than to redistribute the abundance of riches that is available to them. Dominant ideology prevents a redistribution of military resources to the provision of health services together with housing and employment opportunities to a large proportion of the world's population. Harvey (2005, p. 2) has defined the latest ideological phase of global economic development in the following terms:

> Neoliberalism is in the first instance a theory of political economic practices that proposes that human well-being can best be advanced by liberating individual entrepreneurial freedoms and skills within an institutional framework characterised by strong private property rights, free markets and free trade. The role of the state is to create and preserve an institutional framework appropriate to such practices.

Such a neoliberal approach marked a radical change of economic direction following the 'welfare state' period of 1945–1975. During this time, the major economies of the world generally reflected the aspiration of the majority of peoples for a peaceful and dignified life that involved working together for the public good. However the need for capitalism to constantly expand and find new markets for exploitation meant that by the 1970s new forms of human exchange were required with new theoretical and political underpinnings. In broad terms, the economics of Friedrich von Hayek and Milton Friedman provided the former, while the 1979 election of Margaret Thatcher in the United Kingdom and the 1980 election of Ronald Reagan in the United States provided the latter. Over the following 30 years, neoliberalism has not only dominated global economic systems but, on the surface, appears to have dominated relationships between people as well. The real question here is: why has neoliberalism taken such an apparent hold on the population worldwide? Whether or not neoliberalism is similar to other occasions in history, where imposed ideology has been exerted to manipulate and manage the population, only to be rejected at a later stage, remains to be seen.

For the major economies during the neoliberal era to date, education budgets have expanded to allow for more children to stay at school longer, the development of secondary education and for more highly qualified teachers. University student numbers have also increased, particularly in response to the growing economic strength of the People's Republic of China and of India and the perceived need of other competing economies to increase their base of research and skills. However, formal education in schools and universities is a key mechanism of economic influence and ideological control and increased budgets amounting to billions of dollars being allocated to formal education every year could only be tolerated by ruling elites if outcomes remained in their interest.

A social and educational contradiction has thus emerged. On the one hand, the neoliberal economy requires relatively small numbers of educational outcomes in specific areas for maintenance and robustness. This is particularly the case where many national economies are increasingly less self-sufficient, globalised and derived from elsewhere. On the other hand, the general population has come to expect the right of all citizens, regardless of background, to complete schooling and to access privileged and recognised knowledge accordingly. This contradiction is supervised by two main strategies: first, support for privatised and exclusive education for the minority with appropriate social and cultural capital. Second, for the public majority, a delicate balance between centralised control of curriculum content and standardised assessment procedures for students (and increasingly for teachers) while allowing for certain areas of professional autonomy and innovation. In some countries, a national curriculum is the main vehicle for educational control of this type.

Proposals for public policy require that families and children who fall into the minority and majority categories, as mentioned above, need to be identified. Appadurai (2006, p. 168), for example, suggests that on a global scale, 'The lower 50% are not even in the knowledge game, because they are starving, dispossessed or economically marginal'. He comments further that about 30 per cent may be enabled to obtain professional and vocational jobs, but with little prospects for advancement, while the top 20 per cent have educational and vocational options based on 'their capacity to benefit from high-end knowledge about knowledge. Such meta-knowledge is the true mark of the global elite'. In specific countries, Appadurai's 50/30/20 breakdown may hold, while in others, a ratio of 10/80/10 may be more accurate. In the more wealthy countries, the majority of people may exist between the poles of poverty and wealth and it is this 80 per cent who find themselves in public schools.

Abject poverty makes it extremely difficult to participate in school and other social institutions and all societies struggle to develop a suite of policies to assist this group to any significant extent. Where family wealth is ample, attendance at schools that are expressly designed to promote the 'meta-knowledge' and ideology of different elites or constituencies is possible.

Children of the 80 per cent majority comprise a diverse social mix, having working-class and middle-class backgrounds with parents and other family members who have a variety of manual, managerial and professional occupations. Over more recent years, family members in this group have been staying at school longer and following school have been engaged in work, job training or higher-education pursuits. Formal schooling and the regular curriculum now need to accommodate large numbers of students from this 80 per cent majority grouping, many of whom are expected to complete secondary schooling and to at least consider university studies as an option. This is a new social and educational phenomenon that neoliberalism would prefer not to confront and certainly not to fund.

To illustrate the dilemmas facing educational public policy in the strong and middle-order neoliberal economies, two brief cases are provided below. Both cases illustrate family backgrounds of the majority of the population so defined. Policy makers can ignore the detail of each case, or they can find themselves in the position of responding to public demand for an appropriate education for all children not dependent on family financial resources. They can attempt to develop a curriculum for the 80 per cent majority that meets neoliberal interest of content and assessment and which at the same time nominates specialist programs for the marginalised and dismissed. This type of approach will need to be sanctioned by the small number of wealthy and powerful families who have access to more elite and private schools, perhaps involving globalised curriculum trends and mass-testing regimes.

Case 1: Stanley, Seaside Secondary School

Stanley is 15 years old and attends Seaside Secondary School in a medium-sized country town near the coast. Seaside is co-educational and was built in the 1960s. Stanley's father completed secondary school followed by a carpentry apprenticeship and has worked at a local building firm for almost 20 years. Stanley's mother also completed secondary school and works part-time as a bookkeeper for a small electronics company. He has a younger brother and sister in primary school who tend not to irritate him too much. The town has a strong sporting reputation, with football in the winter and swimming in the summer being favourites with most families. In general, Stanley likes school and sports and usually obtains reasonable test results. His family has always been involved with reading and he has strong memories of attending the local public library with his mother to collect her monthly bundle of mystery books. He tolerates mathematics at school, finding it somewhat tedious, but enjoys the interesting ideas of science, especially the experiments that the teacher organises every so often. As well as the local library, Stanley occasionally visits the small regional art gallery that is attached to the Town Hall. There are new exhibitions every few months and he is impressed by local artists who paint the beach and other places familiar to him. His father has mentioned joining him as a carpenter one day, but Stanley isn't too sure what he might do on leaving school. His best friend Jack wants to be a professional golfer.

Case 2: Susan, Suburban Secondary School

Susan is 16 years old and attends Suburban Secondary School in the large capitol city of her state. Suburban has a long history, being one of the first co-educational secondary schools built after the war to encourage families to consider university for their children. Susan's father obtained an economics/law degree at university and now manages a legal practice in town. Susan's mother worked part-time while studying for an arts degree and now works for a local welfare agency. An older sister, Stephanie, has left home and from all accounts is progressing well in first-year pharmacy. Susan has worked hard at school and her test results are near the top, generally reflecting reliance on a good memory. Her family has always spent time together and Susan has enjoyed getting out of the city to visit her grandmother on the farm, for trips to the snow and sometimes for opening nights of the latest musical wherever it is playing. She would like to spend more time practising the flute, but other things always seem to get in the way – more recently, the school's debating team. In her quiet moments, Susan is worried that she will have a heavy study load next year and she must choose her subjects carefully if they are to form a pathway to her degree. Stephanie has said that things will work out, but Susan is concerned that her parent's preference for a business degree is not what she wants. Her counsellor at school is not sure either at this stage, but is seeking advice on course options from her university contacts.

These cases depict two students who are progressing through secondary school. Stanley comes from a small country town and a family that has not had extensive contact with schooling as a continuing and major feature of life. He has access to a coastal environment and experiences reading, art and sports. Susan comes from a big city and a family who has been to university and expects her to do the same. She goes on frequent trips, enjoys the theatre and music and mixes with adults who have social contacts. Both attend public schools which offer a similar curriculum experience (and perhaps teachers with similar backgrounds and similar teaching techniques). There are no reasons to expect that the social and educational backgrounds of Stanley and Susan would impact to a different extent on their schooling achievements, either substantially or in a positive or negative sense. As a common indicator, the income level of their fathers certainly does not.

In discussions of this type, the distinction is often not made between students like Stanley and Susan, that is, those who come from different backgrounds but within the 80 per cent of the majority of families who attend public school. What is often discussed is the differences between those living in poverty compared with the majority, or those who access extensive resources compared with the majority. While Stanley and Susan are able to obtain some experience of the arts, museums, galleries and the like, this is more extensive than one group and perhaps less extensive than another. The simplistic assumption here is that such access has a marked impact on the formal outcomes of schooling either directly, or by somehow aligning this experience with the experience of school. The simplistic assumption here also is that access to the arts, museums, galleries and the like is constant – indeed, unremitting – for those of the wealthy group, at least in comparison to Stanley and Susan, an assumption that can be stoutly questioned. These issues and assumptions regarding the capacity to learn are the issues and assumptions of the sociology of education.

Knowledge and the sociology of education

In his seminal book *Knowledge and Control,* that introduced Pierre Bourdieu to the English-speaking world and contained a chapter by Basil Bernstein, Michael Young opened up a historic debate regarding the nature of knowledge and the sociology of education. He claimed that contributors to the book 'make' their own issues for the sociology of education rather than merely 'take' (for granted) what has gone before. In this way, knowledge itself becomes problematic, leading to enquiries into 'the social organisation of knowledge in educational institutions' such that the 'sociology of education is no longer conceived as the area of enquiry distinct from the sociology of knowledge' (Young, 1971, pp. 2–3). Central to this continuing debate is whether knowledge is universal and once 'discovered' is to be accepted by all, or whether knowledge is socially constructed by diverse groups with their own (class, race, gender, poststructural) perspectives and experiences. This dichotomy draws a line between a universal epistemology of knowledge and a relational sociology of knowledge whereby sociology explains and critiques the social basis of knowledge. In many respects, this is a false dichotomy, as knowledge that arises from specific experience can be referred to knowledge that arises elsewhere for comparison and generalisation. Whether all metals expand when heated and contract when cooled can be investigated and theorised by a female engineer in Argentina, a male technologist in Scotland and an African scientist in Nigeria. It does not follow that hard-and-fast principles will necessarily accrue from these studies, or that interpretations will necessarily be imposed.

Discussions raised by *Knowledge and Control* tended to give epistemology a bad name. That is, epistemology was defined as knowledge generated by powerful groups – ruling class, male, scientific – which is then imposed on others, especially through formal schooling systems, whether public or private. Marginalised and disenfranchised groups – working class, female, ethnic – together with postmodern and poststructural perspectives of knowledge were seen to be excluded and struggled to be heard.

Bernstein's chapter in *Knowledge and Control* (Bernstein, 1971) considered how the school curriculum organises knowledge and whether subjects are separated and insulated from each other, or whether they are integrated in relation to each other. He used the term 'classification' to mean whether the boundary between different forms of knowledge is strong or weak. The term 'frame' was used to denote the amount of control that teachers and students have over how subject knowledge is selected, considered and taught in the classroom relationships that have been arranged.

In later work, Bernstein (2010) also discussed the notion of horizontal and vertical discourses of knowledge. In horizontal discourse, a set of strategies are involved that are 'local, segmentally organised, context specific and dependent' (p. 159). In contrast, vertical discourse involves strategies that 'takes the form of a coherent, explicit and systematically principled structure, hierarchically organised' (p. 159). These concepts are significant when it comes to how knowledge is acquired and how the learner can move within and across various knowledge structures.

Bernstein notes that efforts to make more specialised knowledge accessible to all students of differing backgrounds can involve the recontextualisation of segments of horizontal discourse that are then inserted into school subjects for vertical discourse. If the vertical structure and discourse of specialised knowledge are hierarchical, then the use of segmented horizontal discourse needs to be transformed into vertical knowledge (as distinct from 'knowing') at the point it is used.

Issues of knowledge classification, framing and discourse cannot be removed from the context in which that knowledge is located, but this is a different question as to whether knowledge can only ever be context-dependent. Is there a female understanding of the states of matter that is different to male understanding? As Table 1.1 indicates, the socio-political tensions of knowledge production impact strongly on the purpose, nature and interpretation of

Table 1.1 Intersection of political–democratic tensions of knowledge

	Capitalist	*Socialist*	*Religious*	*Scientific*
Economic, power	Private profit, property Differentiated access Possibility of force, aggression	Collective gain Distributed across society Communicative, shared	Faith Authoritarian	Evidence Autonomy
Decision making	Individual, status-driven Private good	Collective Public good	Dictates	Research, knowledge
Aspiration	Private gain	Public, social gain	Life meaning	Explanation
Culture, knowledge	Personal betterment, expression	Collective Contribute to humanity	Closer to deity Give thanks, celebration	Understanding
Philosophy, theories	Explain Interact with reality	Explain Interact with reality	Promote word of deity Morality	Explain Interact with reality
Public, private	Private gain Ruling class	Public gain Proletariat	Private or public Specific group, humanity	Private or public Humanity

knowledge and how it is modified in relation to other knowledge at partic
moments in history.

It is difficult to see how knowledge production can proceed in a soc
vacuum, totally removed from the factors outlined in Table 1.1. In their dis-
tinguished paper regarding such matters and debates within the sociology of
knowledge, Moore and Muller (1999) reject the proposition that knowledge
does not have generalised epistemological understanding and arises only from
the specific interests of specific social groups. They conclude their discussion with three points. First, they suggest that 'voice' discourse, or the view
that knowledge is always and only relational to particular groups, is essentially
designed to 'debunk' epistemology as dominant knowledge claims that support
the interests and ideology of dominant groups. Second, criticism of science
(often argued to be a key determinant of the Enlightenment and therefore of
elite, male dominance and knowledge) as imposed law is misplaced, as modern science has always accepted that its claims are neutral in the sense of being
applied generally, but are produced within socio-political contexts and need to
be seen and critiqued accordingly. Third, 'voice' discourse has proceeded from
an insulated, self-serving position of its own and claims of authenticity 'cannot
reveal the principles whereby these authors produce the world within which
they locate themselves' (p. 203). Moore and Muller provide a basis for the
sociology of knowledge redefining and reconsidering the relationship between
epistemology and the production of knowledge by different groups so that a
more generalised understanding of the social and physical worlds can be made
available to all peoples regardless of background. Access to appropriate phar-
maceuticals for mothers in the village to combat the epidemic ravaging their
children may need to draw upon the scientific construction of new molecules
in the laboratories of a land far away.

Almost 40 years after the appearance of *Knowledge and Control,* Young
(2008) provides a contemporary and comprehensive overview of how he now
sees knowledge as being socially produced but how it must also demonstrate
its independence from powerful and manipulative forces. He comments that:

> The sociology of knowledge reminds us that history and experience inevi-
> tably enter into all forms of knowledge, whether or not it is produced by
> specialists within particular disciplinary traditions. The fact that the inescap-
> able role of experience in the production of new knowledge is often denied
> is itself a problem for both sociology and epistemology and may or may not
> have practical implications (p. 11).

Young goes on to argue for a 'social realist' approach to the sociology of education as distinct from the 'social constructivist' view. The idea of 'social' recognises the role of humans in the production of knowledge and the idea of
'realist' is taken to mean that ultimately 'knowledge' (compared with 'knowing') must be context-independent for use everywhere. He is concerned that
social constructivism, while providing teachers with a rationale for respecting

the experience of local families and for evaluating the viewpoint of students not necessarily in reference to knowledge inflicted and gained elsewhere, also enabled the privileged and recognised knowledge of history and disciplines to be ignored, or to be downplayed as unnecessary. Do our students really need to engage with Shakespeare, Frost, the neutron, calculus, or Van Gogh?

In some respects, this argument mirrors that of inquiry and child-centred learning, where critics claimed that outcomes were relative and were accepted as valid knowledge without challenge. However it is difficult to find examples of this view in the literature, with most teachers utilising inquiry as a means of investigating key concepts and principles, as noted in curriculum documents. The same argument applies to the simplistic process-versus-product debate: is expression more important than spelling? In considering that social constructivism has a number of flaws, Young supports Durkheim's two insights of knowledge, first that 'the sociality of knowledge does not undermine its objectivity and the possibility of truth, but is the condition for it' and second, 'the key role that he gives to differentiation (for him between the sacred and the profane) as the origins of speculative thought and the growth of knowledge' (p. 217). What Young does not explore to any extent is the contextualisation of neoliberalism, the role of social class in the construction of knowledge and the detailed nature of epistemology.

Neoliberalism versus democracy

Given that different groups in society have vastly different life experiences, it follows that the characteristics of social life will establish a different relationship with the characteristics of schooling and learning for the members of each group. This is a complex relationship when broad socio-political and contextual issues of, for example, morality, science, law, aesthetics and critique are taken into account. From a Marxist perspective, the socio-economic base of society is dominant, relating to the social superstructure of regulation and procedure. This view establishes a series of social classes determined by the linkage of members to the productive enterprises of the country. Such classes include the international and national bourgeoisie, who own the key means of production, the middle bourgeoisie, consisting of senior managers and investors who maintain the means of production, the petty bourgeoisie, who are engaged in and are related to smaller-scale production and its physical and ideological maintenance and the proletariat, consisting of manual, industrial and professional workers who provide the necessary labour for production. This type of relationship, that is based on ownership or lack of ownership of the productive forces of society, gives rise to different worldviews and different ideologies, consciousness or aspiration that create tension and antagonism between different social strata. The owners of the mine see the world differently to those who work deep underground. Evans (2006, p. 10) writes about the class nature of education in Britain and suggests that:

This is how social class in Britain works: it is about an ongoing relationship between people grouped according to occupational status, in which the relative value of each group is worked out on the basis of a continuous differentiation of value and consequent reward. The basis for this differentiation is established at school, consolidated in the workplace and finally symbolised by relative wealth.

Evans provides a somewhat simplistic analysis of social class, focusing on the nature of jobs rather than the lack of productive ownership. However, she does note the interrelatedness of school, work and society and how the accumulation of wealth (productive capacity and/or financial capacity) can enable movement across classes. The tripartite interrelatedness of school, work and society for each class (bourgeoisie and proletariat) can be taken as the essential determinant of knowledge and learning, as depicted in Figure 1.1:

Under this conception, arising from the industrial revolution and the era of imperialism and colonialism, social class remains as the major feature of modern human society. This means that other features, such as race, gender, ethnicity, sexuality and disability, need to be considered separately, replacing class in a diagram such as Figure 1.1, or be considered in relation to class and be added to the diagram. Each of these features could be included in the diagram while

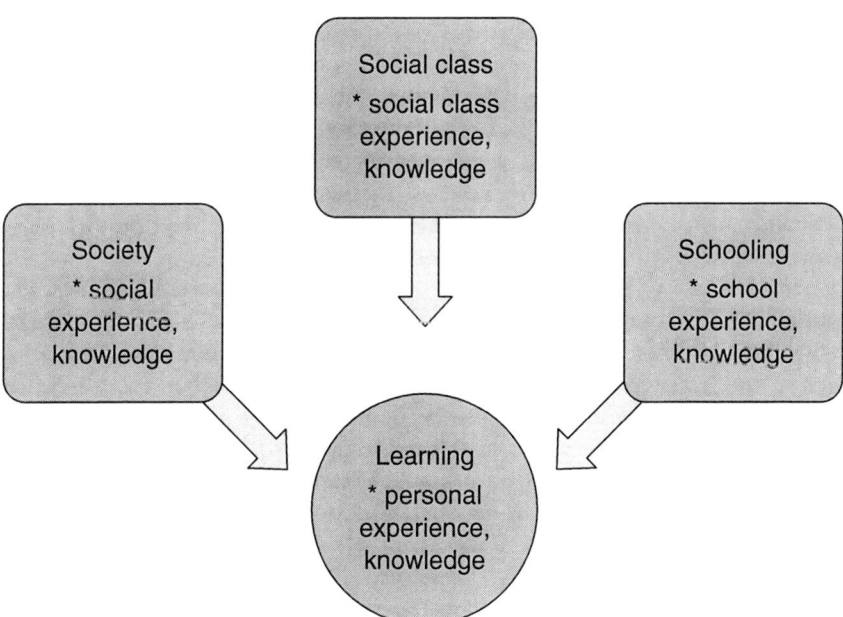

Figure 1.1 Relationship between school, work and society

maintaining class as the foremost feature. The diagram does not preclude other features becoming of central concern at particular times as conditions alter, but this occurs within a class environment.

In terms of a class analysis, however, learning and knowledge are generated for each social class and individual member through the ongoing relationship of school, work and society (while at school), with each having its own understandings and processes. As a guide, the diagram suggests that there are different knowledges involved from each of the three areas of human activity and that overall learning and knowledge (whether epistemological or sociological) are produced, changed and re-changed through this constant interaction.

Questions of neoliberalism, power and the like, as listed under society above, must be considered in relation to the philosophy and practice of democratic life. This is because the continuing struggle and contradiction between private profit and public good have pivoted on the notion of democracy throughout the modern era as the citizenry has demanded progress towards the assembly of human meaning and satisfaction. For some, democracy is seen to exist in parliamentary systems of representative government adhering to the principle of universal suffrage and of one person, one vote. While such systems are immensely better than dictatorships and the use of violence for control, parliaments are still open to graft and corruption and exploitation of power for private benefit. Democracy is much more than parliamentary process and the vote, with its central feature being the capacity for 'associated living' and an honest engagement with experience, knowledge, culture and history in ways that encourage deep and evolving understanding. A creative human inquiry of this type is always amenable to insight and challenge and a developing framework of credibility and truthfulness. Hooley (2009, p. 21) has compiled a list of democratic parameters (Table 1.2), reworked since originally published, that contrast markedly with the features of neoliberalism and clearly indicate why the democratic fire burns brightly in the collective breast of humanity worldwide:

A discussion of this point will be presented in more detail later, but the outline of democracy in Table 1.2 has very clear implications for systems of schooling. If there are different classes of people in all communities and if democratic arrangements are central to all communities, then it follows that schooling and learning should also be democratic for all children. As mass schooling has developed during the industrial era, the question of democratic schooling for all has been impossible to achieve, especially regarding knowledge and learning. This may be a function of time as history rolls on, a recognition that more advanced forms of schooling must be built from prior experience. More likely, however, is the political twists and turns that have eventuated over the past 150 years or so as the bourgeoisie has constructed structures of economy and power to suit their own interests against the interests of the proletariat. The neoliberal has little interest in the democratic.

Table 1.2 Parameters of democracy

Institutions of respectful, non-coercive dialogue amongst the citizenry regarding what it means to be human, the development of a public moral life and allied values and the relationship between public and private interest

Economic, cultural and employment arrangements that set up horizontal rather than vertical processes of authority, responsibility and relationship as the basis of autonomy, reciprocity and personal dignity

Resource allocation that meets the needs of people from all social classes within an appropriate framework of principle and enhancement reliant on humanity and citizenship rather than false prosperity

Decision-making structures that are inclusive, participatory, persuasive and consensual and that are intended to support the interests of the entire group for home, work and socio-political concerns

Aspirations that include continuing social progress and change in all fields for purposes of human satisfaction

Approaches to the quality, equity and meaning of daily life that are holistic and integrated regarding work, family, culture, learning, political and recreational activity

Theories of society and theories of practice that emphasise the continuing unfolding of history, the role of all citizens as agents of change, the unity of practice and theory in all phenomena, a compassionate science and technology, protection of the natural environment and critical and participatory processes of investigation

Similar to Harvey's definition above, Ball (2012, p.18) comments that neo-liberalism 'is used to refer to a family of ideas associated with the revival of nineteenth-century economic liberalism'. He goes on:

> It is characterised by a strong commitment to methodological individualism and the principles of private property, alongside an antipathy to centralised state planning – or *minarchism* as it is sometimes called, the idea that government should be limited to defence, adjudication and a very limited provision of public goods and based on an anti-rationalist epistemology.

Unlike an earlier time, Ball contends that the operation of neoliberalism is difficult to pin down, not so much involving clear lines of authority, contact and communication, but more a series of loosely connected networks whose 'relations are opaque, consisting in good part of informal social exchanges, negotiations and compromises that go on "behind the scene"'. The tension therefore created between neoliberalism and the nation state (undertaking parliamentary governance) makes a neoliberal list of knowledge characteristics as per Figure 0.1 doubtful and the democratic characteristics of Table 1.2 most improbable. The networked organisation of neoliberalism makes analysis difficult and in a strange way brings to mind the Foucauldian notion of looking at disconnected localised events rather than threads or themes that pattern across human experience. What this means for public education is continuing adherence to the principles of democratic and decorous life in opposition to debauched and ruthless plundering by the market.

'Left' and 'right', epistemology and ontology

Application of market doctrine to education as a commodity warps the concept of education and diminishes student experience and learning. It assumes that schooling is nothing more than an offshoot of economy, where students are placidly prepared to find their allotted spot in the economic and political systems of the day. Marx was not advocating of course that the dominance of the prevailing economic base should be meekly accepted, but rather it needed to be replaced by systems that more accurately supported human aspiration. For example, Feinberg (2012, p. 3) notes the view of Aristotle that a public school was responsible for students grasping the idea of their role as public citizens and that, under the control of a public organisation, the school promoted public virtues such as reason. According to Feinberg, Aristotle contended that 'as a deliberative body seeking to advance a common good, the public has a reality that is more than the sum of the individuals who comprise it' and that 'a public refers to a process of rational deliberation about a common fate' (pp. 3–4). This philosophy of human purpose and intelligence places emphasis on the collective rather than the individual, on society rather than the family, and looks for modes of activity that buttress the public good. Having a different purpose, on the other hand, locates neoliberalism as a right-wing political and economic ideology (Figure 1.2) that is prepared to fund education for bourgeois and minority intent behind a facade of common interest.

A more detailed consideration of epistemology will be found later, but at this point it is necessary to begin to explore connections between the sociology of schooling and the epistemologies of knowledge for different social classes and strata of children. A distinction needs to be made between ontology, or the essence of human being, and epistemology, or human knowledge and how humans go about learning and participating in knowledge in all its forms. From a social class perspective, ontological questions will involve consciousness or awareness regarding class background, characteristics of being of a particular class and relationship to the natural and social worlds. From a social class perspective, epistemological questions will involve the nature of knowledge, where knowledge comes from within social class existence and how

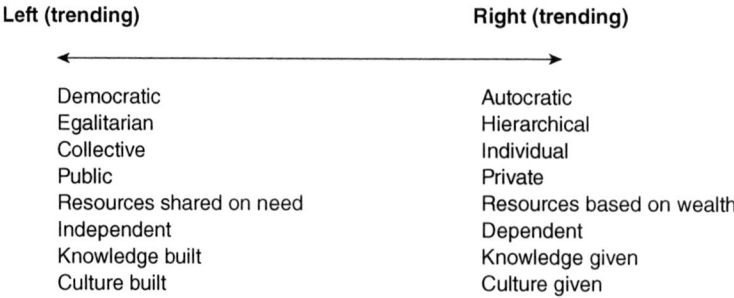

Figure 1.2 Characteristics of 'left' and 'right'

learning interactions with the physical and social worlds occur. From a middle bourgeois perspective and based on the items of Figure 0.2, an ontological question could delve into the employment position a person holds within the hierarchy of a company and what individual advantage is to be served by applying for promotion. An epistemological issue for the middle bourgeois could involve reliance on expert systems or senior colleagues for instruction on how to proceed with issues and problems. Conversely, a working-class approach to ontology could involve focusing on doing productive work for the common good, regardless of employment position. Issues of epistemology from a proletarian perspective are approached from a position of principled and independent thought and action, not in relation to false seniority or authority. These are complicated examples, as situations are not clear cut, with many factors constantly impacting and changing. The central point that is being made, however, involves the universal understanding of ontology and epistemology that gives rise to different applications being made every day from a social class standpoint. In education, the dominance of neoliberalism on these applications can be easily seen in relation to the funding of public and private schooling, the development of curriculum, approaches to teaching and the emphasis on narrow measurement and testing of student performance. Sociology has described these phenomena, but cannot provide a way of resolving them in the interests of all children. That remains an epistemological problem.

Following his discussion of neoliberalism as a loose arrangement of networks with 'opaque relations' and where 'informal social exchanges, negotiations and compromises' are difficult to discern, Ball (2010) turns his attention to current trends in education policy within this socio-political context. In particular, he notes 'related developments in the governance, reform and privatisation of knowledge production in the field of education policy' (p. 124), meaning that 'Education policy communities are thus being reconstituted and new policy discourses and narratives are flowing through them' (p. 134). What this shows is that education policy and practice are being dominated by forces outside the education profession and that the strength of neoliberal imperative has swamped educational debate regarding sociology, epistemology and ontology.

During the welfare state period, a 'left' (Figure 0.2) view of economy and education was in accord with post-war majority understanding of a humble and dignified life for all, but as the changing requirements of the economic system shifted radically to the 'right' (Figure 0.2), pressure on education to do the same became relentless and immense. While there has been community and professional resistance, political and managerial compliance has been substantial. Difficult questions of sociology, ontology and epistemology have not been emphasised and theorised enough by the profession to provide democratic and creative alternatives to the neoliberal, not necessarily entirely, but at least sufficiently, to adapt and modify neoliberal practices to a change of character. In this sense, knowledge itself has not been subject to a class analysis, bringing it into alignment with privileged and more abstracted school knowledge, so that the beauty of knowledge and the pleasure of learning and finding out can be made available to all.

Knowledge as practice

In his famous essay *On Practice,* Mao Tse-Tung (1968) commented that 'Every process, whether in the realm of nature or of society, progresses and develops by reason of its internal contradiction and struggle and the movement of human knowledge should also progress and develop along with it' (p. 17). This approach, known as dialectical materialism, places central importance on social and productive practice as the key determinant of knowledge and the means of combating dogmatism and subjectivism. Knowledge and truthfulness arise from repeated cycles of perception and conception as ideas are brought into correspondence with the outcomes of practice, as distinct from proceeding on a purely subjective basis, or the authoritative opinion of experts. Theory too is generated by practice and serves as a guide to further practice not by imposing what must be accepted, but by providing a framework for thinking, reflection, new ideas and new theorising.

Beginning from the standpoint of practice and of combining practice with theory as an active process of theorising for changing reality is the main tenet that distinguishes progressive from conservative philosophy and is therefore one of the key issues that separates democratic from neoliberal approaches to education. In all areas of education, including all curriculum areas, the standpoint of practice means that knowledge is constructed by humans acting together in the context of the social and physical worlds, including the general ideas of reality that have already been investigated by others at a different time and place. All humans come to their own understanding not by denying generalised consensus or codes, but by grappling with the concepts involved. Here again is the difference between the sociology and epistemology of schooling, where the former, for reasons of equity, concentrates on ensuring that the curriculum contains topics on the states of matter, whereas the latter, for reasons of practice, ensures that all students can investigate states of matter through cycles of experiment, discussion and reflection.

In one comment regarding knowledge, or more specifically 'theory', Willis (1977, p. 57) writes that there is:

> a massive feeling on the shop floor and in the working class generally, that practice is more important than theory . . . that theory is only useful insofar as it really does help to do things, to accomplish practical and change nature. Theory is asked to be in a close dialectic with the material world.

On the other hand, Willis contends that the middle class can see theory 'partly in its social guise of qualifications as the power to move up the social scale. In this sense, theory is well worth having even if it is never applied in nature'.

Such views have generated the divide between academic and vocational programs (and between communities, schools and families) that unfortunately also appears to be accepted by the teaching profession.

Where have these notions of social reality and division come from? This split between practice and theory is somewhat surprising, given that the working class utilises a range of theoretical ideas every day. It is difficult to conceive of practice and theory being separated by humans in their thinking and how they then engage the complexities of daily life. If formal mass education has managed to cement this dichotomy in the minds of learners, then it is one of the most astounding achievements of the modern era and quite contrary to the intent of the Enlightenment. This is particularly so, as the working class does not have an inherent or historic interest in the legitimation and preservation of the dominant ideology. Further questions arise regarding how such dominance actually happens in classrooms and how the authority of the teacher – and knowledge – is exercised across the curriculum. The success of the conservative curriculum in promoting such a rigid view of knowledge, its production, application and measurement, is a testament to the ideology of economic and political privilege.

Despite the above, it remains epistemologically unclear as to why children from different social groups obtain different test results concerning traditional school knowledge, particularly the majority 80 per cent mentioned previously. Children from diverse working-class families have a deep and abiding interest in the cause of solar flares, the nature of the charge on an election, the dawn breaking through yonder window, why war continues and why their baby sister is sick. They have contact with their communities through work, sport, music, drought and flood, accidents, crime and the fascinating stories from grandma. They are constantly solving problems regarding food, flat batteries, broken windows, new shoes and household budgets. They vicariously read books, newspapers, magazines, council notices, political announcements, insurance statements and technological devices. They attend libraries, museums, galleries, concerts, festivals and valued schools with qualified teachers. This is an active, changing discourse of practice, of materialist social life, that demands a construction and reconstruction of experience. If the paradigm of knowledge privileged by formal schooling is not aligned with this creative and cultural practice, then learning will be distorted and frustrated. This is not to say that sanctioned test results will automatically be of this type for all working-class children, but it does stipulate that getting the right answers and meaning from the conservative discourse of school and prearranged, imposed, symbolic subject content will be constantly aggravated and thwarted. For working-class families, what is important is not so much the amazing discovery of a philosophical 'truth' by an absent genius that must be accepted and repeated, but the personal and philosophical investigation of ideas and practices to make them their own. In fact, this is central for all families and whether formal, simplistic schooling provides this for the elite and wealthy, regardless of test results, is also highly doubtful.

2 Progressive pedagogies

Waves oscillate and disappear
defining moments on the shore
while words endeavour to emerge
constructing thought and being
along corridors of imagination
threading tangled beauty and power,
ecosystems of cognitive perplexity.

How teachers go about organising teaching and learning depends upon their explicit or tacit understanding of epistemology, that is, the nature of knowledge, where it comes from and how humans participate with its production, use and meaning. Every act of a teacher in a classroom can be traced back to this understanding, whether intended or not. However, a common and broad distinction that is often used in schools is that between 'abstract' and 'concrete' knowledge. Here abstract is taken to be knowledge that is removed or abstracted from direct experience of the learner, while concrete knowledge is situated or immersed in the experience of the learner. Deriving an equation in trigonometry to find the length of a side of a triangle is abstract knowledge, while hitting a golf ball is more concrete. The Swiss epistemologist Piaget suggested that children are superb concrete learners and that therefore a key role of the teacher is to make the abstract concrete. Unfortunately, the notion of concrete learning is often confused with knowledge and learning that are of a lower order to abstract knowledge and learning and can be related to children in schools who are seen to be more practically oriented, perhaps with weaker intellects. This viewpoint has a long history in philosophy, where Greek thinkers such as Plato and Aristotle considered that knowledge existed independently of personal experience. Those people who had a practical life would be subject to constant change in understanding the world whereas those who had time and resources could embark upon a process of contemplative reasoning that would access ongoing truth. Experience was not to be trusted as it relied on bodily senses, pleasure and pain, in contrast to reason that sought to access general ideas and principles.

This view held for many centuries until the modern era, when major developments in politics, science, technology and industry saw the need to question authority that is handed down by others, in favour of a more autonomous citizenry, experimentation and trial and error. Theory (abstract) and practice (concrete) were therefore reversed or at least brought more into balance so that practical knowledge became more rational and scholarly. Many teachers may not take these issues into account when they walk into a classroom.

When schools or educators separate theory and practice and consider some students more capable of abstract thought compared with other students, learning becomes distorted. It is difficult to think of learning as being entirely theoretical or practical with each not drawing on the other to some extent and at the same time. It could be of course that schools for many decades lacked specific resources to encourage a more integrated form of learning and, complicated by the restrictions of large class sizes, resorted instead to the technologies of paper, pencil and textbook. The father of educational computing, Seymour Papert, recognised that access to desktop computing in the early1980s had the potential to liberate children from the tyranny of teacher-dominated teaching and imposed knowledge and that the computer could assist in making the abstract concrete by providing 'objects to think with'. Papert and others suggested that children should not be confined to an epistemologcial prison, but should be able to learn with 'epistemological pluralism' (Turkle and Papert, 1992) appropriate to their preference and the topic at hand.

In this regard, the notion of pluralism in learning built upon one of the central theories of Dewey, that of 'continuity'. Dewey suggested that theory and practice, or nature and experience, were not separate, but were forever connected, continuous and co-operative. For example, a child swimming or playing in the shallows at the beach has an intimate relationship with water and comes to understand water as it responds to each action of arms, legs, lungs and the like of the mind and body. When the child leaves the water and is playing on the foreshore a similar close relationship develops between mind, body, air and sand; stories and castles are designed and built, embellished by seaweed and shells, waves erode interesting footprints and drawings in the sand. In both locations, the child is thinking, making decisions, talking with adults and other children, using known and invented words to suit the situation and is becoming a different person than before the beach visit. The child has been swimming in water, swimming in air and swimming in words and thought, or has been as one with the natural environment. This is Dewey's notion of continuity between ideas and action, between knowing and doing, between abstract and concrete. If continuity is broken and 'objects to think with' are lacking then learning becomes alienating for all humans.

Dewey was heavily influenced by the development of modern science during the late nineteenth and early twentieth centuries (Dewey, 2012). This was a time for people to think for themselves and to develop new revolutionary ways of investigating the physical and social worlds. Darwin had challenged a religious view of human origin, Marx and Engels had proposed a new view of social change and development and Freud had outlined a confronting theory of human imperative and consciousness. Given the philosophical emphasis of the Greeks on physical substance and material, Dewey (Boydston, 1989/2008, pp. 104–105) was interested in how physics was offering new concepts of the composition and structure of matter and how this might impact on human understanding of knowledge and learning. For example, he noted that:

> Aristotle's physics was a great achievement in its time, but it was built around 'substances'. Down to Galileo men of learning almost universally held, following Aristotle, that there exist things which completely, inherently and hence necessarily, possess Being; that these continue eternally in action (movement) under their own power – continue, indeed in some particular action essential to them in which they are engaged. The fixed stars, under this view, with their eternal circular movements, were instances.

In essence, truth ultimately existed in the substances of the universe, a most conservative philosophy that saw motion (and ultimately what is) as a fixed entity. Detecting significant changes in science, however, Dewey (p. 101) discussed three levels of inquiry: those of self-action (things acting under their own powers), interaction (causal interconnection) and transaction (systems of description and naming employed to deal with aspects and phases of action). These different registers of 'action' moved away from truth being fixed and enabled humans to consider different situations as being different, union when union is required, separation when separation is required. Interestingly, Dewey (pp. 108–109) points out that Einstein himself may have been caught up in the transition from self-actional and interactional to transactional science in that, while Einstein had a transactional view of physical phenomena, he retained a self-actional view regarding the human role in science. The issue at stake here is how humans think about and describe the physical phenomena they observe and how accurate this is in relation to the actual reality of physical phenomena. How do humans conceptualise the nature of atomic particles in relation to their actuality? This explains why Einstein had doubts about the emerging field of quantum mechanics and the many strange issues and questions it was posing scientific thinking of the time.

What this discussion shows is that, for teachers and educators, learning environments need to be constructed for children of all backgrounds that enable an experiential continuity to be established between knowing and doing, or between abstract and concrete knowledge, so that transactional experience is possible (Moll, 2014). Rather than *teaching and learning* situations (as distinct from a physics textbook) specifying truth of some type, such as the direct correspondence between physical reality and physical quantity, classrooms need to encourage the creation of ideas and knowledge by learners at a particular time that are steps along the way to more expansive learning. School classrooms are similar to the physics or chemistry lab to the extent that both are operating within generally agreed frameworks of ideas and guidelines to investigate interesting problems and puzzles. People of any age or social background come to appreciate the idea of flotation, or current, or tide by being as one with the ocean, of coming to their own understanding as experience is gathered. A musician becomes engrossed with sound and rhythm to express meaning and emotion. Paint, colour and form enable the artist to convey the misery or exultation of human progress. The word 'concrete' can be replaced by connected or continuity if need be, but the notion of humans being always immersed in experience as the basis of reflection, communication and theorising needs to be retained in all classrooms. Schools are places of learning, not places where all children must have the correct adult view at all times and where for the learner, the names–knowings–knowns related to phenomena are open for investigation and transaction. On this basis, ways of organising knowledge and activities to enable the learner at all times to 'swim and gambol with knowledge' brought into relationship with the experience of personal culture and daily life demand the availability of diverse and imaginative pedagogies of practice in every mind and every act.

Continuities of practice

Over recent times and parallel with the neoliberal era, a number of professional areas of activity and study have been challenged regarding their exact composition and emphasis, their place in the academy, their autonomy and their specialised knowledge (Schatzki *et al.*, 2001). Areas such as nursing, teaching, administration, counselling, social work and business fall into this category. It is therefore necessary to be able to theorise these areas of human activity not only to meet continuing ideological challenges, but to be able to strengthen the work of each for the best possible outcomes. In relation to professional practice, an emerging international trend can be discerned of returning to the ideas of Aristotle regarding the human virtues of techne, episteme and phronesis, the latter meaning the human disposition of practical wisdom and prudence (Kemmis, 2009). Additionally, the notion of praxis refers to human action in pursuing phronesis, or ethically informed action for the public good (see below). With these broad concepts in mind, it is clear that teachers and educators are involved with learning practices and praxis every day, in every classroom, acting in the interests of their students and communities. Paulo Freire was a more recent philosopher who also accentuated human action and praxis in his writings as a key way of how we come to investigate and understand the world.

According to Freire (1972b), different forms of human consciousness exist depending on the social and economic conditions that dominate. These conditions generate intransitive, semi-transitive and naïve-transitive thinking and states of mind that can be transformed into critical consciousness. Different states of consciousness are fragile and, while they can be converted into more progressive arrangements, can also slide backwards or be distorted. Freire (1972a, p. 78) argued that 'Critical consciousness is brought about not through an intellectual effort alone, but through praxis – through authentic union of action and reflection.' In bringing together the debate on education and freedom, Freire continues that 'Such reflective action cannot be denied to the people. If it were, the people would be no more than activist pawns in the hands of a leadership which reserved for itself the right of decision-making.' In relation to schools and approaches to teaching, the 'people' noted by Freire could be students and the 'leadership' could be teachers. He maintained that a central element of critical knowledge was dialogue amongst the people.

Freirean dialogue can be described as participatory, open communication focused around critical inquiry and analysis, linked to intentional action seeking to reconstruct the situation (including the self) and to evaluated consequences. Referred to as 'conscientisation' by Freire, becoming critical involves a struggle and dialogue against the dehumanising structures, regulations, practices and knowledge of society such that reflection on everyday activity can bring about progressive critique and change for the collective good. Becoming critical is of necessity initially located, fashioned and challenged by the socio-political parameters of the time, but through tentative and emerging action, dialogue and collective critique can be transformed into new aspiration and possibility. It cannot be expected that every writer or theorist can answer all questions completely and Freire certainly did not, especially in relation to the more detailed analysis of teaching and learning. However his emphasis on dialogue and critical consciousness remains a major contribution to educational theory and practice around the world.

Progressive models of education and of teaching, that is, those that are committed to ongoing change and improvement for all learners, must be able to locate themselves in the recognised literature, even more so during difficult times when conservative ideologies are dominant. It is necessary to develop approaches to education and teaching that are distinctively educational and not primarily derived from other disciplines and domains. On this specific point, derived models will most likely not be able to engage the issues of schooling for low-income families and the epistemological strategies that are required to open up alienated areas of knowledge across the curriculum. Accordingly, it is important to respect the moral agency of teachers and of knowledge itself such that the culture and experience of all people, regardless of socio-economic background, form the basis of learning and can bridge the privileged knowledge of others. The Scottish philosopher Alasdair MacIntyre (1983, p. 175) added to the delineation of culture, experience and social practice when he spoke of the 'internal goods' of practice, although the concept remains somewhat vague:

> By a 'practice' I am going to mean any coherent and complex form of socially established co-operative human activity through which goods internal to that activity are realised, in the course of trying to achieve those standards of excellence which are appropriate to and partially definitive of that form of activity, with the result that human powers to achieve excellence and human conceptions of the ends and goods involved are systematically extended.

Following MacIntyre, we can recognise the 'internal goods' of human practice as the basis of coming to an understanding of human virtue and how virtue is contested and constructed, rather than have an authoritarian version of the world and of humanity imposed. Attempting to untangle all the possible characteristics of practice one by one is an impossible task. It could also be the wrong task, if the central feature of practice properties is convergent rather than divergent. However if some features or properties of 'internal goods' of social practice can be proposed as language, knowledge, action, thought and interest (all of which can be seen in the example above of the child playing at the beach), then this will enable the liaison between them to be contemplated and the conditions necessary for their complicated existence to be consolidated. It means that educators can change the conditions under which learning occurs so that for each learner intellectual models can come into correspondence with experience, thereby creating new models to guide further learning. This is the epistemological criticism of mass testing, where tests cannot reflect or respect progress in learning that proceeds without being told what is 'correct' by experts, that involves deep experiential attachment with ideas and which connects with human interest that lies at the basis of our knowing and meaning. School mathematics (as distinct from mathematics as it exists and interacts with humans in the universe) is a case in point, generally disconnected from personal experience and expected to be understood from small, rectangular pieces of paper, in grand silence and isolation (see Chapter 5). As already mentioned (and will no doubt be repeated later), children are wonderful learners and it makes no sense at all that they are alienated from knowledge, except if the procedures imposed by adults are alienating and confusing. Much of the learning achieved by children is in fact 'invisible' and misrecognised or overlooked by adults because the epistemologies, knowledge structures and systems assumed by adults may not apply for that child at that time, subsequently distorting the adult's view of children's learning. It is the adult who has failed the child's test.

Consider the practice of learning to ride a bicycle. Aside from the various advice offered by others, the novice must come to grips with all of the factors operating, together, in a related whole. Informal coherence and relationship must be established between (the formal concepts of) balance, motion, gravity, steering, speed, force, torque, direction, weight, without calculating the correct answer from an equation. Such magnificent learning generally occurs without cost, without direct instruction and with complete immersion of the learner. In other words, the internal goods of this practice are not explicitly named and taught, are strongly mathematical and connect with the human interest of the learner through experiment. Practice properties are engaged at the time with the intellectual structures that exist and impact on those structures so that experience is constructed and reconstructed for each person. Each person has to work out how to ride a bicycle for themselves and therefore learning involves literally reinventing the wheel for everyone. Most teachers of school mathematics are not mathematicians and find the generation of mathematical learning environments for all children difficult. They generally do not approach the learning of mathematics in the same way as learning to ride a bike. This does raise the epistemological issue of whether certain areas of knowledge are different to other areas of knowledge, or whether knowledges as defined are similar. Is all knowledge socially constructed from culture, experience, history, language, community, heated debate and the like, or are structures of (formal, defined) knowledge predetermined, meaning that some learners are included and others excluded?

Taking language as a proposed 'internal good' of social and educational practice means that specific features of language need to be identified, perhaps a feature such as 'credibility of language forms and how used (grammars, procedures, expression)'. This raises broad understandings of language, as suggested by Chomsky (2004), particularly that of generative grammars, an ability to generate infinite sentences or expressions and then to connect them to thought systems and to sensory motor systems. In this respect, the term 'grammar' is not used as school rules to be taught, but how humans interact with and express their experience (generally and in all school subjects). The concepts of 'grammars' and 'rules' need to be seen epistemologically rather than as hegemonic classroom procedures by which language is taught. Habermas (1984) also concentrated on language as he attempted to theorise how humans can more accurately interpret the world and formulate critical, indeed emancipatory, perspectives. He proposed a set of validity claims regarding speech so that what is stated is true, what is said is comprehensible, the speaker is sincere in what is said and that it is right for such speech to be enacted. Ultimately, this process of 'ideal speech' communication enables a consensus to be reached about what is true. The very notion of an 'ideal speech situation' indicates that the views of Habermas are somewhat idealistic, but they do offer a framework for democratic relationships between groups of people as they pursue understanding. Language then, as a generative property (or grammar) of practice, needs to be a key aspect of enhancing the student experience of consensual learning.

From the above discussion, it can be argued that a weakness or absence of generative and experiential language as 'internal goods' of classroom practice will diminish learning. This brings into serious question the efficacy of the lecture, the silent classroom, the specified content and teacher-dominated classroom, the linearity of expert knowledge and individual or heroic rather than community emphases. Conversely, it suggests that on balance, formal educational programs need to ensure that communicative action pervades all studies and that discourse frameworks are well known for all participants. All human conversations are unique, producing many meanings and interpretations, but if students and others are excluded, or are forced to work within an imposed narrow rigidity, connotation and sense are markedly distorted. Describing himself as a 'curious being' who changed every day, Paulo Freire defended the right of all citizens to use their own beautiful language in their search for meaning and in accessing the language and privileged knowledge of others. This approach would seem to offer an improved learning environment for improved test results, a more substantial way of proceeding than more of the same testing. MacIntyre's notion of practice and its 'internal goods' as the basis of human virtue, together with Dewey's concept of 'continuity' between all aspects of learning provides some of the missing epistemological and theoretical links that distance many students from schooling today.

Practice, phronesis, praxis

If education and learning are social practices occurring at the interface of sociology and epistemology (see Figure 0.1 in the Preface), then the exact nature of this practice needs to be explicated. While Figure 0.1 is a simplified diagram of the complicated matrix of factors impacting on learning and formal schooling, it does highlight the major items of study that surround issues of educational quality that emerge from sociological and epistemological analysis. As outlined above, notions of continuity (concrete/abstract) and internal goods (such as language) provide a means of detailing practice, making it available for constitution and change to meet the needs of diverse learning populations. Other philosophical properties of practice to consider at this point are phronesis and praxis.

Much of the current debate regarding schooling, teaching and learning takes place within a neoliberal political and economic context that assumes its imperatives can be directly imposed on education. While the nation state will usually adopt this position for each economic system prevailing, it must be recognised that a range of reference points are possible in relation to the public good of teaching. When questions are asked regarding the purpose and nature of schooling and teaching practice, we are going to the heart of what it means to be human, to be broadly educated and to live well. Aristotle was concerned with these issues and spoke of three rationalities or intellectual virtues that can assist our understanding: the virtues of techne, episteme and phronesis. Techne is taken to be context-dependent, variable and is based on an instrumental rationality oriented towards technique or craft. Episteme is context-independent, invariable and exhibits an analytical rationality that today would be associated with a scientific approach. Phronesis is ethically framed rationality or disposition regarding what is good and appropriate; it is based on a system of values rather than rules or laws and requires judgements to be made. Praxis is the action arising from phronesis to pursue such values and intent. Aristotle proposed that experience and particular cases rather than universals are crucial for phronesis. He noted accordingly that some people without generalised knowledge are more adept in action than others because of this close connection with social practice. Phronesis and praxis embody prudence and practical wisdom at both the personal and societal levels.

In his influential book regarding the nature of social science, Flyvbjerg (2001, p. 60) suggests that a phronetic methodology involves 'analyses and interpretations of the status of values and interests in society aimed at social commentary and social action, i.e. praxis'. He goes on to propose four 'value-rational' questions that will pursue this end:

1   Where are we going?
2   Is this desirable?
3   What should be done?
4   Who gains and who loses?

Flyvbjerg argues that social sciences are fundamentally different to the natural sciences and therefore they should not seek the explanatory and predictive capacity characteristic of the natural sciences. This raises issues about definitions of theory and epistemology in the social sciences and whether they are, or can be, 'scientific'. In referencing Aristotle, Flyvbjerg (p. 57) supports the notion of phronetic social science in that:

> *Phronesis* thus concerns the analysis of values – 'things that are good or bad for man' – as a point of departure for action. *Phronesis* is that intellectual activity most relevant to praxis. It focuses on what is variable, on that which cannot be encapsulated by universal rules, on specific cases. *Phronesis* requires an interaction between the general and the concrete, it requires consideration, judgement and choice. More than anything else, *Phronesis* requires *experience* (original emphasis).

A rigid division between the social and physical sciences may be inaccurate (creating serious problems for educational practice at the interface), especially if the above four questions are taken into account and how physical science is actually practised. It may be thought that to propose some similarity between the two disciplines is a form of rampant intellectual imperialism on the part of science, but the above four questions are not the exclusive domain of social science and modern science does not usually proceed by the unyielding application of predetermined theory or rules. For instance, both Popper and Kuhn have developed philosophies of science that would contest this view. Modern science works within a broad framework of accepted constructs that guide continuing experiment and theorising and which are available for constant disputation and renovation. It is not the case that generalised principles such as $F(orce) = M(ass) \times A(cceleration)$ or $A(rea\ of\ circle) = \Pi \times R(adius)^2$ are believed as being totally accurate or to be used unthinkingly, but they provide a good guide to action through the 'consideration, judgement and choice' of Flyvbjerg. Practitioners of the social sciences in education managing the interface between sociology and epistemology are understandably wary of the possibility of generalised 'law' being endorsed, such as 'many working-class children are deficient in formal mathematics' or 'public schools lack a system of articulated values found in private schools'. However it could be suggested that both the social and natural sciences operate within a broad schedule of dialogue, codes, principle and theorising that guide further investigation of their respective interests and which assist progressive and moral human purpose. There are significant philosophical questions at stake regarding objectivity, truth and value in all areas that are activated when the child is sick, when the child feels isolated in the classroom, or when a child's bicycle is being designed.

Birmingham (2004, pp. 321–322) relates phronesis to her own work as a teacher in three specific ways. First, she notes the personal aspects of teaching and the potential of phronesis 'to broaden the moral vision of teaching' beyond the personal to the institutional. Second, phronesis raises the issue of community in terms of the Aristotelian view that 'a virtuous life is necessary for a happy life', both of which depend on sense of community. Third, she continues that, in a time when educational measurement primarily is supposed to give meaning, phronesis instead reminds us of 'personal virtue bound to the particulars of situations and embedded in a community'. Of course, the value judgements of practitioners involved here can be either 'good' or 'bad' depending on their definition and the context within which they are made. The three virtues noted above of techne, episteme and phronesis therefore exist within the political, economic and cultural features of the day and constitute a never-ending struggle between different worldviews. In modern education, for example, questions of equity, social justice and the learning of different groups of students will be strongly contested and require different application of different virtues. In this regard, public education in all countries will benefit from a reference point of a progressive phronesis or praxis. Current conservative debate supposes the direction and organisation of schooling are adequate and that teaching quality is reflected in the passage of predetermined knowledge from teacher to student. Under the ideology of techne, some students will absorb this knowledge, while many will not. It may be that humans do not learn primarily in this way, but engage the world actively from the point of view of their own interest, changing the world in the process. Aristotle held that phronesis cannot be reduced to techne, but that techne can be found in phronesis. If schools and teacher education do not take account of these rationalities and their relationship, then there is little surprising in the frustrations and tensions that are found in many classrooms.

In general terms, we could consider a school's curriculum as involving the three intellectual virtues or knowledges as art/craft, sciences and ethics (see Part II for a more specific discussion of curriculum detail). Using current terms and to connect with current school subjects, these could be detailed and slightly expanded as studies in arts, humanities, sciences, technologies and philosophy. The purpose here is not the mere accumulation of packets of information, but to investigate 'how to live well'. Epistemology asks questions of the type: what is knowledge, how is it possible, why and how do humans learn? These surely should form the basis of a modern education system for all students underpinning all subjects – and being fascinated by such dilemmas is not determined by family income. But we can now add questions of the type: what is good character, in whose interests do we act and how do we think about the virtues of courage, compassion, generosity and solidarity constructed over a lifetime?

The fact that education is constantly drawn away from the beautiful and the virtuous is testament to the dominance of the political and economic system and a corresponding diminution of the true nature of learning. Reclaiming phronesis/praxis will support all teachers, students and citizens in their historic

Table 2.1 Key ideas of educational configuration

Principle	Description
Democracy	Forms of associated living involving shared experience, communicative and participatory relationships and organisational respect that enables culture, traditions and explanatory structures to belong to the citizen/learner and not be disrespected or dismissed by others
Social justice	All members of society having equal access to the public opportunities, procedures and resources of that society for democratic purpose, alleviating inequality and sharing in support for the public good
Educational equity	Fair, reasonable and consistent approaches in meeting the educational needs of all families and students regardless of socio-economic and cultural background
Partnership	Negotiated social and educational arrangements between schools, universities and communities of collaborative practitioner inquiry that support teaching and learning for the mutual benefit of all concerned
Practice	Professional activity to achieve particular educational consequences and governed by a set of theorised parameters to ensure consensus of participants
Phronesis/praxis	Cycles of ethically framed action or rationality regarding what is good and appropriate, based on a system of values rather than rules or laws and requiring judgements to be made – providing authentic experience, reflection and changed practice to improve teaching and learning, that link with community issues and that involve principles of democracy and equity
Critical praxis	Cycles of ethically framed action or rationality regarding what is good and appropriate, based on a system of values rather than rules or laws and requiring judgements to be made – bringing together the ideas of ideology critique, self-reflexive consciousness and emancipatory action for improved teaching and learning and the public good

undertaking of 'good' work. Specifically, this means the values of democracy, social justice and educational equity for all students, including those from low-income families, and upholding the educational principles of partnership, practice and praxis. Neoliberal ideology needs to be resisted as it oozes into every niche of social life on the basis of market reach, efficiencies and accountabilities and the inappropriate, shallow and erroneous measurement of human progress. A statement of educational intent is therefore required that clearly outlines a shared understanding of key ideas and which guides the purpose and direction of new organisational configurations, ideas that have been briefly discussed above and are summarised in Table 2.1.

Critical praxis for educators seeks to move beyond the constraints of formal teaching, knowledge and curriculum and instead encourage communities, teachers and students to work together in producing new understandings and practices for majority interest, located within, but critical of, the socio-economic determinants of the time. Initially, this involves rejection of various deficit pathologies directed at low-income, ethnic and other groups of students in relation to genetic code, cultural and economic deprivation and inadequate socialisation, and refocuses on the incorporation of community wisdom, prudence, interests and practices in school classrooms and programs. Intensive critique of current privileged school knowledge (sometimes configured as 'disciplines') such as mathematics, science, literature, language and history is also necessary to the extent that new arrangements of knowledge may be required that include new forms of investigation. As a collaborative participant in knowledge production, the teacher enables and challenges thinking by introducing external comment and evidence from national and international projects so that ideas are not confined by the boundaries of location.

Pedagogies: traditional, progressive

It should be expected that what happens in classrooms every day will be based on the broad concerns discussed above, that is, pluralistic epistemological arrangements regarding the nature of knowledge and learning and philosophical questions such as 'What can we learn?' and 'How do we live well regarding ourselves and others?' Such general arrangements are called pedagogies, defined here as the science or theorised understanding of teaching and learning practice involving all social and educational conditions that impact on teaching and learning of all children from all socio-economic backgrounds. In these terms, pedagogy is a key factor at the interface of sociology and epistemology and impacts decisively on the creation of dynamic social justice conditions for students. The incorporation of different pedagogies for different purposes with different children is an indispensable strategy for inclusion in all subject areas, rather than relying on the same approach regardless of the class, topic or students. However while having a range of pedagogies at their disposal, it is realistic to expect teachers to usually operate within a broad epistemological framework that reflects their overall approach to teaching and learning and which has been reasonably successful in the past and to then use professional judgement when introducing other strategies to meet different circumstances as they occur. As mentioned previously, large class sizes (especially if located in small classrooms) and lack of teaching resources (including dilapidated buildings) have prevented epistemological pluralism, but as these constraints are overcome, a range of pedagogies becomes possible. This does not automatically occur, as smaller class sizes can mean more teacher time with students implementing the same approach, more time in working from the textbook. What is required around the world is systematic transition from traditional to progressive pedagogies.

John Dewey was the central figure in identifying and explaining the difference between what he termed traditional or conservative approaches to education and pedagogy compared with progressive education and pedagogy. For this impertinence and his general theories of pragmatic and inquiry learning

(Bruce and Bloch, 2013), he was strongly criticised in the United States. Dewey (1966, p. 76) saw learning as growth and stated that, rather than an

> unfolding of latent powers from within and of the formation from without, whether by physical nature or by the cultural products of the past, the ideal of growth results in the conception that education is a constant reorganising and reconstruction of experience.

In this way, Dewey was advocating that the child was not born with intellectual attributes (present to a greater or lesser extent) that lay dormant and needed to be galvanised, or that the child depended on being inculcated by adults into predetermined truths and traditions, but that the child's intellectual capabilities were bolstered over time as broad experiences were continuously brought together. Emphasis was redirected from deficiencies of the child to the social and educational conditions of learning that surround the child both at school and at home. Learning was therefore 'progressive' developing, moving and changing as the child actively explores the world.

On this basis, Dewey's famous definition of education was composed: 'It is that reconstruction or reorganisation of experience which adds to the meaning of experience and which increases ability to direct the course of subsequent experience' (p. 76). Dewey noted that continuous experience enables new connections between the elements of experience to be perceived, thus revealing or constructing the tentative meaning of the experience and bringing the learner into a new relationship with experiential objects that possess that meaning. Climbing a tree at any age and feeling the texture of leaves, moss and bark high from the ground causes a new perception of 'tree' to be formed.

Dewey does not support the dualism of mind separated from the social and physical objects of mind so that subject content in schools has already been decided by others as a pre-classified arrangement of information and facts. He cites topics in science such as zoology as an example of material that has 'already been subjected to intelligence; it has been methodised' (Dewey, 1966, p. 165). Methods of approaching teaching, argues Dewey (p. 179), must arise from the experience and observations of teachers rather than be imposed artificially on students:

> Method is a statement of the way the subject matter of an experience develops most effectively and fruitfully. It is derived, accordingly, from observation of the course of experiences where there is no conscious distinction of personal attitude and manner from material dealt with. The assumption that method is something separate is connected with the notion of the isolation of mind and self from the world of things. It makes instruction and learning formal, mechanical, constrained.

This is a considerable challenge for teachers who have a number of classes each week with many students involved in total. The fact that it is a difficult challenge does not mean that it should be denied in favour of less-defensible and conservative approaches. Rather than structuring teaching or pedagogy around the arrangements of subject content already decided, learning environments need to be flexible enough to permit teachers to implement different strategies of learning as they observe students and work with them on practising difficult and emerging ideas.

In other words, teaching method involves the constant rearranging and reconstruction of experience by teachers and students as they investigate meaning in all its forms, together. Literacy is a good example of this. There is a very strong line of demarcation between literacy as teacher-directed, stepwise instruction into the predetermined structure of language and literacy as language experience involving all human activity. One does not necessarily preclude the other, but the proportion of each approach adopted in the classroom will determine its character. The agreed and imposed curriculum may demand that certain subject content be covered and formally assessed, often in short time spans of less than one calendar year, but this can produce enormous dissatisfaction and confusion if topics are not 'experienced' and 'known' deeply, to the extent that learners do not accept that they are developing new understandings for themselves. Cutting the textbook in half so that double the time can be allocated to experimenting with a smaller number of ideas can be justified epistemologically at any staff meeting. Assessment (or, more correctly, assistment) of learning arising from more open, flexible environments will also require more open and flexible techniques than generally available at present.

Will education conducted within neoliberal societies favour more traditional or more progressive approaches to knowledge and pedagogy? Given the contradictions that exist in all societies, a definitive answer cannot be given, but trends can be identified. From a purely marketised, globalised or 'anything goes' point of view this may not be a significant question, as it would be assumed that whatever system is in place, there will be winners and losers and that there will be sufficient winners of quality to keep the economic system healthy. Teachers therefore could fall anywhere in cells 1–4 of Table 2.2. Traditional teachers will most likely be located in cell 1, although it is possible for them to adopt more progressive teaching to reach the same outcomes. Recognising the strength of neoliberalism, progressive teachers will most likely be in cell 2, with excursions into cell 3 whenever possible. On this analysis, it could be expected that the majority of teachers will fall into cells 1 and 2, with smaller numbers in cells 3 and 4. Those teachers who consistently arrange their teaching in cell 4 will be a slight minority, at present.

Table 2.2 Relationship between approaches to knowledge and pedagogy

	Traditional pedagogy	*Progressive pedagogy*
Traditional knowledge	1	2
Progressive knowledge	3	4

From a social justice viewpoint, a more progressive approach to knowledge and pedagogy, as represented by cells 2 and 3, will advantage students from diverse socio-economic families and settings. This enables students to draw upon their culture and interests as much as possible while retaining access to privileged knowledge for reference. Maintaining traditional knowledge and pedagogy does not allow conditions of continuity, experience and internal goods of practice to be enhanced, thereby limiting learning. Establishing environments of both progressive knowledge and pedagogy should not be confused with unwarranted or extreme conditions as, while these are the usual characteristics of natural learning, they are usually not the conditions of school learning. All teachers are in the position of making difficult decisions regarding the conditions of knowledge and pedagogy they seek to establish in each of their classrooms and will find themselves situated in some position amongst the four cells relative to the other three. In Table 2.3, line A shows traditionalists and progressivists who can operate to a limited extent in other domains, line B shows progressivists who want to extend their reach as much as possible, while brackets C indicate a pluralist approach to both knowledge and pedagogy whenever possible. These are social justice considerations at the interface of sociology and epistemology.

Table 2.3 Relative relationship between approaches to knowledge and pedagogy

	Traditional pedagogy	*Progressive pedagogy*
Traditional knowledge	1	2
Progressive knowledge	3	4

3   Schooling for the majority

To be human is to breathe, to learn, to err
not within narrow confines artificially set,
but to jump fearlessly outside the boundaries
challenging the unknown, an experiential
knowledgeable citizenry and new humanity
anticipated by the explosion of courage.

Education systems around the world reflect the political and economic systems of each country as well as come under pressure to change as social conditions alter. In the more wealthy countries, primary and secondary education have become expectations for most citizens, although the exact format of each is constantly debated. How schooling is organised, how subject content is structured and the approaches adopted towards teaching and learning, generally speaking, remain entrenched in past practices even as class sizes have been reduced and new resources have become available. More recent advances in technology have caused some change to occur but, in many cases, such change is superficial. Fundamentally new forms of schooling on a mass scale have not as yet emerged from this long transitional period with original structures, meaning that there may be a serious philosophical mismatch between the lifeworlds of students and the schools they attend. There is a (long-held) tendency in some countries to cope with this phenomenon by attempting to identify different types of schools for different groups of children (see below), but this generally results in a misrecognition of the children concerned and an overall fragmentation of the curriculum. There are also serious ethical questions regarding labelling children as being 'different', particularly from an early age, based on highly dubious psychological assumptions. Designing systems of education that enable all children to participate fully with challenging knowledge and to develop their own learning interests and passions is difficult work in progress that requires a rigorous theoretical framework enabling appropriate epistemologies and pedagogies. To this end, the educational practices and reasoning of Pierre Bourdieu are now briefly considered.

Pierre Bourdieu was a highly respected French social philosopher who had wide interests in anthropology, sociology, philosophy, economics, politics, culture and education. He emphasised the connections between theory and practice and how these impacted on the nature of research and the conduct of sociology itself. He also developed a set of theoretical constructs such as cultural capital, habitus, field, symbolic violence and reflexivity for use in a broad range of social analysis. Bourdieu's first articles published in English appeared in *Knowledge and Control* (Young, 1971) where, in one paper, he discussed the relationship in general terms between creative and artistic work and the social and intellectual environments in which the work is located. He noted the role of schools in this process and commented that 'These institutions are entrusted with the functions of transmitting consciously (and also in part unconsciously) the unconscious. More precisely, the school produces individuals who possess this system of unconscious (or extremely obscure) schemes constituting their culture' (Bourdieu, 1971, p. 185). By his use of the term 'unconscious', Bourdieu was drawing attention to how schools not only transmit obvious subject content that is considered central to the dominant culture, but through their explicit organisation, procedures and sanctions support non-obvious social dispositions that are entirely political and biased. Bourdieu described this general process of society maintaining itself as 'reproduction' and, writing with his colleague Passeron, defined what became a celebrated educational concept in sociology (Bourdieu and Passeron, 1977, p. 54):

> Every institutionalised educational system owes the specific characteristics of its structure and functioning to the fact that, by the means proper to the institution, it has to produce and reproduce the institutional conditions whose existence and persistence (self-reproduction of the system) are necessary both to the exercise of its essential function of inculcation and to the fulfilment of its function of reproducing a cultural arbitrary which it does not produce (cultural reproduction), the reproduction of which contributes to the reproduction of the relations between the groups or classes (social reproduction).

In this passage, Bourdieu and Passeron propose that schools must of necessity engage in 'self-reproduction', or protect their own interests and influence as institutions, given their central position in the economic and cultural system and the consequently substantial funding received from the state to support this position. They then comment that schools participate in 'cultural reproduction' by sustaining a culture that is 'arbitrary' or not predetermined by non-critique of knowledge, teaching and learning practices often imposed from outside schools and the profession by the dominant culture. Finally, they point out that the processes of self-reproduction and cultural reproduction that maintain the relationships between groups of people from different cultural and economic backgrounds establish 'social reproduction' across society generally, thereby maintaining power and economic differentiation. The theory of reproduction shows how societies and their institutions are capable of protecting and regenerating themselves as conditions alter without recourse to naked repression and violence, the protection of economies and major banks during the continuing global financial crisis being apposite. Of course, account must be taken of conditions and events such as the French Revolution, the Paris Commune and the riots of May 1968 in Paris as social and political tensions become extreme, indicating that forces and contradictions stronger than benign reproduction are at work. Under customary political circumstances however Bourdieu noted that the relative autonomy of schools is determined by their relationship with other social institutions and power brokers, although this is not always easy to discern. If primary education is generally accepted as being concerned with the well-being and basic literacy of young children and secondary education is seen as vocational preparation for many and elite knowledge for some, then cultural and social reproduction is assured.

In his book *Pascalian Meditations*, Bourdieu (2000) discusses what he calls the 'scholastic fallacy' connected with the notion of *skhole* or leisure, the existence of free time to remove oneself from the difficulties of the world. As a senior academic within France, he was keenly aware of his own privileged position in this regard and was clear that his critical thinking of society, culture and education that developed over time should also apply to himself. As the word 'meditation' would suggest, the book is a musing by Bourdieu on a series of issues concerned with how various citizens, including sociologists, view and interpret the world. For example, in expansive mood, he writes about 'symbolic capital', defined as 'social importance and of reasons for living' (p. 241). He suggests that economic, social and cultural capital exist as symbolic capital 'in its relationship with a habitus predisposed to perceive it as a sign' (p. 242). The notion of habitus developed by Bourdieu (1990a, p. 53) describes how practice and practical reasoning can establish a relationship between objective and subjective knowing:

> The conditionings associated with a particular class of conditions of existence produce habitus, systems of durable, transposable dispositions, structured structures predisposed to function as structuring structures, that is, as principles which generate and organise practices and representations that can be objectively adapted to their outcomes without presupposing a conscious aiming at ends or expressed mastery of the operations necessary in order to attain them. Objectively 'regulated' and 'regular' without being in any way the product of obedience to rules, they can be collectively orchestrated without being the product of the organising action of a conductor.

As a broad descriptive model of human learning, habitus provides a means of thinking about the production of knowledge without being locked into a fixed, step-wise connection between the structures of learning and the field of activity impacting on those structures. Economic matters do not have to determine our thoughts regarding art, the natural environment, or other people. Instead, there is a fluid relationship between habitus/structure and fields/action so that one does not dominate the other. As a result, Bourdieu firmly locates himself as a structuralist but in such a manner that the structures are ill defined, apparently flexible without being rule-based and non-determinist regarding human activity. The concepts of habitus, field and various capitals therefore have a direct bearing on how we understand the practices of social agents and subsequently, how learning actually takes place. These considerations, whether tacit or overt, are not only present in all schools but indeed exist in society as well. According to Grenfell (2004, p. 198), Bourdieu was intimating that habitus, field and capitals are internal rather than external to humans that result in a new 'knowing' being possible in the social and collective search for truth. If so, processes of this type should be accessible to all children in every neighbourhood school.

Public/private education

A major educational division at any level in many countries is that between public and private provision. This divide represents a significant philosophical difference regarding the purpose of schooling and the nature of learning, aspirations for children regardless of political, economic and cultural affiliations and ultimately, what it means to be human. Table 3.1 outlines the trend characteristics of public and private education:

Within the private sector, a distinction needs to be drawn between elite, long-established, high-fee-paying schools and schools with a more modest fee regime, between religious and non-religious schools and between small,

Table 3.1 Characteristics of public and private education

Public education (trends)	Private education (trends)
State-funded and supported, secular, open to all without fees	Private and state-funded, religious and non-religious, mainly exclusive, fee paying
Learning for democratic public interest and culture	Learning for private interest, ideological, individual
Inquiry learning, democratic values incorporating practice, cycles of reflection on experience that transforms perceptual knowledge into conceptual understanding	Transmission of predetermined knowledge, dogma, culture, values
Epistemological unity of practice and theorising, knowing and doing, learning and labour, personal connection with products of learning	Epistemological separation of theory and practice in support of preordained truth and faith
Knowledge that is collective in the interests of the general community related to nature, society, work	Knowledge that is specified in the interests of specific communities related to ideology
Inclusive, integrated curriculum combining practice, reflection, theorising, critique	Curriculum that is differentiated in organisation between scientific and metaphysical, not subject to critical critique

non-systemic schools that have been established for particular reasons such as community or family-type schools. It is often the case that debate on the benefits and outcomes of private schooling tend to focus on the elite schools that by definition are small in number, compared with, for example, a much larger number of unpretentious schools such as parish Catholic schools. Debate also often focuses on the notion of parental choice between sectors, whether this is a religious choice or not. However there are many protocols adopted by society for the common good that override the liberalism of individual and private choice, particularly where children are concerned. It should also be the case that the wealthy countries can comfortably afford a high-quality public education system for all children provided that there is an equitable distribution of resources over time. At a philosophical level therefore, the six major principles for constructing a public system of education and which generate the characteristics shown in Table 3.1 should involve:

1   democratic as a public right for all citizens and as a central component of active citizenship for a civil society
2   democratic in organisation and in approaches to teaching and learning
3   inclusive of all children, regardless of socio-economic background
4   secular, in accord with the separation of church and state
5   equitable in relation to participation and learning progress
6   transformative and open-minded regarding the investigation of knowledge and understanding.

In democratic countries with forms of representative democracy, universal suffrage and taxation, with a separation between church and state and with a similar separation of powers between the executive of government and an independent judiciary, then all citizens are equal under the law with equal rights and expectations (Salazar, 2013). With such a constitution and legal system, all institutions and procedures that support the public good are similarly aligned and democratic. It is difficult to define a democratic right in terms of the capacity of citizens to pay fees for its application. Those who struggle to pay and who cannot therefore access facilities are not able to exercise their democratic right, making health, education and legal costs important areas of reform.

Once agreed, a democratic right and process does not depend on funding. However, as mentioned earlier, an educational democratic right for all citizens could be funded and established in many countries around the world by not going to war and by purchasing two or three fewer fighter aircraft in each budget. The easy production of trillions of dollars during the recent global financial meltdown also showed clearly the amount of money that is available.

In a country that is not a church state, schooling must not be used to promote religion or, more accurately, to impose a view of existence. For schools to enforce a particular religious ideology on children is immoral, in the same way that insisting on a particular scientific interpretation is immoral. This is the reason why all schools should be secular and inclusive of all viewpoints.

Deciding on approaches to knowledge, teaching and learning is tricky for everyone concerned, taking into account the political and economic conditions that exist. Whichever way is adopted will involve a particular philosophical view that has been contested over long periods of time, perhaps throughout the centuries. Some social groupings will seek to pass on predetermined knowledge and demand acceptance by students, mainly through informal and formal testing. Others will encourage students to inquire into knowledge and form their own conclusions.

There are many assumptions buried deep within the principles and characteristics of public and private schooling that will be taken up in later chapters of this book. Placing the question of a religious grounding to schooling aside, a major issue concerns doubting the capability of all children to learn and to learn profoundly.

In relation to making schools more appropriate for diverse learners, Cozolino (2013) discusses issues of social neuroscience, emphasising the relationship between social networks and neural networks for the learning of children. He suggests that formal classrooms should be similar to 'tribal' conditions on the basis that 'the more the environment of a classroom parallels the interpersonal, emotional and motivational components of our tribal past, the more our primitive instincts will activate the biochemistry of learning' (p. 239). In stressing the role of language in learning for everyone, Cozolino notes three types of language that contribute to self-reflection. Reflexive social language enables social connections to be made and often involves automatic, spontaneous responses found in daily use. Internal dialogue is a private, internal conversation that occurs regarding how to proceed, particularly when there is inner dispute. Self-reflective language allows for quiet contemplation of issues, somewhat akin to an executive function that guides other thoughts and actions. If teachers attempt to plan their classroom activities so that students are enabled to participate with different internal and external languages in learning then their experience 'supports an expansion of self-awareness, emotional regulation and a scepticism towards "obvious" truths' (p. 196).

An excellent example of classroom organisation that encourages active and integrated languaging and no doubt 'a scepticism towards obvious truths' is provided by the fifth-grade class of Esquith (2009) in Los Angeles. His entire book is structured around a visit with his class to a baseball game, the interaction with students during the game and his reflections on the complicated journey and experiences of the children that have taken them to this point. The book is an exposition of continuity between concrete and abstract learning and the intellectual growth of children from different cultural backgrounds, especially as varieties of language are actively engaged.

Both Cozolino and Esquith encourage the view that all schools should be able to involve all children in bridging an array of culture, interest and ideas, making the public–private educational divide a fiction.

Philosophy has attempted to guide human thinking and values on these matters. For example, Socrates asked 'how should we live?' Descartes pondered 'what can we know?' Newton, Einstein and Hawking have discussed 'what is the nature of the universe? why does the universe exist?' Questions such as these, including 'how do we learn?', can be investigated in schools and form the baseline of all studies. Some private schools might argue that they are well placed to pursue these philosophical issues, but whether they do so democratically in a genuine search for knowledge wherever that might lead is most unlikely. Thomas Aquinas might hold that humans can investigate the mind of God but in recognition that all that we know by so doing is religious revelation. Conversely, establishing a set of values enabling open-minded democratic inquiry of all philosophical questions is the central task of public schooling. Like any organisation, its essential features and overall purpose need to be closely examined rather than be distracted by minor issues, however useful or laudable. Private schooling exists to support generally minority partisan interest and to assist the advancement of those who are dominated by private rather than public pursuits. Public schooling exists for public interest and to benefit all citizens of the democratic republic without fear or favour. It is difficult to see how schools that exclude rather than include, that request fees in exchange for knowledge, that have a predetermined view of truth and which see their essential role as reproducing the values and culture of specific groups of people can meet the six principles outlined above. From this philosophical standpoint, private schools cannot be justified; they are inherently undemocratic. Of course, if the world is viewed from a position of privilege, power and religion then a different argument ensues.

Models of schooling

It has been extremely difficult for many countries to implement systems of comprehensive schooling, particularly at the secondary level. The notion of comprehensive schooling is taken to mean a broad curriculum that involves experience of major ideas in the major areas of knowledge and which is available to all students regardless of background. Key learning areas generally involve subjects drawn from the academic disciplines and associated fields, such as mathematics, sciences, languages, history, arts and physical education. Appreciation and implementation of comprehensiveness are more likely in primary schools where knowledge is often integrated, activity-based and linked together by language experience. At the secondary level, subject-based learning becomes more important, especially in the middle and senior secondary years, when future pathways to employment or post-school study are considered. Universities often exert formal or informal pressure on the curriculum of secondary schools related to their entrance requirements and their academic approach towards knowledge and learning. Problems concerning the development of comprehensive education are both sociological and epistemological in essence concerning, in the first instance, inaccurate understanding of the lifeworlds of the vast majority of families and children and in the second, inaccurate assumptions regarding the learning capabilities and deficits of children.

It is indeed strange that connections are made between family income and education futures as well as between family income and intellectual scale; both need urgent recalibration by the public and by the profession. Postulating that family income of itself manipulates the concept of beauty experienced by a child when viewing a sunset, when reading a poem, or when looking through a microscope cannot be justified. Suggesting that a child born today will have trouble with senior-school mathematics many years later because of family income is absurd. It is doubly absurd when the epistemological paradigm that dominates most schools is very seldom analysed for appropriateness as a learning situation for low-income and culturally diverse student populations.

When comprehensive education is rightly or wrongly criticised for not meeting the needs of all children, other forms of organisation are often proposed. It should be pointed out that these proposals generally refer to public schools, rather than the small number of elite schools that are assumed to continue as they have done forever, following traditional approaches to organisation, teaching and learning. While it cannot be assumed that children of high-income families will be high achievers, it is often supposed that elite schools are automatically of high quality. For public schools then, and in contrast to comprehensive education, technical schools arose in response to the demands of manufacturing economies and, while having a similar basis to their regular curriculum in terms of included subjects, have a more practical orientation. They usually have a number of trade subjects and associated workshops that provide background for a range of apprenticeships that often result in strong support from working families for their children to gain employment opportunities. Supporters of technical education argue that the curriculum is not necessarily entirely vocational but gives a more balanced approach to learning across the curriculum, incorporating what are seen as academic/abstract and applied/concrete subjects.

Over recent years and the decline of manufacturing in many countries where it was previously strong, due to neoliberal free trade policies and the impact of new technologies, technical education has also declined in favour of a more perhaps ill-defined general education for all students. However this has reduced the opportunity for students to experience the many attributes of technical learning as an integrated aspect of overall learning, such as working with industrial equipment, personal and detailed understanding of the properties of materials and the construction of real items of use rather than facsimiles only.

A range of other structures have been attempted to provide education to different groups of children. These often involve attempts at becoming more independent of systemic regulation and bureaucracy and in encouraging greater parent and community participation. Academies and free schools in the United Kingdom and charter schools in the United States are examples of this trend. In some cases, school governance is the responsibility of a school council or board consisting of parents, teachers, students on some occasions and other representatives such as employers. Accountability for the overall operation of the school may exist within a loose framework of central regulation, or exist outside of any external control.

The Harlem Children's Zone in the United States is a somewhat controversial and well-known example of a charter school that emphasises the role of the community and values that include 'the importance of higher education, personal responsibility and hard work required to succeed in school' (Cozolino, 2013, p. 261). The approach is conservative with the school day and school year extended, traditional instruction and with remedial, after-school and Saturday classes. Apart from being seen as conflicting with public schools and being endorsed by conservative political figures for political reasons, this type of anti-public and anti-systemic movement generally supports highly traditional approaches to teaching and learning, with a strong emphasis on educational success being measured by test scores.

The educational philosophy behind comprehensive schooling on the other hand gives weight to the learning, interest and passion of the child for knowledge, wherever that might lead. In addition, the philosophy would suggest that, rather than being contradictory, a comprehensive education is the best vocational preparation of all. On the other hand, Meier (2002, p. 4) provides evidence of also working within the public system of Harlem and poses the challenge: 'The question is not, is it possible to educate all children well? But rather, do we want to do it badly enough?' She then develops this aspiration further:

> But there's a radical – and wonderful – new idea here, the idea that every citizen is capable of the kind of intellectual competence previously attained by only a small minority. It was only after I had begun to teach that public rhetoric gave even lip service to that notion that all children could and should be inventors of their own theories, critics of other people's ideas, analysers of evidence and makers of their own personal marks on this most complex world. It's an idea with revolutionary implications. If we take it seriously.

Meier is providing a different set of social and educational values to those who advocate the neoliberal ideology of 'anything goes', where any one or any group can establish their own school in their own private interest. A summary comparison of democratic and neoliberal trend values is shown in Table 3.2. Of course, it is correct that large systems create large bureaucracies that can take on a life of their own, but this is a matter of the appropriate profession and of communities being active and keeping bureaucracy in check, rather than denying altogether the necessary support that bureaucracies should provide. We need to be reminded that, under the British Westminster system of government adopted by many countries, there is the principle of ministerial responsibility for policy supported by the public service for without fear or favour advice and operational detail. Under this system, the bureaucracy does not have a policy function and cannot direct practitioners such as schools.

It is unfortunate that this principle has weakened of late under governments of all persuasions and its strengthening has not been vigorously supported by the profession or bureaucrats themselves. The values shown in Table 3.2 need to be able to take into account the changing and complicated nature of society and ensure that social diversity as indicated by class, race, gender, ethnicity, disability and geography can be accommodated. Not only do these values find expression

Table 3.2 Comparison of selected democratic, neoliberal values

	Democratic values (trends)	Neoliberal values (trends)
Nation state	Public philosophies, diversity, individual responsibilities, rule of law, regulated markets and fair trade	Private property rights, individual freedoms, rule of law, free markets and trade
Liberty	Collective and personal freedoms within legal guidelines	Unrestricted individual and economic freedoms within legal guidelines
Equality	Personal, social and legal	Influenced by market and status
Governance	Democratic, participatory, collective	Minimised, influenced by and enabling of market forces
Justice	Equal before the law	Rule of law, influenced by and enabling of market forces
Citizenship	Democratic, participatory, public good	Market-oriented, competitive, individual good
Family	Community network	Basic social unit
Religion	Unrestricted, separation of church and state	Unrestricted, separation of church and state
Education	Public, democratic, humanity	Private, commodity, individual

in society, they are also encountered and evaluated by citizens in their daily lives, being accepted, redrafted or rejected as experience and reflection dictate. Given that public schools have open, inclusive doors, they must establish agreed frameworks that enable the values of their communities to be respected, while at the same time ensuring that generally endorsed principles and procedures are maintained. A democratic approach allows this requirement to be met. Neoliberal schooling also has a loose framework of values to support its political intent, but this can be unencumbered by any notion of diverse, collective democratic life.

Questions of diversity in society raise issues of multiculturalism and the movement of large numbers of people around the world, particularly in response to the ravages of war and oppression. As the composition of societies has altered due to globalisation, immigration and refugees, it is inevitable that, apart from the benefits such movement brings, social tensions, including racism, will also continue to exist and ultimately, find their way into schools. For most teachers, the multicultural classroom is to be welcomed because of the new cultures, languages, ideas and histories that enrich relationships between children, enabling different perspectives to be brought to bear on different subjects. However this is not an easy task for the teacher, demanding a broad and compassionate cultural background and access to resources. Steinberg and Kincheloe (2009, pp. 3–5) contend that 'There isn't one paradigm, nor one taxonomy, nor one way of diversifying and multiculturalising citizens and school curricula'. They go on to detail five positions regarding multicultural education and pedagogy:

1   conservative diversity practice and multiculturalism or monoculturalism
2   liberal diversity practice and multiculturalism

3   pluralist diversity practice and multiculturalism
4   left-essentialist diversity practice and multiculturalism
5   critical diversity and multiculturalism.

This arrangement shows the difference between a useful, but perhaps superficial, approach to multiculturalism that may focus on issues such as clothing and food, to a pluralist approach sharing value positions and the study of different groups in the curriculum, to a critical analysis that raises issues of politics, power, exploitation and domination. Steinberg and Kincheloe point out that conservative multiculturalists usually do not look for connections between culture, economics and education and often see 'unattached individuals' remote from the complex networks of influence that envelop them. This analysis directs its attention to individual characteristics rather than the social conditions that prevail, similar to an emphasis on the psychology of deficient children and not on an unequal society of prejudice which families and children have to confront.

Associated with the concept of multicultural education, Kincheloe (2009) discusses urban education in the United States from the perspective of inclusion. He notes that urban education came to prominence during the civil rights movement of the 1960s and the desegregation of schooling in the United States, but that many problems continue to plague the field. In attempting to move away from a 'one size fits all' approach, Kincheloe cites his own collaborative work in relation to what he terms *metropedagogy,* that is, pedagogy described as maintaining a 'rigorous and contextually specific professional education for teachers and administrators who operate in urban settings' (p. 380). He notes that critical pedagogy understands that 'every aspect of schooling and every form of educational practice are politically contested spaces'. In highlighting the specific problems of urban education, Kincheloe's insightful 'metropedagogy' brings together the combined thinking of critical theory and multiculturalism so that the culture, language and community of large cities can inform the curriculum, teaching and learning of their schools. Multiculturalism is a permanent reality in most countries, providing difficult situations and exciting opportunities for more progressive approaches to inclusive and democratic schooling to be implemented for all children.

In a powerful reaffirmation of democracy as the way forward against the ideological and practical pillage of neoliberalism, McLaren and Jaramillo (2007, p. 111) argue:

> Today, it is urgent that we develop a coherent philosophy of praxis, but equally important must be our determination to live in our daily lives, our dialectical self-reflexivity, as we navigate the perils of everyday existence and enact a politics of refusal and transformation.

This is a call to arms, whereby ordinary people are able to make the abstract concrete, are more than capable of analysing the connections between issues and undertake a program of activism in pursuit of the historic civil society. For education, such a philosophy can be lived in relation to the provision of democratic public schooling for all students and for the continuing construction of high-quality comprehensive schooling appropriate to particular circumstances. The notion of a 'coherent philosophy of praxis' also draws attention to and in the main the lack of any progressive philosophy developed by the education profession and a philosophy that has an epistemological compass of ethical practice for the public good. Compelling words such as these need to be put into effect in ordinary classrooms around the nation/s and some examples will be suggested in later chapters. A final consideration of schooling for the majority regarding political intent now needs to be given to the comparative tables above of democratic and neoliberal characteristics and values.

Sorting through a 'left' view of schooling

In political terms, the notions of 'left' and 'right' have become more than a little confused as the influence of neoliberalism has overwhelmed political debate. Strictly speaking, they refer to the relationship adopted between the economic system and particular societies, groups and individuals, with 'left' referring to socialist and collective practices and 'right' referring to capitalist and individual practices. In those countries where there is broad acceptance of the prevailing economic system, 'left' is taken to mean those practices that constitute major change and trend towards more community-based approaches, compared with 'right' practices that minimise change and trend towards more individual approaches. Other words commonly used to signify these movements involve 'progressive, radical' and 'conservative, traditional' respectively. The word 'liberal' is usually defined in terms of a strong preference for individual rights and actions, to the extent that 'anything goes' unfettered by government and regulation (provided that regulation supports market operation). It is generally the case that neoliberal economies are 'centre right' or 'right', although they often remain under strong community expectation that adequate resources will be provided for public amenities such as health, education and transport and to support employment opportunities in both public and private sectors. Neoliberal advocates are irritated by the proportion of national budgets that are allocated to public undertakings and generally support low-taxation regimes and small public financial borrowings. At the same time, and in obvious contradiction to the principle of minimum interference in the market, they arrange budget, taxation and financial matters for private and minority interest. Political and economic practices such as these are the context within which education for the majority needs to be developed in every country.

A left view of education seeks maximum change to benefit all children and their families regardless of socio-cultural circumstance. It is cultivated within the general economic and political framework of the day and will alter as conditions alter. As noted above, other political persuasions are also interested in change to a greater or lesser extent, but usually for specific interest groups. Often this is a backwards-looking rather than a forwards-moving shift. Above all, the left is interested in this question, of how to encourage action and reconstruction, to act on the world in order to change it for the better. By so doing, activists learn from uncertainty and risk about what is possible in spite of what they are told. Many techniques are used to restrict the scope of people's action, ranging from minor regulation and legality to brute force of the (secret) police and military.

Ultimately the educational left attempts to overthrow reactionary schooling and curriculum and strives to create the new vision in practice rather than merely describe it. The nature of educational proposals for a left change must be thoughtful, realistic and clearly defined. Proposals and programs can be elaborated around principles that outline the purpose of education and its public character, procedures for supporting educational democracy, how equity is to be achieved, approaches to knowledge and pedagogy, the role of the profession and the values that underpin public systems of schooling.

For the general citizenry rather than the neoliberal, education serves the people. Primary and secondary schooling exists to enable young people of all backgrounds to explore their interests and surrounds to the maximum extent. Bowles and Gintis (1976, p. 104) puncture this aspiration in a manner that remains exact today when they note that 'Throughout history, patterns of privilege have been justified by elaborate facades'. Continuing, they write:

> Dominant classes seeking a stable social order have consistently nurtured and underwritten these ideological facades and, insofar as their power permitted, blocked the emergence of alternatives. This is what we mean by 'legitimation': the fostering of a generalised consciousness among individuals which prevents the formation of the social bonds and critical understanding whereby existing social conditions might be transformed.

Again, the continuity of practice and theorising is imperative, essential for the 'legitimation' of what is, but also necessary for what can be imagined and transformed. To be human cannot be denied, to learn and to err not within narrow confines artificially set by false authority, but to jump outside the boundaries regardless of the unknown. Education and schooling that establish an active, fearless and knowledgeable citizenry of this type contribute to a new humanity. Clearly, the left supports a public view of education where the state must not discriminate towards the wealthy, the privileged and the private, but act for the benefit of everyone. Schooling is a public good that enables the full participation of all children and their families on serious issues of knowledge and investigation. Public schools are secular and do not indoctrinate or demand adherence to particular ideological views but open up important ideas for experiment. Based on this standpoint, the public school is one of the most significant democratic institutions in society, a place where all families (many coming from oppressive circumstances) have the right to experience democratic participation and respect every day, including freedom of association and speech. Obviously, there are major contradictions when the school is located within a non-democratic social context. This means that left proposals are always needed to expand the range of democratic opportunity for teachers, students and parents alike.

Of central importance to the vitality and energy of a democratic public system of education is a dynamic profession (see Chapter 11). It is the education profession that implements the principles being discussed here every day, taking into account the complicated conditions that apply. The educational left is therefore very supportive of a strong, autonomous profession that seeks to act on the status quo and create better learning environments for all students and teachers.

Finally, the above discussion and tables articulate a set of left values that frame the development of schooling for the majority. These values constitute schooling that is secular, public and democratic, that establishes procedures for equitable access and quality outcomes, that enables learning to proceed through inquiry where practice and theory are combined and where knowledge and views are not imposed. They are progressive values that recognise the autonomous profession as the major agent of change and improvement. It would be going too far to suggest that these values have directed education over the years, but it is accurate to point out that they have been present in educational debates for a very long time. The role of the teacher and the place of the child in learning have been constantly argued and there is enormous conflict between differing views of knowledge, learning and assessment. More conservative approaches that encourage passivity over activity and transmission of knowledge rather than its construction are really debates about power and economics rather than a deep participation of all citizens in the progressive development of knowing.

Like every other social grand narrative, education is still working itself out. Around the world, the narrative involves very heavy conservative criticism of every mildly progressive practice that committed educators have debated and established. In turning a negative into a positive, however, uninformed ideological attacks that do not align themselves with the general interest can provide fruitful opportunity for a reconsideration of what is the essence of a left program for education and a redetermination to pursue it, vigorously.

Neoliberalism has been most successful in promoting its own practices, to the extent that many groupings such as democratic political parties, trade unions, professional organisations and individual critics have found it extremely difficult to be heard; hope for a brighter egalitarian future that flourished following World War II, for example, has been replaced by anguish and despair in many cases. One result of this process has been the lack of articulated political alternatives, including the efforts of countries other than our own that are not available to provide the language, practices, theorising and literature to support left movements elsewhere. McLaren and Jaramillo (2007, p. 55) lay down the challenge for left educators to push as hard as possible for the long-term task of 'dialectical praxis' such that it does not refer merely to 'pernicious trinkets of philosophical verbiage, but is grounded in materialist dialectics. It refers to action in and on the world'. However, in attempting to build immediate programs and systems of schooling that are democratic, public and secular, the educational left acts in the interests of all children, regardless of socio-economic and cultural background. No other political grouping has this noble historic purpose. While it has been very difficult to implement a left-oriented curriculum so far with many twists and turns, it is undoubtedly true that the next century will see progress in this direction, rather than the neoliberal and conservative. Democratic and activist educators committed to a democratic civil society will see to that.

4 Social justice, culture and knowledge

> Listen to the stories of the land
> crafted by endless restless tides
> suggesting what might endure
> against the convulsions of change
> yet seeds germinate in sunburnt soil
> and resonate with the fall of rain.

Attempting to correlate home background with schooling outcomes predominantly measured by high-stakes testing continues to raise many speculative and shadowy sociological issues around the world, such as the effect of family income and schooling histories, the nature of family and community culture, support for schooling by the family and the capabilities of the child, particularly in relation to abstract knowledge. Similar difficulties of interpretation are faced when locating the sociology of education within a social justice framework. If social justice can be defined in general terms as 'all members of society having equal access to the public opportunities, procedures and resources of that society for democratic purpose, alleviating inequality and sharing in support for the public good', then educational social justice needs to ensure access to epistemological resources that will utilise the sociological issues above for affirmative learning purposes. In this sense, educational social justice has moved past mere access (including funding) to the notion of suitable progress in learning for all children. Social justice does not usually imply equal outcomes for everyone given that all people are different and will engage understanding in different ways. All candidates may pass a particular examination, such as obtaining a motor car licence, but each person will have achieved differently. Based on the discussion of previous chapters, it is now possible to give greater detail to the sociology–epistemology interface (see Figure 0.1 in the Preface) through the identification of a series of major epistemological practices that embrace all children and are ubiquitous at school, home and community. It is this network of interface practices (Figure 0.2) that will give necessary definition and structure to the 'speculation and shadow' noted above.

As an opponent of neoliberalism and conservatism, Paulo Freire respected the history and culture of local communities and their right to act on the world in order to know and change it. His theories and experience in working in Brazil and many other countries with literacy and educational issues generally provide guidance in approaching participation with the network of interface practices and a close connection with the 'action' trajectory of the other major theorists already mentioned. Freire's colleague McLaren (1999, p. 51) outlined a summary of Freire's work to assist teachers in developing appropriate pedagogy:

- The world must be approached as an object to be understood and known by the efforts of learners themselves.
- The historical and cultural world must be approached as a created, transformable reality.
- Learners must learn how to actively make connections between their own lived conditions and the making of reality.
- Learners must consider the possibility for 'new makings' of reality, the new possibilites for *being* that emerge from new makings.
- Learners, in the literacy phase, come to see the importance of print and will actually *experience* their own potency in the very act of understanding what it means to be a human subject.
- Learners must come to understand how the myths of dominant discourses are precisely myths which oppress and marginalise them, but which can be transcended through transformative action.

Freire's concept of 'conscientisation' (Freire, 1972a, p. 51) is a way of thinking about McLaren's summary, that is, a process whereby humans 'as knowing subjects achieve a deepening awareness of the socio-cultural reality which shapes their lives and of their capacity to transform that reality'. A key strategy for moving towards critical awareness or critical consciousness is respectful dialogue amongst participants as they set about changing their social conditions for the community good. He comments that 'Dialogical relations – indispensable to the capacity of cognitive actors to co-operate in perceiving the same cognisable object – are otherwise impossible' (Freire, 1972b, p. 53), as an epistemological insight of sociology. This approach was no doubt influenced by Freire's experience of the 1964 military coup in Brazil and his observation that many colonised and other Latin American countries were 'closed societies' operating under a 'culture of silence' (Freire, 1972a, p. 61). He developed a 'humanising' approach to existence, education and pedagogy involving 'the process of becoming more fully human as social, historical, thinking, communicating, transformative, creative persons who participate in and with the world' (Salazar, 2013, p. 126). Freire's emphasis on the capacity of ordinary people to take action in support of humanisation and their social aspiration also characterised his approach towards education, teaching and learning, to the extent that:

> In the midst of reflective action on the world to be transformed, the people come to recognise that the world is indeed being transformed. The world in transformation is the mediator of the dialogue between the people, at one pole of the act of knowing and the revolutionary leadership, at the other. If objective conditions do not always permit this dialogue, its existence can be verified by the witness of the leadership.
>
> (Freire, 1972a, p. 74)

While acting on and changing the world is not always possible, or possible completely or immediately, Freire is suggesting here that what can be done should be done and that there is a responsibility for the more experienced to explain and 'witness' action as it proceeds, even if only minimal steps are viable. Teachers and parents have a serious obligation in this regard as children undertake playful intellectual excursions and experiment and encounter problems or frustrating outcomes. Fischman and McLaren (2005, p. 441) point out that, under pressure of social oppression of various types, critical consciousness must not only be aware of the conditions that prevail, but also express and act upon an 'unwavering commitment to the struggle against injustice' at all times. This indicates that, as citizens generally and teachers and students specifically attempt to pose and solve problems, they do so in the knowledge that their intellectual stance and worldview will in some way impact on friends and colleagues everywhere and, if conducted fairly, will contribute to historical well-being and integrity.

Freire's advice for progressive educators can therefore assist investigation and theorising of the interface practices of sociology and epistemology by ensuring that 'efforts are patiently directed at creating counter-hegemonic sites of political struggle, radically alternative epistemological frameworks and adversarial interpretation and cultural practices, as well as advocacy domains for disenfranchised groups' (McLaren, 1999, p. 54). Serial practices of praxis, dialogue and critical consciousness need to be integrated across cultural and knowledge formation as the personal and community construction of reality continues.

Nominating a network of interface practices (or accepting the concept in a broad sense) is only the starting point of auspicious learning, although adults and children alike constantly engage such processes every day, a natural process without instruction. Each practice is a complicated arrangement in its own right and does not exist independently, but only in relation to all other practices. For example, language is not isolated in Figure 1.1, but has been previously discussed as an internal good of all practices. The epistemological question here is whether practices have layers or hierarchies of properties that can be considered separately as existing across diverse practices, similar to electrons shared across a molecular structure, for example, or whether each practice and property is unique. For the purposes of educational analysis, it is possible to consider different practices as discrete entities and how they are constructed and operate, but ultimately, the human organism acts in a holistic manner, with all practices taken in relation to all other practices, at once. The spark plugs of a motor car engine have their own properties, but they act in concert with all other engine parts as a coherent whole. At any one time, one or a number of the interface practices or aspects of practice may be taking a leading role in an activity, while other practices or aspects become more ascendant at another time. At the precise moment that gears are changed, the practice of engine becomes dominated by this aspect, while a split second later, the aspect of cylinder becomes dominant. In an analogous way, a child involved in the practice of language may be contemplating the idea of 'wheel' and 'circle' through discussion with a teacher, then through looking at diagrams from a book, then checking a thought from the Internet, then sketching and labelling her own diagram and then experimenting on her ride home after school. Her conclusion is that she 'knows' wheel. How the relationship between all aspects of practice and between different practices occurs is not known, except that it is necessary and, if not allowed, restricts learning enormously. Forming strong epistemological relationships between home and school knowledge is necessary for the strengthening of current knowledge and the construction of new knowledge.

Connecting with funds of knowledge

Schools located in working-class and lower-income communities have an extremely complicated task in connecting the valued knowledge of the mainstream curriculum with the life experience of children and families. Delpit (2006) describes this sort of work as 'cultural brokerage', presupposing that teachers need detailed understanding of local communities and can then build cognitive bridges between the areas of interest of school, home and child. She sees it as something that does not happen automatically but needs to be learned: 'Teachers really are cultural brokers who have the opportunity to connect the familiar to the unknown. We teachers have to work at learning to do that' (Delpit, 2006, p. 226). Studies of 'school effect' (Marks, 2010) attempt to isolate such factors and determine which are more influential. In many respects however this is a false division, as very few teachers work in an intellectual vacuum where connections with what the child is assumed to know are not made with what the school wants the child to know. In their discussion on the meaning of culture, Gonzalez *et al.* (2009) note the various approaches and definitions that have emerged over the years, including culture 'as a holistic configuration of traits and values that shaped members into viewing the world in a particular way' (p. 34). The authors comment on the notion of 'cultural hybridity', where all citizens draw upon an 'intercultural and hybrid knowledge base' (p. 38) as the all-embracing processes of globalisation continue. If this viewpoint offers a useful frame of analysis, then the role of the teacher in navigating and brokering cultural values and practices is exceedingly complex.

In charting problems that impact on unequal schooling outcomes, Darling-Hammond (2010, p. 31) writes that the United States 'has the highest poverty rates for children among industrialised nations' and that, amidst great wealth, social supports and resources are also lacking. According to Darling-Hammond, poverty rates for children in 2007 were 23 per cent in the United States, an increase from 17 per cent in the 1970s. She identifies five factors that need to be acted upon to correct this situation (p. 30):

1   the high level of poverty and the low levels of social supports for low-income children's health and welfare, including their early learning opportunities
2   the unequal allocation of school resources

3   inadequate systems for providing high-quality teachers and teaching
4   rationing of high-quality curriculum through tracking and interschool disparities
5   factory-model school designs that have created dysfunctional learning environments and unsupportive settings for strong teaching.

These factors exist to varying extents in most countries, although figures for the United States are considerably higher than the estimate of 10 per cent of people living in poverty in some countries, mentioned earlier in this book, and a consequently broad and diverse 80 per cent of students in the middle band of income attending schools. High levels of poverty and very low income make participation in all aspects of social life difficult and provide ready-made areas of excuse and criticism. Darling-Hammond (p. 30) comments that 'everyday people, pundits and policy makers often implicitly or explicitly blame children and their families for lack of effort, poor child rearing, a "culture of poverty", or inadequate genes'.

From a learning or epistemological perspective, the five factors of reform noted by Darling-Hammond in response to poverty and institutionalised disadvantage generally can be activated through an emphasis in all classrooms on the network of interface practices shown above. For schools with a proportion of low-income families, this will mean an understanding of the cultural and community life of these families so that connections can be made between knowledge from home and knowledge from school. This process needs to proceed not on the basis of assumptions about working-class life by middleclass policy makers and teachers, but from ongoing investigations of home life and the diversity of culture that exists in communities. As noted by Delpit and also Moll *et al.* (2009, p. 85), identifying the 'funds of knowledge' capacities of ordinary people raises the complicated and non-judgemental issue of how schools value and incorporate culture in its broadest sense:

> Although the term 'funds of knowledge' is not meant to replace the anthropological concept of culture, it is more precise for our purposes because of its emphasis on strategic knowledge and related activities essential to households' functioning, development and well-being. It is specific funds of knowledge pertaining to the social, economic and productive activities of people in a local region, not 'culture' in its broadest anthropological sense, that we seek to incorporate strategically into classrooms.

The sorts of insights into human experience offered, for example, by Darwin, Shakespeare, Einstein and Twain should be accessible to all, regardless of social class, race, gender or parental income. Grappling with the complexities of our common culture is one of the main aspects of schooling. The role of the school is to deal with issues that are central to our culture. Various attempts have been made throughout the twentieth century to resolve the issue of how schools can comprehensively and inclusively interact with culture, such as the development of vocationally oriented technical schools, mentioned earlier. The issues raised by Darling-Hammond suggest that new models, pedagogies and structures are required to enable all children to access the valued aspects of schooling. In connecting culture and education for working-class and lower-economic families and communities, the 'funds of knowledge' approach investigated by Gonzalez and others (2009) attempts to honour the economic, productive and social capacities of local communities and to connect with a broad and accurate view of culture rather than rely on stereotypes and assumptions. For example, if we consider the extensive problem-solving capacities of citizens in their working and daily lives, then we might expect to note a similar rather than contradictory approach to teaching in all classrooms. If we consider a direct approach to practical situations and explanations in terms of interactions, language and communication, we might expect to see a similar rather than contradictory approach to teaching in all classrooms. The issue here is how to take the privileged knowledge that schools and society value and which all working-class families should expect to encounter in public schools and connect meaning and understanding with the 'funds of knowledge' that communities embody. In this way, working-class culture, knowledge and economics are not seen as a deficit or barrier to school learning, but the broad, dynamic experiential base on which reflection takes place and from which new and transforming ideas are composed.

Rodriguez (2013) provides an extensive review of the pedagogical dimensions of the funds of knowledge framework. She describes three themes that emerge regarding the application of funds of knowledge in classrooms (p. 95):

1   engaging students in the co-construction of knowledge to deepen or extend academic knowledge
2   recognising and encouraging the application of multiple funds of knowledge among students
3   moving beyond solely connections between student/family/community, academic knowledge and funds of knowledge to teachers and students acting beyond the classroom.

While such efforts should not be exaggerated, these movements are most significant in dealing with educational issues of inclusion and equity. First, they are epistemological and pedagogical, rather than sociological, meaning that they focus on the 'action' of teachers and students in pursuing learning. Second, they are not content with current arrangements and understandings remaining as is, but seek to reach out beyond classrooms and structures that constrain learning, into the community, to work with new cultures and perspectives and how these might inform, or indeed change, school knowledge.

With a cautionary observation, Zipin (2009) alerts investigators to what he calls 'dark FoK [funds of knowledge]', or those difficult aspects of poverty and community life involving violence and racism that teachers generally tend to avoid except in perhaps more abstract ways. This is an important theoretical point for the funds of knowledge approach, or for any culturally inclusive orientation regarding the realistic possibility of including all aspects of local culture into a comprehensive school program without straying into areas that are very difficult for teachers and students to appreciate and understand – areas, perhaps from an ethical point of view, they should not include.

Rodriguez (2013) raises similar concerns when she discusses funds of knowledge discourses of power and agency in the relationships between school, communities, teachers and students and, despite the best of intentions, whether the school as a powerful social institution will continue to dominate. Teachers are always in this position when designing curriculum or selecting class materials and must use their professional judgement in evaluating their appropriateness and accuracy.

Bourdieu's epic study of poverty and the lives of ordinary people, outlined in *The Weight of the World* (Bourdieu et al., 2002), describes his method of 'reflexive sociology' and his attempts at coping with the power, culture and ideological differences that exist between researchers and participants, particularly in case study and interview situations. Bourdieu *et al.* (p. 613) point out that:

> researchers have some chance of being truly equal to their task only if they possess an extensive knowledge of the subject, sometimes acquired over a whole lifetime of research and also, more directly, through earlier interviews with the same respondent or with informants.

This is a serious challenge for the funds of knowledge school and teacher.

Two scoping cases are now presented to illustrate funds of knowledge in action. The cases are authentic and realistic rather than exemplary and draw upon the experience of Indigenous peoples in Australia and Gypsy/Roma peoples in the United Kingdom. More detailed curriculum projects will be discussed in Chapters 5–8. Case 2 offers a summary of practice and provides a set of draft principles for what the authors have called 'discursive learning', proposed as being culturally and epistemologically appropriate for the engagement of low-income, alienated and marginalised students with mainstream curriculum and for the reciprocal engagement of teachers and mainstream curriculum with different worldviews.

Funds of knowledge case 1: Worawa Aboriginal College, Australia (Hooley *et al.*, 2013)

Situated to the east of Melbourne on the former Coranderrk Aboriginal Station and near the township of Healesville in the tranquil Yarra Valley, Worawa Aboriginal College continues to honour the ideals of its founder, Aboriginal visionary Hyllus Maris. Speaking at the opening of the college in 1983, Hyllus said: 'In this, the first Aboriginal school in Victoria, the educational curriculum has been specially designed to suit Aboriginal students to bring them to their full potential. Aboriginal culture will be imparted not only as a school subject in each class's timetable but as an integral part of everyday life at the school'.

Worawa Aboriginal College is a boarding school for Aboriginal young women in the middle years of schooling who come from Aboriginal communities in urban, regional and remote locations across Australia. Worawa provides a holistic education through an integrated education, culture and well-being approach. Governed by Aboriginal people, the Worawa model of learning is grounded in Aboriginal values and ways of knowing, doing and being. The academic program is based on the policy entitled Victorian Educational Learning Standards that incorporates the new Australian Curriculum while retaining Victorian principles and approaches. The curriculum is delivered through a series of learning centres involving Aboriginal culture, health and sport, creative arts, languages, mathematics and science environment; the education program includes personalised learning plans, partnerships with other schools and organisations, vocational education experience, sport and physical fitness and health and well-being arrangements. The beautiful rolling hills and country setting of the college include the world-renowned Healesville Sanctuary and provide wonderful opportunities for students to interact with and contemplate their relationship with the natural environment.

The College offers a themed approach with realistic pathways to continued education or the world of work. Environmental management through a state-of-the-art horticulture centre provides the opportunity for students to develop knowledge and skills in Indigenous plant use and extends to special projects such as maintaining a koala feed plantation for the Healesville Sanctuary. A strong relationship with the nearby world-renowned Healesville Sanctuary enables students to gain work experience in wild-life care and management and interpretation. A feature of life at Worawa that brings together Aboriginal and non-Aboriginal learning is the exquisite art work created by students. Reflecting stories of community, family and land, the designs of wonderfully expressive paintings are now incorporated into fabric patterns and are displayed alongside original costume jewellery.

The College has a very modern creative arts centre for the visual and performing arts as well as its own art gallery which holds exhibitions that are open to the public. The gallery displays high-quality student art as well as art from the students' home communities and demonstrates the holistic and creative nature of learning for all to see.

Through partnerships with the Wilin Centre for Indigenous Art and Culture at the Victorian College for the Arts, Ilbijerri Indigenous Theatre and Malthouse Theatre and partner schools, Worawa is expanding the reach of its arts program to encompass the performing arts. Aboriginal languages are seen as a focal point and the College will introduce skills development in media through family oral history collection.

Funds of knowledge case 2: Learning within networks of culture and knowledge, UK/Australia (Levinson and Hooley, 2012)

It is now possible to denote a number of strategies to transform schooling to better meet the learning needs of diverse groups of students. Parallels between the two communities with which we work suggest they cannot be treated as isolated phenomena or idiosyncratic problems emanating from the groups themselves. We have previously put forward two broad statements to guide further investigation of these issues:

> Policy: Formal education for nomadic and Indigenous children must respect, include and build upon the culture, history and language of communities and ensure that such culture links with the major ideas of school knowledge.

> Practice: Formal education for nomadic and Indigenous children must ensure that the organisation of teaching and learning enables immersion in practices of learning that are congruent with community perspectives and ways of knowing.

Similar statements are found in various policy documents throughout the world, although a distinguishing feature of the above is their explicitly epistemological intent. What this means is that specific aspects of 'culture, history and language' need to be arranged such that connections can be made with particular knowledge of the regular curriculum. Following that, specific and detailed 'practices of learning' need to link closely with 'community perspectives and ways of knowing'. It seems unlikely that this will be facilitated through the rigid predetermined curriculum and conservative pedagogy of formal, school-based education, but rather open and discursive arrangements that encourage student action, experimentation and intellectual risk.

The notion of a discursive environment for teaching and learning invokes an atmosphere of respect, recognition and reciprocity where participants communicate, question and encourage each other on significant issues. This dialogue will take place within and be mediated by the political climate experienced by schools and communities. Such an approach challenges the normal operation of many schools and classrooms and in particular, the approach adopted towards particular curriculum areas. For example, the incorporation of 'nomadism' as a principle of learning will clash with the idea of 'sedentarisation' characteristic of many classrooms.

Adopting the epistemological stance of the marginalised means that subject content and teaching techniques must change, a recognition that attempts at educational inclusion are likely to fail in the context of known and continued educational exclusion. We now propose in Table 4.1 a series of principles and broad curriculum features to establish a discursive framework of learning for disenfranchised groups.

(Continued)

Table 4.1 Principles of discursive learning

Principle	Curriculum features
Learning requires respect for and recognition of different worldviews of knowledge and learning	Philosophical investigation of knowledge, values, beliefs, viewpoints
Learning connects with the local and general physical and social environment	Country, geography, sacred sites, philosophy, customs
Learning integrates local and general knowledge	Community and family events, oral and written history, stories, artefacts
Learning arises primarily from holistic knowledge, inquiry processes and language practices	Projects, themes, learning circles, celebrations, communication
Learning respects community interest, knowledge and experience	Community and family curriculum decision making, history, events, stories, ideas, interpretations
Learning involves community members and Elders	Narratives and accounts, community visits, guest speakers, revered knowledge and wisdom
Learning occurs within community structures and protocols	Ways of knowing, community codes, ceremonies, conventions, extended time
Learning intensifies when 'community friends' assist knowledge production	Background and cross-cultural knowledge, advice, formal experience
Learning requires appropriate support structures	Community tutors, discussion sessions, meeting places, parent rooms, outreach scaffolding
Learning involves local and general protocols of monitoring, appraisal and consensus	Oral and written descriptions of learning in relation to local and general knowledge over extended time with community involvement

Like all principles, those of discursivity outlined in Table 4.1 will need to be adapted for use across all subjects of the school curriculum. We can imagine them guiding the teaching of mathematics at Year 9, or literature in Year 5.

In total, they emphasise an approach towards learning that privilege culture, community and country and integrate language and history throughout. This will lead to marked changes in curriculum design with a much greater emphasis on negotiated project work and student investigation than specified 'textbook' knowledge. Debate on the nature and positioning of literacy and numeracy will continue, with the line being drawn between integrated or separated knowledge and between inquiry or transmitted knowledge. Rather than envisaging schools as places for the reproduction of subject content and social values, the discursive classroom is seen as supporting philosophical investigations into knowledge and social practices so that children can construct their own views and understandings over extended periods of time. It is surely not a radical proposal to suggest that knowledge should emerge from an active integration of local and global concerns, beginning with the community and culture of the local and broadening to the global in cycles of experience. This approach has been described as 'two-way inquiry learning' (Hooley, 2009) and in similar vein, learning at the 'cultural interface' (Nakata, 2007), where different cultures are respected rather than denied and new understandings are created.

Culture as lived

Because of different life experiences, different groups will have different views of culture, the Indigenous view being different from the non-Indigenous, the Gypsy/Roma view different from the non-Gypsy/Roma, the working-class view different from the bourgeois. In the United Kingdom and continental Europe, Gypsy/Roma peoples may speak of travelling and 'the road', whereas Indigenous Australian peoples may emphasise being as one with 'the land'. These are fundamentally different concepts that give rise to quite separate worldviews, including that of nomadism.

In Australia, the Indigenous academic Langton (2013), argues that the struggle of Indigenous peoples to leave the scourge of colonialism and racism behind as they engage modernity within the context of their heritage and cultural identity is creating a 'new generation of Aboriginal people' that is 'turning dreams into reality: education, economic participation, self-esteem and success are part of this new Aboriginal world and there is no turning back' (p. 149). Langton describes the broad process of many peoples as they are embroiled in social and economic change, but strive to maintain their communities, language and traditions at the same time. She cites the example of Indigenous peoples caring for the land, but deriving economic benefit from mining royalties as a major social, economic and cultural change that is occurring and one that requires judicious management from all concerned.

Indigenous peoples obtaining benefit from the harvesting of trees on their forested land is a similar example that confronts many environmentalists. Langton comments that the European cultural view of 'wilderness' is totally different to that of the Indigenous cultural view. Ideas and practices of culture can be associated directly with the economic system and forces of production, with the value systems of morality, law, science, aesthetics and critique, or be seen to arise from networks of knowledge subject to agreed validity claims. For those with substantial wealth, culture can be apparently disconnected from domination and production and take on characteristics of luxury and abstractness. Recognised literature regarding aggression, exploitation and poverty can be enjoyed for its form and content, rather than for its role in describing and recreating a more just reality. For the proletariat, that does not have such comfort, the key determinants of culture can be listed as:

- lack of ownership of the means of economic production
- survival depending on a capacity to work

- existence that is experiential, demanding a need to know and express meaning
- linking of daily activity with creative interpretation, knowing and doing
- sharing of knowledge and group interest through social practice, communication, artistic form and artefact
- sense of fair play and solidarity with others in a similar situation around the world
- personal and community consciousness that springs from connections with history and the social and physical worlds.

Writing during the burgeoning development of industry and science of the industrial revolution, Dewey needed to incorporate activities such as these into his theory of knowledge and learning. His notion of continuity and opposition to dualisms enabled him to conceptualise human inquiry as always integrated, with practice, thinking and reflection constantly informing each other. According to Hickman (2007, p. 117):

> Dewey argued that inquiry into materials such as was practiced by Galileo precedes and conditions inquiry of a more conceptual variety. It also informs its methodology and terminates its activity in further concrete application. This was perhaps Dewey's most important contribution to the debates concerning the relations between science and technology. Even though the craftsman who thinks in and with materials may not translate that thought into the conceptual sphere and conversely even those who think by means of conceptual tools are frequently unable to bring their work to fruition in practical terms, there is nevertheless no reason to posit a methodological gap between the two enterprises.

This insight is of enormous consequence for educators everywhere. It undermines the deficit assumptions regarding the capability of low-income and proletarian background, it provides the basis for respecting concrete and practical knowing and it suggests the active dialectical relationship between practice and reflection – without one there is no other.

Exactly how democratic situations of experience, continuity and inquiry are established in conservative organisations such as schools in all aspects of their curriculum remains extremely difficult, but it entails the central problem obscuring full inclusion. Hickman (2007, p. 127) quotes from an address given by Dewey on celebration of his 80th birthday, where he comments decisively that 'Democracy is the faith that the process of experience is more important than any special result obtained, so that special results achieved are of ultimate value only as they are used to enrich and order the ongoing process'. In the democratic classroom, students must be able to refer to their own culture as the internal basis of learning while external authority and procedure are the conditions of learning. Enabling this to occur when knowledge results are discontinuous and predetermined by the curriculum becomes almost impossible, especially when mediated by problems of inadequate diet, health and housing, making it difficult for many families and children to turn their minds to more creative educational activity. For example, the child of a train driver may be fascinated by steam engines, but these may not be a part of the school's regular science program because of resource issues, the teacher's lack of knowledge, or other distracting matters such as illness, hunger and home duties. On the other hand, a detailed exploration of the cultural background of students at a particular school may reveal a deep interest in mechanical devices, including steam engines, and perhaps the addition of excursions to a train museum for direct experience. In this way, a broad base of practical experience is built up from which conceptual links are made to language, expression and related ideas, the within-classroom, beyond-classroom funds of knowledge process noted by Rodriguez above.

Social justice and civil society

Poverty is a powerful word that invokes strong meaning and strong response. It relates to the resources, services and opportunities available to citizens with minimal amounts resulting in hunger, bad health, unemployment, inadequate housing and, generally, shame. The term is relative to the economic conditions of different countries, with the poverty level in some being considerably higher than subsistence levels in others. Poverty is often taken as a convenient, usually negative, way of describing the relationship between social classes, particularly when groups in adverse circumstances and low income are criticised for not making more progress, of not lifting themselves out of the mire. Most notably, in the more wealthy countries the bourgeois notion of individual 'prosperity' is emphasised rather than human 'satisfaction', urging citizens to evaluate their lives in personal economic terms and not ethical conduct for the public good. Public wealth through national budgets is therefore directed at supporting bourgeois interest with as little public interest allocation as possible.

Another indicator of the well-being of a country is that of inequality. Wilkinson and Pickett (2010, p. 25) suggest that, rather than absolute levels of wealth, better measures involve the comparative gap between rich and poor, with more unequal societies having higher levels of violence, illness, social dissatisfaction, mental depression and the like. In arguing that it is social positioning in society that is crucial, they state:

> The view that social problems are caused directly by poor *material* conditions such as bad housing, poor diet, lack of educational opportunities and so on, implies that richer developed societies would do better than the others. But this is a long way from the truth: some of the richest countries do worst (original emphasis).

Wilkinson and Pickett conclude that material inequality comes first, as some type of skeleton around which other factors such as class and culture are formed, factors involving identity, clothing, education. This is a difficult distinction to make as class and material very much depend on each other, over time, ideologically and practically. When the genuinely wealthy lose their paper money in the usual cycle of boom and bust, they are still considered to be of a certain class background and social standing, until such time as they recover their financial position. The poverty-stricken have nothing to lose and do not have access to social and cultural capitals for assistance. However those of modest means do have an extensive investment portfolio in human progress towards justice, integrity and solidarity.

Interestingly, in terms of education, Wilkinson and Pickett report more children having low aspiration for higher-ranked jobs in more equal countries (smaller gap between rich and poor) and higher aspiration in more unequal countries. This may be because, in more equal countries, lower-skilled occupations are held in higher esteem than in unequal countries where young people can be attracted to apparent status and celebrity. Again, aspiration is a difficult concept to interpret, as manual work, farm work, trades and manufacturing jobs all involve 'an honest day's pay for a honest day's work' and constitute essential labour in the service of the country. The high esteem in which fire fighters in the United States are held following 9/11 is evidence of this.

It is unclear within this context whether working-class people today see compulsory education as a means of social progress, especially in terms of employment opportunities, or whether they still regard schooling being mainly concerned with personal well-being and 'good' citizenship, as during the welfare state and social reconstruction period. Neoliberalism has certainly emphasised education as a competitive commodity that has market value and which can be exchanged for financial positioning.

Another way of viewing education as a commodity is as 'rite of passage'. This concept relates strongly to the 'interface of practices' discussed earlier, whereby teachers and students come together to investigate the difficult ideas of school knowledge from the perspective of their own understandings and culture. Drawing on the work of van Gennep and his own studies of ritual and symbol in tribal Africa, Turner (1967) described 'rites of passage' as 'liminal' in that they involved transition from one state of awareness to another (see Chapter 8 regarding Indigenous education). According to Turner, rites of passage are found in all societies in various ways, but most emphatically in 'small-scale, relatively stable and cyclical societies' (p. 93) where change is rhythmical and recurring. He outlined three distinct phases of liminality: those of separation, margin (limen) and aggregation. In the separation phase, there is detachment from previously held views and cultural positions; the liminal phase includes some uncertainty and ambiguity regarding both the past and future; and in the aggregation phase, certainty is restored, with new attitudes and practices of a new awareness attained.

In the broad sense, liminality does not only refer to individuals but can involve the changed states of groups, community or nation as socio-economic conditions change, in times of war, for example. Liminality is therefore a useful construct with which to consider the learning interface of practice between sociology and epistemology as it exists in schools and in all classrooms. Consider the biology classroom where the current ideas of students are challenged as they come into contact with new abstractions, symbols and words of taxonomy, confront the implications of evolution and enter the ambiguous world of new thinking. At some point, through reading, experiment and discussion, these new ideas begin to clarify and a state of new meaning is reached. A different explanation regarding the long neck of the giraffe finally makes sense, rather than the much-loved bedtime stories of childhood.

The process of liminality or rite of passage at the practice interface can be embarrassing and bewildering as ideas are formed and reformed, but it is this process of transition that befalls all humans in their never-ending quest for meaning. It seems however that there is little understanding of the actual liminal process of epistemological transition, with attention and examination being given to what is simplistic and visible, not the complicated and hidden that shape confounding alienation in schools.

A common thread that unites all education theorists who emphasise learning as progression, growth and action is that education can be the practice of freedom and democracy. This can be seen in purely political terms (often a conservative criticism), but it is an epistemological concept as well – freedom to think from and change experience, freedom to engage great ideas and knowledge, freedom to design new practices of humanity. Dewey's comment that 'education is not preparation for life, education *is* life' is closely associated with Freire's 'ontological argument that posited praxis as a central defining feature of human life and a necessary condition of freedom' (Glass, 2001, p. 16). In this way, Freire was defining a continuum of history and freedom that relies on the capacity of social conditions and social agents to establish cycles of ethically informed practice and theorising for the public good in all aspects of life. This is the struggle for humanisation mentioned earlier, essential for social justice and the formation of civil society. In civil society, there is respect between different groupings so that resource and cultural differences are minimised and there is realistic opportunity for different social positions to be adopted.

Civil society arranges itself so that citizens of all backgrounds can participate in decision making and that access to services is equitable at least to some extent. Habermas (1992) considered the 'public sphere' as a structure of current and civil society where, as a form of democratic association, citizens freely meet and discuss issues of community importance. Fora of this type are not part of the formal and legal discourses and decision-making processes of society, but are seen as existing between local and national organs of governance. Public spheres enable respectful, non-coercive discussions amongst the citizenry to inform decision making and do not proceed on the strategic and aggressive basis of points of view being won or lost. Habermas spoke of the European coffee houses of the 1600s being public sphere gathering places, whereas today candidates might include trade unions, schools and universities, neighbourhood organisations, environmental and feminist groups. This may contrast with the 'private sphere' discussions of the bourgeoisie, where major decisions are debated and made outside of official structures for implementation inside. Democratic movement towards features of civil society can occur within different economic and ideological systems, although the dominant will always find concessions difficult as they seek to maintain their privilege. The commodification of education under neoliberalism, and the correspondingly high level of resources being allocated to it in an internationally competitive environment, means that public education still has a crucial role to play in humanisation, democratisation and social justice for ordinary people around the world. This historic hope must now be located in progressive epistemology, critical thinking and transformative practice in every classroom.

Part II

Knowledge practices and testing

Investigating the interface between sociology and epistemology and connections between learning outcomes and family income must consider the knowledge paradigms used across the school curriculum. Given the importance placed on national and international mass testing regimes, it also follows that a lack of alignment between knowledge paradigm and assessment will produce highly distorted results and highly inaccurate evaluations of teaching and schooling systems. Chapters of Part II describe approaches to literacy and numeracy, mathematics and science and the humanities and arts, as well as a major area of educational difficulty and equity found around the world, Indigenous education. They explore approaches that respect the cultural backgrounds of families and attempt to connect family knowledge with school knowledge as the basis of theme and principle. Each chapter identifies a 'key idea' arising from the different areas of school curriculum under discussion to provide a practical example around which work at the 'practice interface' can proceed. Examples of 'integrated projects' are also included again as practical mechanisms of how connections can be made between epistemology and sociology. These chapters suggest that the lack of epistemological strategies based on sociological description has created serious estrangement from school knowledge for large numbers of students and that reconfiguration of the culture–knowledge relationship is urgently required.

5 Literacy, numeracy and test distortions

> In due course, we emerge into the lowlands
> expansive grasses replacing luxuriant foliage
> punctuated by the homesteads of settlement
> rusted machinery lying fallow and discarded
> causes pristine residues of nostalgia to linger
> suddenly the distant metropolis silhouetted
> where the problems of today force precedence.

Discussions of literacy – and, to a lesser extent, numeracy – are guaranteed to inflame the educational passions and predilections of commentators, parents, policy makers and teachers around the world. Most unfortunately, educational considerations of literacy have been transformed into the 'literacy wars' (Snyder, 2008), almost akin to military campaigns. There are three main reasons for this. First, as education has become increasingly politicised during the neoliberal years and accounts for a large proportion of national budgets, literacy has become an obvious target for ideological conflict. Different social and political perspectives have different understandings of the role of literacy in cultural formation and expression and place it at the centre of power and influence. Second, similar to eating and breathing, literacy is experienced by most people and is therefore open to comment and criticism from a personal standpoint. Everyone has a view based on how literacy was approached during their school days, plus their need to utilise literacy for enjoyment and work, home and community purposes. Third, the education profession is deeply divided on how best to pursue literacy in school, a debate that has continued for many years and is still some way from settlement. As the profession has become more established over the past century or so and has expanded its practice and literature base, some major developments regarding teaching and learning exhibit contrasting features that require ongoing investigation.

While numeracy is also considered as being significant for its cultural implications, it has not been subject to the same intense scrutiny and criticism as literacy. This may be due to the apparent grasp that mathematics has on the collective minds of commentators, parents, policy makers and teachers around the world regarding the nature of mathematics and how it is taught. In broad terms, mathematics is seen as a set of procedures that are true and that can be passed on to the next generation for acceptance and recall. This generates a conservative approach to teaching and learning of mathematics that, by definition, is difficult to be criticised by conservative ideology. Test results that indicate mediocre uptake by students are therefore explained by student deficits rather than weaknesses in curriculum and teaching (see Chapter 6). On this basis, literacy and numeracy constructs are of deep philosophical and political interest to most societies but are often considered from a superficial point of view.

Literacy can be thought about as a collection of rules that underpin reading. Writing is also a part of literacy but does not excite such passion, particularly as hand writing by children is usually of an acceptable level and the impact of the computer is raising a different set of issues for debate. On this model, the rules of literacy have been developed by adult scholars and experts over the centuries and need to be passed on to children as early as possible, at least as the very first instructional program children receive at school.

Learning to read is like building a brick wall: each rule or brick is put in place one at a time and, in due course, the wall will be completed and children can read. Here, literacy is really an enabling skill, whereby access to the accepted rules and conventions of grammar, phonics, codes and syntax will allow symbols to be understood and placed in the correct order. In this case, the word skill is usually thought of as a somewhat mechanical act that is part of a broader human activity; teachers often draw this distinction through the expression 'knowledge and skills', for example. There is skill involved in typing the word 'elephant', but conceptual acuity in writing 'The elephant has ears like big dinner plates'.

Conversely, literacy can be seen as a social practice where reading arises from experience in the same way as all other social practices (Gee, 2012). Evolution has produced a human disposition to language such that a combination of activity, experiment, speaking, communication, contestation and reading enables meaning to be explored and exchanged with others. This approach does not preclude experience of predetermined rules, but these are incorporated as necessary to meet the developing language of the child.

There are thus two concepts of literacy that propose two different philosophical understandings of knowledge and humanity. The philosophy of phonics views humans as learning under the tutelage of experts conveying ordained rules and knowledge, whereas the philosophy of social practice sees humans as learning from personal experience in community with others as they explore rules and knowledge. Exactly the same argument applies to numeracy. In this symbolic language, ideas are either presented for acceptance in a step-wise manner, or are investigated through personal experience with friends and colleagues. As is always the case, different epistemologies are being played out here regarding the nature of knowledge, the nature of being itself.

There is an important demarcation between literacy and numeracy on the one hand and the study of English (or language) and mathematics on the other.

English and mathematics are considered as broad areas of knowledge, or disciplines, that have their own principles, claims, procedures and processes of validation. In the school curriculum, disciplinary knowledge can often be called 'pure' or more abstract, while a more practical or restricted form of each can be called 'applied'. Literacy is not normally associated with so-called quality and recognised literature, but with reading brief newspaper articles, scanning documents for employment or at home from the bank, or obtaining tickets from the Internet for a sporting event. As has been seen previously, Dewey's continuity principle and his lack of support for non-dialectical dualisms make the distinction between pure and applied, or abstract and concrete, untenable, or, at least, unpromising in learning terms. The notion of merely applying a skill almost without thought or understanding is difficult to justify. That is, the musician merely places notes together and does not think of improvisation, the carpenter merely hammers in nails and does not think of supporting structures, the golfer merely strikes the ball and does not think of distance, force and curvature. Under this narrow outlook, literacy is therefore nothing more than a simplified or pared-down use of language that does not require a totality of knowledge as the President's comments are noted, or reports regarding a sick friend are contemplated. Similarly, numeracy is nothing more than a simplified or pared-down use of symbols that does not require a totality of knowledge as the erosion of a coastline is explained, or the costings of an extended trip are compared with family benefit.

This approach to literacy and numeracy may be inappropriate in heralding the aspiration that schooling can have lower-level literate and numerate outcomes for some, perhaps the majority, but higher-order language and mathematical outcomes for others, perhaps the minority. If such distinctions between knowledge and outcomes were abolished, the school curriculum could then be organised around a series of general studies that attempted to combine action and reflection, problem posing and problem solving and functional and creative activities that make the concepts of literacy and numeracy redundant. Thinking, acting, reflecting and exploring with language and mathematics should be available to all children without prejudice at all levels of schooling.

Theorising literacy: narrative, investigation and structure

Conceptualising literacy as a practice of knowledge at the practice interface of sociology and epistemology demands a radical overhaul of the place of literacy and language within the regular school curriculum. Situating literacy as a practice of knowledge eliminates the concept of literacy as lower-order activity and strengthens language as an integrated practice of learning. New models of language/literacy are required that more accurately reflect the changing nature of society and human activity, the philosophical character of language itself. They need to provide a balanced and coherent approach to language practice and theorising and be inclusive of the interests and backgrounds of diverse student

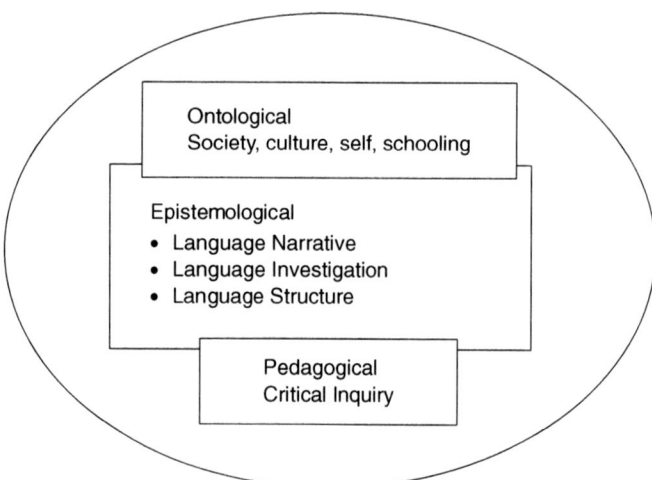

Figure 5.1 School language/literacy

populations. Any model of language/literacy needs to involve an explicit and defensible blend of ontological, epistemological and pedagogical concerns and an appropriate balance of the components of language knowledge. Specific aspects of language are not isolated but are seen as integrated into social and cultural life. A representation of one such model is indicated in Figure 5.1, necessitating a reconceptualisation of the current dominant language curriculum in schools into three major domains of language narrative, language investigation and language structure.

This is a comprehensive and integrated view of language and literacy that seeks to establish a social framework for learning, the compilation of life narratives (Goodson *et al.*, 2010) as the basis of identity and interest, the negotiation of challenging projects between teachers and learning circles of participants and connections with the recognised structure of language to inform, assist and extend personal and learning-circle projects. Learning will be scaffolded through critical inquiry, where learners consider the complexities of language, narrative and communication and the impact of cultural understandings and purposes.

As always, language, literacy and learning take place within an affluent environment of reading, writing and discussion, where the thoughts and experiences of others across space and time illuminate and challenge. As a central element of teaching and learning, the relationship between the known and unknown, the valued and emergent and the different specialisms of knowledge remain issues for ongoing debate within classrooms. The model in Figure 5.1 contends that language, literacy and communication exist everywhere, link with all knowing and are embraced by all children of whatever background. Isolating and disconnecting specific aspects severely distort this concept of humanity.

Freire's view of literacy as a proactive and cohesive act of 'reading the text and reading the context' and 'reading the world and unveiling the world' locates literacy in dialogue, community, experience and the social transformation of ideas and practices. His notion of literacy is embedded within his central concept of 'conscientisation' or the active development of community and personal critical consciousness to critique and change society. He placed importance on dialogue between participants, with the essence of dialogue being the word. Each word contains the two dimensions of action and reflection, or of usage and meaning, and to deny either destroys the praxis that exists between them. Freire (1972a, p. 29) argued that teachers and students need to have a relationship of 'authentic dialogue' and that:

> If learning to read and write is to constitute an act of knowing, the learners must assume from the beginning the role of creative subjects. It is not a matter of memorising and repeating given syllables, words and phrases, but rather of reflecting critically on the process of reading and writing itself and on the profound significance of language.

This stands in marked contrast to national reports on reading (Rowe, 2005; United States, 2008) that recommended a stronger emphasis on phonics. While children following an intensive, decoding-based program based on the principles of 'first, fast and only', for example, can do better on tests of decoding (pronouncing words out loud) when compared to students who had not received such instruction, they do not do better on measures of reading comprehension. Tests of comprehension show that the impact of intensive systematic phonics instruction is generally small and statistically insignificant. Claims to the contrary are often based on tests that require memory and recall. Language/literacy involves the capacity to understand, analyse, critically enact and respond and create spoken, written, and visual communications in different situations with different perspectives; it is not merely the accumulation of segregated skill. For example, when announcing their major concepts of 'new learning 'and 'multiliteracies', the New London Group (Kalantzis *et al.*, 1996) outlined their general approach in the following way:

> Our view of mind, society, and learning is based on the assumption that the human mind is embodied, situated and social. That is, human knowledge is initially developed not as 'general and abstract', but as embedded in social, cultural and material contexts. Further, human knowledge is initially developed as part and parcel of collaborative interactions with others of diverse skills, backgrounds and perspectives joined together in a particular epistemic community, that is, a community of learners engaged in common practices centred around a specific (historically and socially constituted) domain of knowledge. We believe that 'abstractions', 'generalities' and 'overt theories' come out of this initial ground and must always be returned to it or to a recontextualised version of it.

What is significant here is that the learning framework so described applies across the knowledge spectrum and not to one area alone. It applies to music, art, poetry, mathematics, language, science, history, basketball and the like. It provides an integrated and holistic view of knowledge, language and learning as a general guide to human epistemology and ontology. Attempting to straitjacket language and literacy with the one set of constraints denies their philosophical nature and the diverse ways that humans communicate and make meaning. Unfortunately, the public debate on reading has often focused on the structure of language to the exclusion of linguistic and cultural differences and communication patterns across national and international social groupings that involve the textual, visual, audio and spatial. The public debate confuses the specific aspects of language such as phonemic awareness, phonics and grammar with the necessary context within which language occurs and makes sense. Humans come to know through an active process of experience, thought and structure that is constantly considered and refined on the basis of outcomes as experience is acted upon and new experiences constructed.

Theorising numeracy: narrative, investigation and structure

Discussion of numeracy will follow a similar trajectory to that of literacy above, given that both are seen as important aspects of language and learning. Conceptualising numeracy as a practice of knowledge at the practice interface of sociology and epistemology demands a radical overhaul of the place of numeracy and mathematics within the regular school curriculum. Situating numeracy as a practice of knowledge eliminates the concept of numeracy as lower-order activity and strengthens mathematical language and thinking as an integrated practice of learning (NCTM, 2013). This approach will eliminate the conceptual distinction between pure and applied mathematics in schools, where different forms of mathematics are seen to be more suitable for different groups of students. A new integrated and holistic model of school mathematics is therefore required that more accurately reflects the philosophical nature of mathematics itself, provides a balanced and coherent approach to mathematical practice and theorising and which is inclusive of the interests and backgrounds of diverse student populations. The model needs to involve an explicit and defensible blend of ontological, epistemological and pedagogical concerns and an appropriate balance of component mathematical knowledge. A mathematics curriculum can be designed that contains both integrated and specific content knowledge (see below and Chapter 6). Figure 5.2 is a representation of one such model, necessitating a reconceptualisation of the current mathematics curriculum into three major domains of mathematical narrative, mathematical investigation and mathematical structure. Emphasis on the making of mathematical meaning will require a reduction in current subject content to provide time for experiment and projects.

In pursuing the epistemological similarity between literacy and numeracy, the notion of Freire above regarding dialogue and literacy can be adapted as:

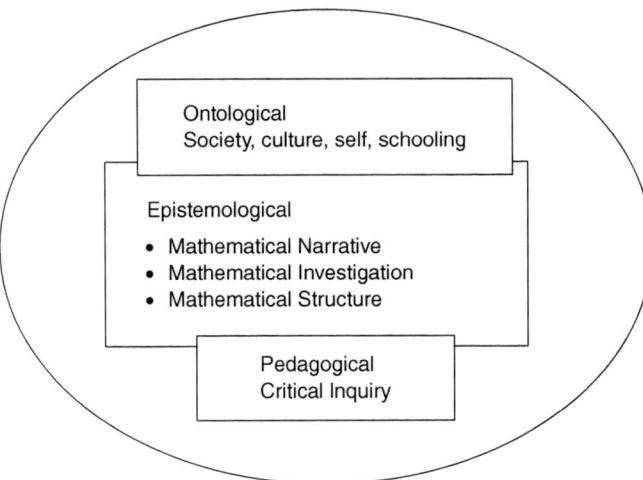

Figure 5.2 School mathematics/numeracy

If learning to think and act mathematically is to constitute an act of knowing, the learners must assume from the beginning the role of creative subjects. It is not a matter of memorising and repeating given formalisms, words and phrases, but rather of reflecting critically on the process of mathematics itself and on the profound significance of mathematical language.

It is for these reasons that Figure 5.2 emphasises mathematical narrative, investigation and structure as key epistemological practices. That is, children are encouraged to discuss, write about and depict the wide range of activities in their lives that involve mathematics (broadly defined), conduct various experiments and investigations regarding particular mathematical ideas and relate their understandings to more formal explanations (see Chapter 6). This type of mathematics then constitutes a philosophical investigation of the world (and therefore creation of childhood identity), strongly advocated by Seymour Papert (1980). Papert is commonly known as the father of educational computing and, after working with Piaget in the early 1960s, he developed the computer language Logo that enabled children to experiment with the key ideas of computer science. Papert's first, classical and inspirational book *Mindstorms* influenced a generation of teachers around the world as the new technologies began to flood into schools.

Like his mentor, Papert's concern has been about expression, not instruction. He described Logo, for example, as a *language for learning,* meaning that children can both learn the language of Logo and learn in a general sense through the language. He envisaged the computer environment as featuring *objects to think with* and worked with the Lego Company to design robotic projects now to be found in many schools.

With two doctorates in mathematics, Papert has attempted to find ways of combating the alienation of many children from this significant area of knowledge in schools. He noted that the word 'pedagogy' is used to indicate the art of teaching, but for children, there is no corresponding word to mean the art of learning, especially in a Piagetian sense. In order to fill this gap, he advocated the use of the word 'mathetics'.

Mathematics comes from a family of Greek words related to learning and means 'disposed to learning'. The word 'polymath', for example, does not mean someone who has studied many types of mathematics, but someone who has a broad knowledge across many domains. It is thought that mathematicians were so confident that their branch of knowledge was the true and absolute road to understanding that the word was appropriated and used worldwide. In attempting to create a new way of thinking and talking about mathematics in school, Papert (1992, p. 85) suggested the word 'heuristics' to support the 'sound and feel' of learning mathematically. Heuristics, or 'the art of intellectual discovery', would combat the problem that 'School gives more importance to knowledge about numbers and grammar than to knowledge about learning' and connects strongly with Dewey's inquiry and Freire's dialogue.

In addition to this notion of mathetics, Papert also wrote about the idea of intuition and the views of the French mathematician Henri Poincaré. The idea that mathematics develops intuitively is one of its great philosophical pillars. Poincaré, for example, would work through a problem and then put it aside so that the way forward would occur to him when he was not consciously thinking about its resolution.

Thinking intuitively in this way also raises the question of aesthetics (see Chapter 7). It has long been argued that mathematics exhibits inherent beauty, especially for those who are intimately concerned with its practice. There is a strong connection between beauty and truth, both of which can be considered absolute or human constructs, depending. Dewey considered aesthetics to be based on experience like all other learning and involved the coalescence of meaning and values drawn from both previous and current experience. This experience does not only relate to art but to the aesthetic quality of life generally. For Dewey, the distinction between high art for the elite and low art for the ordinary person is false and socially constructed (reflected in the notions of pure and applied forms of knowledge). These distinctions are important as they raise questions of form and content as well as creator and audience in all human activity. There needs to be engagement between all of these quantities if aesthetics is to signify the capacity of citizens to participate in all aspects of society, including knowledge. The participants need to be active, evaluate, discriminate, compare, critique and produce as independent social agents who are not to be dominated or duped. They can make their own thinking.

Key idea: assessment and testing

Assessment of student learning is one of the most contentious issues facing education at all levels and in all countries. It is a central aspect of the teacher's professionalism as a formal indicator of teaching and learning progress and of the teacher's status and authority in society. As mentioned previously, assessment has been commandeered by politicians as an instrument of their policy success and as a means of exerting pressure on schools to meet political ends. It is used by conservative and neoliberal critics to attack public education and to pursue a conservative ideological agenda. While there is a wide range of assessment techniques available, the preferred conservative and neoliberal approach is that of mass or population standardised testing that allows for simplistic measures to be taken. Measures of this type may have public appeal as they can be related to community experience such as surveys (How will you vote in the coming election? On a scale of 1–10, how would you rate your city council?), true/false telephone interviews (Do you have a large-screen TV at home? Are you interested in solar energy?) or previous school tests (spelling lists, punctuation exercises, plotting graphs). Rather than testing all members of a particular population, such as all Grade 4 students in a specified region, testing of a sample can be undertaken involving representative numbers of male/female, lower/higher income, public/private schools, city/country and the like. With any organisation of testing, there are issues of accuracy, reliability and validity that must be satisfied. That is, what assumptions are made regarding knowledge and learning, do the tests measure what we want to measure, can they be applied fairly and consistently across different groups and how accurate are the results? Testing, after all, is based on the dominant views of knowledge and learning.

Former President of the United States, George W Bush was well aware of the ideological significance of student assessment when he initiated the No Child Left Behind (NCLB) program very early in his presidency. In summary, NCLB involved an extensive system of state-based reading and mathematics testing of Grades 3–8 intended to show yearly progress until 2013–2014, when 'proficiency' of all students was to be reached. Schools that did not show adequate progress faced the possible prospects of students leaving to attend other schools, principal and staffing changes and a program of restructuring and conversion to a charter school. In her vigorous criticism of NCLB at her time of writing, Ravitch (2010, pp. 110–111) commented:

> NCLB was a punitive law based on erroneous assumptions about how to improve schools. It assumed that reporting test scores to the public would be an effective lever for school reform. It assumed that changes in governance would lead to school improvement. It assumed that shaming schools that were unable to lift test scores every year – and the people who work in them – would lead to higher scores. It assumed that low test scores are caused by lazy teachers and lazy principals, who need to be threatened with the loss of their jobs. Perhaps most naively, it assumed that higher test scores on standardised tests of basic skills are synonymous with good education.

This is a damning criticism of how testing can be used to manipulate schooling and the interpretation of learning in schools. Given that the NCLB legislation was supported by a large majority of all federal politicians in the United States, it was either seen as an important bipartisan plank of (neoliberal) nation building or, as Ravitch notes, it constituted a very 'naïve' view of schooling and the role of tests. It may have represented a heart-felt view that here was a chance to pursue knowledge, to act in the interests of all Americans, especially those who are falling behind at school.

If the triangle is an important piece of knowledge, then all children will have an inherent interest in it, regardless of economic standing. The esteemed American educator, Jerome Bruner (1979) agreed with this outlook in his famous statement that he could teach any intellectually defensible knowledge to any child at any time. Bruner did not mean that he could teach the intricacies of nuclear physics to a pre-schooler, but that he could begin the process of learning in a spiral manner, revisiting key ideas over time. He went on to say that there were two reasons for deciding what is worth knowing: whether it provides intellectual delight and whether it enables going beyond the information given. Learners will decide these questions for themselves, but teachers can provide an environment to optimise the process. In the case of the triangle, this will involve as much experience as possible with the triangle in natural and built settings and using the triangle for 'worthy' purposes.

Merely imposing predetermined views on children will not work. In his extensive analysis of 'discovery' learning, Bruner suggested four benefits that accrue for the learner. These were an increase in intellectual potency, the shift from extrinsic to intrinsic satisfaction, learning about the discovery of knowledge itself and improving memory. To support this approach, he said, teaching should be more 'hypothetical' or open and active, rather than 'expository' or closed and passive. For example, surprise and the reduction of surprise are essential components of Bruner's 'intellectual delight'. The mixing of two clear solutions to give a coloured cloudiness may astonish at first, but when simplified through discussion of the different chemicals involved and how they react provides a much deeper understanding of the universe. Few children do not show human interest at this phenomenon.

Bruner here is developing the view that to be human is to learn and that there is profound human interest in all aspects of our surroundings. It makes no sense at all to argue that some children are not interested in the triangle, let alone because of economic background. What does make sense is that the triangle needs to connect with the process of meaning making for the child. If Bruner is substantially correct in his notion of discovery learning, then how teachers teach, how the school curriculum is arranged and how assessment occurs should reflect this approach as well. If this is not the case, then children will be engulfed by structures that do not support their favoured mode of learning. The whole basis of learning and of testing will be misdirected, giving highly distorted results.

It seems strange to argue that motor mechanics know little about the properties of liquids and gases, that construction workers are ignorant of materials and structures, that farmers are not aware of yields and pesticides. Working families live history, science, mathematics and literature, quoting poetry and speeches, managing budgets, dealing with regulations and bureaucracy. They live with and create generations of knowledge and experience. If there is a viewpoint that low-income families do not appreciate the tragedy of war, the beauty of a rainbow, the emotion of a story, the meaning of a painting or the song of a bird, then it is seriously misplaced. These are human experiences that apply to everyone and which enable our understanding to constantly grow and develop. They are experiences that are not restricted to only some.

The problem here is not that working families are uneducated and uninformed but that, in general, the curriculum of schools does not respect and include the culture and knowledge that local communities possess. Rather than building knowledge from the combined experience of the child and community, schools tend to abstract learning and draw upon the experience of others from another place and time. This is not to say that the recognised knowledge contained in textbooks is unimportant, but that it must connect with the direct knowledge of learners.

Bruner commented that an educated person needs to know what knowledge is like, how it integrates with other broader knowledge and how learning occurs. This is personal learning, not artificially contrived outside of experience. Testing knowledge and learning in a way that does not draw upon personal culture and experience is like being coached in tennis and being tested on swimming. Of course the results will be inaccurate and distorted. The capabilities of children from low-income working families are surely the same as anyone else and must be recognised and respected. It is traditional testing that is deficient, not the learning of children. In summary:

- Knowledge in formal educational programs is often considered from a logical positivist perspective mainly or only. While not necessarily the case, this assumes a linear progression from knowledge that is presumed to be known accurately, taught, learned, assessed and graded accurately. Experiential knowledge, on the other hand, involves cycles of practice where knowledge is built, discussed, monitored, evaluated by consensus and is ungraded as a guide to further learning. Knowledge does not establish a one-way conduit of truth, but a two-way investigation of doubt over long periods of time. Students should not be excluded from different forms of knowledge and should have access to programs that model each form.
- Assessment that assumes one approach to teaching and learning imposes an ideological and epistemological view of knowledge that assumes power and control by those who know. This makes it extremely difficult for teachers to adopt approaches that best meet the learning needs of students, those who do not know. Learning is then restricted for a proportion of students in every class, including those who prefer to learn in an interdisciplinary way drawing upon aesthetic, scientific and communicative experience. In diverse classrooms involving a range of multicultural, cultural, economic, historical, community and personal interests, it is undemocratic and inequitable to impose one view of learning and knowledge on all students.
- Different approaches to assessment itself are possible involving assessment *for* learning, assessment *of* learning and assessment *as* learning. This last

approach of assessment as learning integrates the monitoring of assessment as a learning program proceeds, enabling feedback and discussion to occur on a continuing basis and for both the program and individual projects to be altered along the way. This is much more congruent with a criterion-based view of assessment than assessing items at the end of a program, often after students have departed from that unit or study.

- Structural changes arise from an epistemological view of knowledge and how participation with knowledge can be best arranged. The notions below all support the direction of criterion-based knowing and assessment as learning:

  - cluster arrangements where groups of staff work with groups of students
  - learning circles where small groups of staff and students work in semi-autonomous teams to decide and implement activities
  - flexible learning involving burst mode, occasional large groupings, online communication, podcasting
  - partnership work to emphasise professional dialogue and practice
  - praxis inquiry that seeks to integrate the practice and theorising of change and significant ideas.

Integrated project

A fundamental change for schooling – indeed, for society – has been suggested above, that is, a conceptual reconstruction of literacy and numeracy to the extent that current modes of operation cease to exist. Words such as mathetics, heuristics or even bricolage (see Chapter 9), philosophy and epistemology could be used to denote this new field. For the purposes of this discussion, the notion of literacy and numeracy will be replaced with the practice of philosophy. Reconceptualisation (which can occur to a greater or lesser extent) does not mean that original aspects are necessarily disregarded, but are available and incorporated when necessary. Forms of assessment would not rely on the recall of formalisms and rules, but would expose progress with meaning. It may be that if the new field is accepted as being primarily concerned with learning, experiment, play and thinking rather than specified content, then formal assessment will not be required. Identified content could be included in other subject domains as a practice rather than being organised as a separate entity. Specific workshops to consider particular content could be arranged throughout the week or semester, resulting in an integrated curriculum model, as shown in Figure 5.3. The essential feature of this approach is epistemological, where students are participating in an explicit and defensible paradigm of experiential or pragmatic knowledge and learning.

With a small number of integrated studies being the preferred epistemological model, there will be less subject content involved compared with traditional curriculum designs. The amount of content included is always a selection from what is available, with less content demonstrating the intention of delving deeper into meaning rather than skimming across the surface of knowledge. This will be reflected strongly in the philosophy workshops that will investigate understanding of language and mathematics concepts, their origins and use.

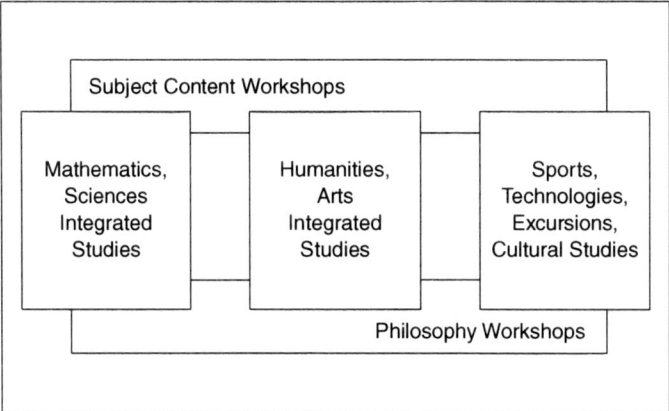

Figure 5.3 Philosophical model of curriculum

As an epistemologist, Piaget raised philosophical issues with young children, such as 'Where does the wind come from?' and 'Why does the ball roll downhill?', encouraging them to think and propose creatively about their worlds. Their comments are not wrong and are not assessed, but form the basis of their expanding knowledge base. As dialogue and experiment proceed, the adult can introduce other ways of thinking about experience perhaps through measures, symbols and physical relationships: 'How *long* does it take the toy car to stop?' 'What does *that* word mean about the dragon?' '*Why* do words rhyme?' 'Can we *think* of different ways of telling the time?' 'What *might* happen if we use a larger wheel?' These questions can be approached philosophically through discussion and related to other accepted information and conventions from teachers, granddad, books, posters or the Internet. Philosophy workshops and content workshops arise from the integrated studies, with Table 5.1 showing a draft outline of an integrated project that emphasises literacy/numeracy or language/mathematics:

This integrated study of people and cultures enables language and mathematics to be underscored throughout and for particular aspects of these practices to be consolidated in the separate philosophy workshops. Focus questions will generate issues around migration and refugees, traditions and customs, community languages and the social values that are generally agreed as being important. Small groups or project teams of students will investigate these questions under the guidance of teachers but will be as independent as possible. Obviously, the role of the teacher is crucial, participating with students as a team member and offering advice and avenues to pursue within the overall epistemological framework of the study. Arranging issues, ideas, conflicts and the like will require careful tabulation and community checking for accuracy. Outcomes from the project are available for assessment and include public exhibition and discussion of findings as well as Internet communication for comment and feedback. Other aspects of the study can be identified for

Table 5.1 Overview of Integrated Project 1: People and Cultures

Level	Middle years 5–9
Topic	People and cultures
Interface practices	Language/literacy knowledge
	Mathematics/numeracy knowledge
Focus issues	What are the features of a contented community?
	How do communities cope with major change?
	Why are some members of the community held in high regard?
Activities 1 (weeks 1–2)	Formation of project teams; general discussion and clarification of focus issues; collation of background materials; initial contact with community members
Activities 2 (weeks 3–4)	Collect stories from interviews, newspapers, reports; initial documentation of ideas, issues arising
Activities 3 (weeks 5–6)	Identification and categorising of community knowledge
	Drafts returned to community for accuracy and suggested amendment
Progress outcomes (week 7)	Public exhibition and discussion of findings
(for assessment)	Contribution to blog, social media
	Communication with community groups
Ongoing studies (week 8)	International contact with countries of origin
	Involvement with community language
	Comparison of geographies

ongoing work depending on progress made and the time available. As integrated projects of this type accumulate across each year level and across schools in general, it will become possible to consider 'exemplars of knowledge' as the basis of the curriculum, generated locally rather than from the textbook.

Knowledge exemplars

As integrated projects are completed, parents (through community meetings or learning circle discussions), teachers and students can begin to reflect on their composition and any themes or features they see emerging. These themes can then be detailed on a matrix involving key aspects as agreed by participants. Indicators of each aspect can then be suggested so that there is a clear display of the nature and quality of the work undertaken. Table 5.2 shows a matrix or 'knowledge exemplar' (for a more extensive discussion, see Hooley, 2009) arising from the people and cultures integrated project and concerns the issue of 'family' that could be identified as being central to the study.

Four indicators are provided for each feature of the knowledge exemplar. With the 'ideas and knowledge' feature, for example, there can be seen a strong influence of family in shaping knowledge, the significance of ceremony of various types and the learning that takes place through employment. The final two rows of the knowledge exemplar show how links can be made to the regular school curriculum. That is, beginning with the local knowledge of students around negotiated key issues of importance to them and their community,

Table 5.2 Overview of Knowledge Exemplar 1: Family

	Indicator 1: Family and country	Indicator 2: Importance of family	Indicator 3: Community events	Indicator 4: Work
Community	Connections with local area; stories by Elders	Kinship; support; memories	Historical tributes; festivals	Employment; new/old industries
Community culture and artefacts	Newspaper articles; historical reports; stories by Elders	Photographs; family stories	Interviews; reports	Implements used; photographs; stories
Ideas and knowledge	Achievements of family; significance of landscape	Influence of family in community	Meaning of song, dance, ceremony, customs	Interactions between work mates
Reflection	Discussion with family, Elders	Discussion with community groups, Elders	Interview with local newspaper, participants	Recorded interview with employers, retired employees
Making public	Parent–teacher nights, newsletters	Exhibitions, displays at school	Articles in newspapers, social media	Articles in work newsletters
Links to school curriculum	Local history, geography, language	Local history, geography, language	Science, arts, humanities, mathematics	Science, arts, humanities, mathematics
Implications for school curriculum; language/ mathematics	Projects include dialogue, narrative, teamwork, themes, patterns, meaning, environment	Incorporates timelines, groups, relationships	Raises categories of values, themes, conflicts, customs	Significance, trends, budgets, local resources

a process of investigation ensures connections with school subjects and, for this exemplar, the incorporation of reconceptualised literacy/numeracy as language/mathematics, or, better still, philosophy.

As mentioned above, the accumulation of integrated projects and knowledge exemplars over time could form the basis of the regular curriculum, thereby shifting the intellectual centre of gravity from the general to the local, at least in the initial stages of investigation.

As a final step in the process, ongoing monitoring of teaching and learning progress and quality can be undertaken by application of an interface practice index (Table 5.3) for each knowledge exemplar. Brief definitions of each index

Table 5.3 Interface practice index for Knowledge Exemplar 1: Family

Practice	Definition	Index 1	Index 2	Index 3
Continuity	Dialectic between abstract, concrete knowledge; antidualism	Establishes projects that feature family, practice, reflection	Encourages links between outcomes and perspectives	Supports creative thinking about new ideas, cause, effect
Inquiry	Open-ended, based on personal interest	Investigates own practice for improvement	Participates as team member	Incorporates local and global studies into practice
Praxis	Cycles of ethically framed action for change and public good	Implements description, explanation, reflection and change of practice	Develops curriculum and cross-curriculum praxis approaches to learning	Constructs learning environments of ethically informed action for the public good
Dialogue	Democratic, open discussions for consensus	Compiles and discusses family artefacts of personal learning over time	Participates with family artefact, knowledge that show meanings of practice	Engages discourses that clarify practice and illuminate the reflection of practice in practice
Habitus	Human dispositions and structures that relate to activity	Identifies family, personal viewpoints	Reflects on reasons for personal views	Considers other views based on personal practice
Fields	Human activities that relate to habitus	Recognises family, personal learning from immersion in personal practice	Supports communities of practice for improved learning environments	Critique of practice for changed conditions to formulate new practice
Capitals	Cultural, economic, social features of human influence	Identifies features of family cultural, economic background	Considers range of cultural, economic factors	Critique of culture, economic factors for new practice
Reflexivity	Relationship between habitus and field	Activates, connects with families, local communities	Integrates family, community culture and knowledge into curriculum	Participates with community groups to investigate local history, knowledge, language
Internal goods	Set of practice properties that enable human knowledge, virtue	Incorporates language, family interest, activity throughout practice	Develops awareness of language and other practice properties	Encourages enhanced use of practice properties
Knowledge	Defensible human understanding arising from inquiry and reflection	Participates in discussion of project artefacts, outcomes	Considers different reasons for project results	Compiles ideas for continuing studies based on agreed project conclusions

practice (column 2) can be adapted to meet local circumstances, including current approaches and curriculum planning being implemented by teachers, although the problem of knowledge relativism must be borne in mind. The interface practice index applies to knowledge exemplars and therefore enables curriculum evaluation rather than for assessment purposes regarding individual students. Using the index makes it possible to chart progress year by year, or to moderate curriculum development and improvement across different schools if required. Table 5.3 has been designed for the Family knowledge exemplar above.

The interface practice index is constructed so that the separate indices provide an increasing gradation of complexity from left to right. A more detailed gradation could be arranged through the provision of additional columns and more particulars in each cell. The items included above refer to the curriculum for a secondary Year 9, or middle years project, but have general applicability across different subjects and year levels. This is a matter of professional judgement and interpretation for the teachers concerned. A point has been reached therefore where curriculum design incorporating a combination of integrated studies, content and philosophy workshops, knowledge exemplars and the interface practice index has provided a progressive and pragmatic epistemological paradigm in which to locate a more appropriate understanding and practice of literacy, numeracy and student assessment for all children.

6 Reconceptualising mathematics, science and technologies

Hidden amongst the clutter of suspicion
enclosed by hues of lavender and mauve
spherical brilliance probes the landscape
challenging our notions of sense perception
while new ideas are preamble to amendment
against a reference honed by intuition;
if beauty is a figment of the imagination
must mathematics be invented for explanation?

Education is about how to live in association with others, to live well, about participating with the best society has to offer, about exploring, constructing, reconstructing and critiquing knowledge of the social and physical worlds and about contributing to productive and critical citizenship. These human aspirations flow across the curriculum at all levels of formal education and should not be denied; they apply to all school knowledge rather than being restricted to some. It is similar to the notion of scientific morality that arose during World War II and the development of the atomic bomb for a greater purpose. Should we suppose that scientists are mere technicians working on essentially technical problems in a remote, disinterested fashion, or are moral beings subject to the same considerations of what ought to be of benefit to humankind? Is there a type of 'moral equivalence' across all sectors of society? Do we suppose that teachers or, more particularly, certain teachers of certain subjects are mere technicians or clinicians passing on encoded knowledge in a disinterested way, or are moral beings and activists in the philosophical construction of knowledge, learning and meaning? Can it really be said that the study of the natural sciences and mathematics is devoid of moral and ethical intent?

School mathematics surely has a moral dimension and purpose (Leslie and Mendick, 2014). In enabling humans to describe phenomena, patterns and their relationship, it facilitates the investigation of ideas and practices by children and opens up the nature of the universe to explicit question and experimentation. By so doing, children come into contact with the big ideas of beauty, elegance, order, ambiguity and connection, all of which are at the centre of the human imperative to know and understand. Like all other knowledge, mathematical thinking and schema arise from social practice and are therefore subject to design and redesign, refinement and deletion and argument and consensus throughout differing periods of time. This is the moral dimension of mathematics, to immerse humans and children in continuing interaction with their social, physical, aesthetic and cognitive frames so that what is possible remains a characteristic of daily life. In presenting the Presidential Medal of Freedom to Professor Stephen Hawking, US President Obama said that 'From his wheelchair, he's taken us on a journey to the farthest and strangest reaches of the cosmos'. The sciences and mathematics must surely include all citizens on this journey, whereby 'No barriers of race, gender, or physical infirmity can restrain the human spirit and that the truest test of a person's life is what we do for one another' (President Barack Obama in awarding the Presidential Medal of Freedom to 16 recipients, August 2009).

In conceptualising school mathematics as a moral and philosophical field of inquiry into mathematical ideas, principles and practices (Ernst, 1998), it is necessary to disgorge current conservative epistemological shibboleths and establish new constitutions that open up rather than close down learning. In extending the model detailed in Chapter 5, school mathematics and science could consist of three integrated domains at all levels, involving the construction of personal narratives of interaction with mathematical and scientific ideas in the broadest sense, ongoing investigation of negotiated and integrated mathematical and scientific projects in small teams and application of recognised mathematical and scientific procedures and knowledge that inform investigations. These three aspects of study need to occur within discursive and respectful environments of critical inquiry where the philosophy and history of ideas together with cultural and community interest are constantly met, discussed and reviewed. The moral dimension and purpose of mathematics and science in enhancing humanness and of the negotiated projects of students become explicit through the nature of inquiry, language and collaboration.

This three-pronged approach to school mathematics is obviously incommensurate with the dominant paradigm of logical positivism. It will require a restructuring of pedagogy and time, with a greater emphasis on meaning and understanding across fewer content areas. Not only will teachers need to integrate appropriate principles into projects as appropriate, but they will need to have at least a general understanding of different philosophical approaches to knowledge and mathematics to ensure that these infuse the broad experience of all children. This should however be a commonplace for all teachers. It will be necessary for children to be reflecting upon their own mathematical experience through the compilation of descriptive and systematic narrative formats so that they become aware of the ubiquitous nature of mathematics in the world and in their own worlds.

All classrooms contain diverse experience, culture and capabilities that need to be brought to bear on significant issues and problems, rather than be discarded as being unimportant. The absence of narrative understandings across the curriculum and in particular mathematics and science, is a severe weakness of schools that needs to be reinscribed to inform and enhance the child's participation with structure, relationship and generality. Lakatos (1976) defined the 'formalist' school of the philosophy of mathematics as identifying mathematics 'with its formal axiomatic abstraction' (p. 1) and commented that 'informal, quasi-empirical mathematics does not grow through a monotonous increase of the number of indubitably established theorems, but through the incessant improvement of guesses, by speculation and criticism, by the logic of proofs and refutations' (p. 5). Similar debates between dogmatism and scepticism are to be found in the philosophy of science.

Mathematics, free at last

Many children who are studying mathematics at secondary schools around the world will be familiar with the theorem of the Greek mathematician and philosopher Pythagoras. They will readily inform us that, for all right-angled triangles in the universe, the square on the altitude plus the square on the base of the triangle will equal the square on the hypotenuse, or symbolically $A^2 + B^2 = H^2$. It will not surprise if they also mention the building of the Pyramids in Egypt and the ratio 3:4:5, a phenomenon which has prompted Bellos (2010, p. 85) to remark that this understanding is the 'jewel of our mathematical patrimony, an intellectual artefact of great power, elegance and concision'.

There are two philosophical issues at stake here. In the first instance, it is interesting why this equation seems to remain in the minds of many children and adults alike, whereas many others, or most, do not. Does it have something to do with the story that is usually told regarding its use, the history and intrigue surrounding the building of the Pyramids, also included in most curricula around the world as well as in many films, books and museums? In the second instance, however, there is a similar occurrence with most other school mathematics and that is the unexplained and total acceptance of its truth and accuracy. While it may be that the ratio 3:4:5 holds as isolated numbers in our heads and approximately for a length of rope stretched roughly between pegs in the ground, is the ratio exactly true for real triangles? Tiles, for example, need to have a space between them, meaning that three tiles each of 1 cm^2 will be slightly larger than a line 3 cm long. It can be shown abstractly that the sum of the two squares on the triangle is equal to the square on the hypotenuse, but how accurate is this in practice? Usually the mathematics teacher 'proves' this relationship with one or two examples by using graph paper, or by drawing triangles with paper and pencil, or by using a computer program. Apparently we are prepared to accept a general rule about the universe on such flimsy evidence, without a hint of philosophical question and investigation.

There is debate regarding the nature of the mathematical universe of which all students should be aware. Plato argued that there is the real world that humans perceive through their senses and there is the abstract world of concepts, of perfect shapes and ideas. Does a circle exist in the real/concrete or perfect/abstract world of shapes? This Platonic view means that mathematical facts exist independently of humans and await discovery rather than invention in the human mind. In contrast to the absolutist belief, the fallibilist or constructivist position considers mathematics as a social practice and therefore subject to construction, change and revision over time.

Inexplicably, the absolutist view has a strong hold on school mathematics, where philosophical differences amongst the profession are seldom debated. However in what may prove to be a major and progressive development for schooling worldwide, the internationally respected National Council of Teachers of Mathematics (NCTM, 2013) in the United States has released a statement on mathematics learning. Entitled *Curriculum Focal Points from Prekindergarten to Grade 8,* the document is a compilation of the most important knowledge and concepts that is considered appropriate throughout the primary and early secondary years. Significantly, the statement attempts to reduce the amount of mathematics content that traditionally suffocates many classrooms.

There are three curriculum focal points at each level. For Grade 7, these are listed as being number and operations and algebra and geometry; measurement and geometry and algebra; and number and operations and algebra. Clearly, there is still a lot of content here, but the actual topic load is being reduced. Some commentators in the United States have welcomed the focal points as a 'back to basics' movement, but this is a serious misrepresentation of the case. The focal points are not seen as a listing of individual topics that are to be taught syllabus-fashion in quick succession. Instead, they comprise a mathematical landscape of understanding that needs to be encountered for student thinking and practice to be grounded and thorough.

Release of the curriculum focal points is a further step in the development and change of school mathematics that has been encouraged by the NCTM for many years. In 1980, *An Agenda for Action* recommended a shift to active problem solving rather than mere rote learning. In 1989, the famous *Curriculum and Evaluation Standards* focused on an inquiry approach to mathematics where students investigated and wrote about their understandings through to Year 12. *Principles and Standards for School Mathematics* was published in 2000 and attempted to clarify content and approaches for the new century.

In particular, many teacher organisations, if not teachers around the world, are familiar with the 1989 document and there is some resonance between it, curriculum frameworks and the current emphasis on essential content learnings. Whether or not the vast majority of mathematics classrooms have actually adopted an inquiry framework that encourages less content, student initiative and creativity is however doubtful.

Of course, the new statement is not revolutionary. We are talking about mathematics after all and incremental change. But any approach that attempts to establish a way of thinking about and discussing school mathematics, instead of issuing extensive lists of passive goals, objectives, standards and social expectations to be imposed, must be a huge step forward. Curriculum focal points are intended to be studied within the context of the processes of mathematical inquiry, such as communication between all learners, including the teacher, active engagement with key ideas that strengthen mathematical reasoning and connections between concepts and the posing and solving of problems that have a basis in the child's experience and culture. Under these circumstances, mathematics has a coherence and authenticity that links with and challenges curiosity and interest.

As usual with statements of this type, the tendency may be for teachers and, perhaps more tellingly, textbook writers, to take the curriculum focal points and immediately specify the old and seemingly endless content. This will be most unfortunate. The NCTM intends that the statement will launch a wide-ranging discussion amongst the profession on the issues it has raised, to guide the development of innovative and exciting curriculum and to push back oppressive boundaries for all teachers and students. Practising mathematicians certainly do not work with the constrictions we place on children; their work embraces the processes mentioned before and generally, as well, the passion, intrigue and uncertainty that characterise all other human activity. Why do we see school mathematics as only a long trail of predetermined slices of subject content that have been discovered elsewhere external to the child and which are arranged in so-called hierarchical order? Mathematics and science generally do not proceed in this way, nor children playing in the sandpit, experimenting with words, or observing the seeds of wheat growing in cotton wool. All of these experiences involve mathematical queries, imagination and reflections.

Children do not learn in the way that many mathematics classrooms display. Why it is expected that active, energetic and insightful learners will engage with apparently sterile, disconnected and abstracted formalisms is a mystery. All students need to be able to work within a liberating framework of inquiry that enables them to employ a range of strategies as they see fit around the questions and meaning they want to investigate. As human learners, all children from all backgrounds are inherently interested in understanding their world and the dilemmas they face. Rather than the inquiry framework restricting opportunity, the realm of learning is expanded and opened up for engagement. All children are deeply interested in the relationship that we describe as $A = L \times W$ and, when presented with it in due course, embrace it eagerly. If the NCTM vision is pursued, curriculum focal points will assist parents, teachers and students to do the same. That is, to seek out new fields and models of mathematical practice for classrooms that inspire and confound, that expose and demonstrate the amazing patterns that constitute our universe. As the American psychologist Jerome Bruner (1979) said, the construction of intellectual delight and going beyond the information given is really the basis of all curriculum activity.

Expeditions of scientific certainty and uncertainty

Stephen Hawking's name is very well known around the world for his groundbreaking work in theoretical physics, especially concerning black holes.

Hawking (2001) proposed that the extremely strong gravity that exists in black holes would prevent any information that had been trapped escaping. However the consequence of this view poses a problem in relation to any information that has fallen into the black hole being destroyed as the black hole collapses and dies. This process is in contradistinction to the principle of quantum physics that information cannot be destroyed. Many physicists, including Hawking himself, are attempting to resolve this problem and to rethink current understanding of black holes and the nature of the astonishing fundamental particles of the universe.

The history of modern science has been written in stories such as this – scientists around the world conducting experiments, having heated discussions and disagreements, proposing different explanations and attempting to understand how things work as best they can. In addition, the Oxford mathematician and Hawking colleague, Roger Penrose (2004, pp. 1038–1039) has noted the concepts of 'beauty and elegance' influencing the direction of theoretical research, including that found in Euclidean geometry, Newtonian dynamics, Maxwell's electromagnetism and Einstein's general relativity. Penrose then goes on to comment:

> Yet, we may question whether the undoubted mathematical beauty in these schemes is something that would shine independently, simply as pure mathematics, had it not been for the remarkable fact that they accord so well with the workings of our universe. How would they stand comparison as just mathematical structures with some of the gems or beacons of pure mathematics? I believe that they would stand up rather well, but not overwhelmingly so. There are many bodies of pure mathematics, with no discernible relations to the physical world, whose beauty equals or even exceeds that of the physical theories that we have yet come across.

This is surely the philosophical argument for the role of mathematics and science in schools and of their inherent interest that grips all children. Mathematics and science do not impose immutable thought of reality and truth on children but, on the contrary, open up ways of thinking about and investigating the world so that their own constructs of meaning can be formed and reformed. All children in all cultures wonder about the beauty of the moon at night, the elegance of spherical raindrops, the brilliance and shape of a rose petal and the changing colour of the ocean. At some point, their curiosity and imagination will tentatively embrace the notion of quarks, leptons and hadrons for their explanatory power and will wonder at talk of Higgs bosun. They can also wonder at the beauty and grace of an equation, about why it works and why the universe appears to be arranged in such a way to allow it to work (whether accurately or approximately).

For the primary and secondary science teacher, this is the task at hand, to provide avenues of intellectual opportunity that bridge personal interest and experience with the great ideas and conundrums of humanity. What is the charge on an electron? Why do some animals have many legs? What do fossils tell us? Central to this task is the question of personal experiment, when seeds germinate, the microscope introduces new visions, salts are dissolved and a small steam engine drives a piston. Of all subjects in the modern curriculum, science should excite and challenge and enable children to conduct their own investigations of what they observe and are told. Reflection on classroom experiments so that broader thinking is encouraged occurs during and following experiment as a major purpose of science education, to not only come into contact with ideas in practice, but to format new ideas of your own arising from practice.

In a similar approach to the NCTM guidelines regarding mathematics curriculum mentioned above, the National Science Teachers Association (NSTA, 2013) has released the *Next Generation Science Standards* in the United States. Drawing upon the *Framework for K-12 Science Education* published in 2011, the standards 'promise to help students understand why is it that we have to know science and to help them use scientific learning to develop critical thinking skills which may be applied throughout their lives, no matter the topic'. It is unfortunate that some students still see science (like mathematics) as an area where facts and ideas have to be memorised, but the new document supports integrated inquiry and the covering of fewer ideas in more depth such that 'students come away with a much richer understanding'.

There may be many reasons why school science has found it difficult to break with conservative approaches to teaching and learning, but the centrality of experiment should have at least emphasised student practice. People such as Copernicus, Galileo, Kepler and Newton worked in the field of 'natural philosophy' and it was not until some time later that 'science' was clearly separated from religion, philosophy and other domains. Francis Bacon from England in the sixteenth and seventeenth centuries is credited with development of the distinctive and inductive 'scientific method' involving experiment, observation, the collection of facts and the subsequent formation of generalisation. Bacon's work was important in providing knowledge with a scientific rather than imposed authoritarian basis, although a strictly empirical approach became associated much later with a positivist view, whereby only scientific knowledge was seen as valid.

Austrian-born Karl Popper in the twentieth century differed from the inductive view in that he proposed modern science develops from a series of conjectures that the scientist then sets about falsifying. Under this approach, truth is never finally determined but is closely approached as falsification continues.

Thomas Kuhn was a philosopher of science in the late twentieth century who theorised that science progresses through a series of major changes or revolutions as a break with past practices and understandings is made. He proposed that a 'paradigm leap' occurs as experiment, observation and theorising create new ways of viewing the world, such as occurred with the Copernican revolution, Newtonian mechanics, relativity and quantum mechanics.

These developments in the nature of science demonstrate that there is little excuse for school science to lock students into a fixed quotidian view of science itself and of scientific knowledge. Stephen Hawking could definitely advise on such matters.

Mercuric oxide, or HgO, is an orange powder. When a small amount is placed in an ignition tube and heated gently over a Bunsen flame, a remarkable transformation takes place. At one moment, the tube contains an orange powder, while at the next, instantly, the powder is converted into a grey fluid, sloshing around in the glass bulb. This is a dramatic event and never fails to engage students of any year level. Why would it not? The student from any social and cultural background is just as engaged with that 'learnable moment' as any other student, fascinated by this amazing property of the universe: 'What's happened here, did you see that, have we done it right?' 'Where did the powder go?' 'What's this grey stuff?' and perhaps best of all, 'Can we do it again?'

Some students will have come across the word 'mercury' from their involvement with the bathroom thermometer when sick, so there is a reasonable chance that the teacher can immediately attempt to link their home and school knowledge. The new piece of thinking will be in relation to how the mercury and oxygen atoms might be connected and what impact the added energy from the Bunsen burner flame will have. There is a conceptual shift to be made when the teacher suggests that the molecular bond is broken, driving off the oxygen and leaving the mercury behind. This knowledge will be returned to again and again in various ways as physics, mathematics, chemistry and romance are combined.

Key idea: information and communication technologies

Desk-top computers began to find their way into schools in the major economies in the early 1980s. Before then, some senior secondary classes had access to mainframe computers for programming purposes, often involving large stacks of punched cards in different computer languages. Miniaturisation of computer equipment was a consequence of the cold-war period and the space race between the United States and Soviet Union, but as smaller equipment became available, other uses in many areas of society became feasible. As is often the case when a new technology is invented, it is initially incorporated into current usage and it may take some time for the technology itself as well as human ingenuity to seek application in more creative ways. For schools, the first generation of desk-top machines were often bought and initiated by teacher enthusiasts with programs that usually consisted of reproducing the textbook on the screen together with traditional approaches to teaching; for these reasons the term 'computer-assisted instruction' or CAI was introduced. Computer games were also limited given the capacity of the equipment and the lack of experience with innovative design.

A major development occurred in 1984 with the release of the Apple Macintosh machine, its new user-friendly interface and the mouse controller. It was many years before schools began to have access to non-CAI materials and the term 'learning technologies' appeared. The term was mainly aspirational as the software remained essentially instructional, with few degrees of freedom for the child, the Logo program of Papert (1980) being the main exception. Over more recent years in schools the phrase 'information and communication technology' (ICT) has become prevalent, based on the field of cybernetics and involving the study of physical and biological systems that are changed through feedback mechanisms as the environment changes.

Information and communication have specific cybernetic meanings that apply across fields as diverse as engineering, neuroscience and psychology. Within education, the phrase generally refers to computer-based systems that enable students to interact with knowledge for learning purposes. While the Internet, laptops, tablets, hand-held devices, blogs, wikis and social media are now common throughout the world and are familiar to many children and teachers, it is probably accurate to claim that the organisation of schools and the dominant pedagogies have remained substantially unchanged. That is, the curriculum design is the same, the topics covered are the same and the relationships between knowledge and students and between teachers and students are the same.

Seymour Papert and his colleague Marvin Minsky (2010) are major figures in the field of artificial intelligence (AI), having attended the initial 1954 conference at Dartmore in the United States. AI has important commercial and military applications, but could also be most significant for schools and learning. Broadly defined as computer-based technologies that relate to humans in an apparently human way and which have similar responses to humans, the potential is enormous.

There are serious ethical problems at stake however if the AI process is taken too far and machines are able to replace rather than supplement humans. An indication of this was depicted in *2001: A Space Odyssey,* when the computer Hal commented on 'human error'. Isaac Asimov had of course predated this eventuality when he developed his 'three laws of robotics'.

Papert (1980, p. 157) discussed AI as being concerned with 'extending the capacity of machines to perform functions that would be considered intelligent if performed by people' and, by so doing, raised the question of knowledge 'representation'. According to Papert, it was not the role of new technology to merely place the textbook on the screen, or to add colour and movement to what was already possible with paper and pencil, but to enable the user to interact with 'objects to think with' in different ways for the engagement of different perspectives not normally available. This would allow humans to gain a better understanding of knowledge and learning and of themselves. Papert went on to explain that 'to make a machine that can be instructed in natural language, it is necessary to probe deeply into the nature of language. In order to make a machine capable of learning, we have to probe deeply into the nature of learning'. To achieve this situation, knowledge needed to be 'represented' in some way through the development of 'mental models' that could be programmed into the machine and would provide a learning environment for the child that could be altered at will or, in Papert's terms, be 'debugged' when changes were required. Children would therefore be involved in investigating learning and their own mental models.

The question of computer-based knowledge representation and mental models for adaptation and experimentation by children is the key feature of educational computing and returns us to the knowledge theories of Bernstein. This is particularly important when considering the teaching and learning of school mathematics and science given the alienation felt by large numbers of children. To review, Bernstein (2010, p. 159) discussed the notion of vertical and horizontal discourses of knowledge. Vertical discourses were to be found in the sciences as a 'coherent, explicit and systematically principled structure, hierarchically organised' and horizontal discourses were to be found in the social sciences as 'a series of specialised languages with specialised modes of interrogation and specialised criteria for the production and circulation of texts'. Bernstein suggested that vertical discourses are circulated through 'explicit recontextualisation and evaluation, motivated by strong distributive procedures'. On the other hand, horizontal discourses entail 'a set of strategies which are local, segmentally organised, context specific and dependent, for maximising encounters with persons and habitats'.

It is possible for teachers to take such definitions and transfer them directly into schools; for example, the physics classroom and the literature classroom. Knowledge covered in the physics classroom will often be considered as hierarchical and independent of location, with packets being distributed for acceptance without change. Knowledge in the literature classroom will usually be seen as having inherent value, but is open to local circumstances and recategorisation by teachers and students; there is public discussion of the latest texts, but little on the equations of motion. It is probably the case that school mathematics has a confused and ill-defined philosophical heritage involving murky concepts of numeracy and pure and applied understandings.

While Bernstein's insights of knowledge are important for teachers in constructing their programs, there are two important implications that will challenge their teaching. First, if schooling is about children's learning, then there is no obligation on schools to structure knowledge in the curriculum in the same way as knowledge outside of schools has been theoretically structured by adults. The latter may be reasonably accurate, but the role of teachers is to find ways for all children to lively participate with knowledge, not to have it rigidly imposed. Second, if learning generally is a social practice, then the obligation of schools is to provide learning environments that enable social practices to be experienced and changed as need be to meet human interest of the classroom.

From a social practice point of view, the innovative and epistemological role of information and communication technologies is to enable all children to conduct personal philosophical investigations into knowledge, including mathematical and scientific knowledge. Given that the nature of school mathematics and whether it has a strictly vertical or horizontal structure is unclear, teachers can utilise ICT applications in an integrated way, opening up school mathematics to culturally inclusive and experiential appreciations. School science is of course much broader than formal physics (a favourite example of Bernstein) and chemistry, with the structure of biology, geology, ecology, general science – and sometimes, controversially, psychology – being more fluid and combinatorial when in the pragmatic hands of teachers. In the general science and mathematics classes of the primary and early secondary years, there is little argument for adopting a strongly hierarchical structure, with division into separate subjects in the senior years being undertaken for political rather than educational reasons.

Integrated project

Discussion of integrated projects and knowledge exemplars will be similar across the curriculum (Chapters 5–7). Arising from consideration of mathematics, science and technologies, a further fundamental change for schooling – indeed, for society – has been suggested above, that is, a conceptual reconstruction of Bernstein's discourses. Rather than the concept of vertical and horizontal relationships amongst knowledge, all school subjects are now seen as a network of knowledge discourses that are engaged when necessary by students to pursue their learning, scaffolded as social practices in classrooms and in the process of thinking itself. Some discourses may be essentially vertical or horizontal at a specific point for specific children, but at other points for other children, the discourses may be much more interactive. It is not necessary to discard the terms mathematics and science but, in keeping with the 'network of discourses' proposal, reconceptualisation (which can occur to a greater or lesser extent) does mean that the domains are seen as broadly integrated, holistic and connected, drawing a clear line of distinction with current designs. Similar to language/mathematics, forms of assessment would not rely on the recall of formalisms and rules, but would expose progress with meaning. It may be that if the new fields are accepted as being primarily concerned with learning, experiment, play and thinking rather than specified content, then formal assessment will not be required. Identified content could be included in other subject domains as a practice rather than being organised as a separate entity. As discussed in Chapter 5, specific workshops to consider particular mathematics and science content could be arranged during the week or semester, resulting in an integrated curriculum model, as shown in Figure 5.3.

With a small number of integrated studies being the preferred epistemological model, there will be less subject content involved compared with traditional curriculum designs. The amount of content included is always a selection from what is available, with less content demonstrating the intention of delving deeper into meaning rather than skimming across the surface of knowledge. This will be reflected strongly in the philosophy workshops that will investigate understanding of science and mathematics concepts, their origins and use. For example, a range of issues can be informally raised to encourage students to think and propose creatively about their worlds: 'Do numbers exist?' 'How accurately can human equations reflect the natural world?' 'What is energy?' Their comments are not wrong and are not assessed, but form the basis of their expanding knowledge base. As dialogue and experiment proceed, the adult can introduce other ways of thinking about experience perhaps through measures, symbols and physical relationships: 'What is a *force*?' 'Will we ever be able to *see* dark matter?' 'Why was the symbol *zero* invented?' 'Do all triangles always contain *180* degrees, exactly or approximately?' These questions can be approached philosophically through discussion and related to other accepted information and conventions from teachers, granddad, books, posters or the Internet. Philosophy workshops and content workshops arise from the integrated studies, with Table 6.1 showing a draft outline of an integrated project that emphasises mathematics, science and technology.

This integrated study of climate change enables science and mathematics to be underscored throughout and for particular aspects of these practices to be consolidated in the separate philosophy workshops. Focus questions will

Table 6.1 Overview of Integrated Project 2: Climate Change

Level	Middle years 5–9
Topic	Climate change
Interface practices	Mathematics knowledge
	Science knowledge
	Technological knowledge
Focus issues	How is climate trending internationally?
	What are the main areas of disagreement regarding climate?
	What initiatives are being taken to cope with changes of climate?
Activities 1 (weeks 1–2)	Formation of project teams; general discussion and clarification of focus issues; collation of background materials; initial contact with climate groups
Activities 2 (weeks 3–4)	Small-scale experiments
	Collect data from interviews, newspapers, reports; initial documentation of ideas, issues arising
Activities 3 (weeks 5–6)	Identification and categorisation of issues regarding climate change
	Drafts circulated to climate groups for feedback
Progress outcomes (week 7) (for assessment)	Public exhibition and discussion of findings
	Contribution to blog, social media
	Communication with climate and community groups
Ongoing studies (week 8)	International contact with climate groups
	Longer-term experiments with outside assistance if possible
	Participation in ongoing debates, e.g. United Nations

generate issues around the climate change argument, how science is being used or misused in support of a particular viewpoint, the nature of appropriate evidence and the social values that are generally agreed as being important. Small groups or project teams of students will investigate these questions under the guidance of teachers but will be as independent as possible. Obviously, the role of the teacher is crucial, participating with students as a team member and offering advice and avenues to pursue within the overall epistemological framework of the study. Arranging issues, ideas, conflicts and the like will require careful tabulation and community checking for accuracy. Outcomes from the project are available for assessment and include public exhibition and discussion of findings as well as Internet communication for comment and feedback. Other aspects of the study can be identified for ongoing work depending on progress made and the time available. As integrated projects of this type accumulate across each year level and across schools in general, it will become possible to consider 'exemplars of knowledge' as the basis of the curriculum, generated locally rather than from the textbook.

Knowledge exemplars

As integrated projects are completed, parents (through community meetings or learning-circle discussions), teachers and students can begin to reflect on their composition and any themes or features they see emerging. These themes can then be detailed on a matrix involving key aspects, as agreed by participants. Indicators of each aspect can then be suggested so that there is a clear display of the nature and quality of the work undertaken. Table 6.2 shows a matrix or 'knowledge exemplar' (for a more extensive discussion, see Hooley, 2009) arising from the climate change integrated project and concerns the issue of 'environment' that could be identified as being central to the study.

Four indicators are provided for each feature of the knowledge exemplar. With the 'ideas and knowledge' feature, for example, there can be seen a strong influence of country in shaping knowledge, the significance of weather as it concerns local animals, plants and crops and the learning that takes place through community discussions. The final two rows of the knowledge exemplar show how links can be made to the regular school curriculum. That is, beginning with the local knowledge of students around negotiated key issues of importance to them and their community, a process of investigation ensures that connections with school subjects and, for this exemplar, the incorporation of reconceptualised literacy/numeracy as language/mathematics, or better still, philosophy. As mentioned above, the accumulation of integrated projects and knowledge exemplars over time could form the basis of the regular curriculum, thereby shifting the intellectual centre of gravity from the general to the local, at least in the initial stages of investigation. As a final step in the process, ongoing monitoring of teaching and learning progress and quality can be undertaken by application of an interface practice index (Table 6.3) for each knowledge exemplar.

Table 6.2 Overview of Knowledge Exemplar 2: Environment

	Indicator 1: Connections with country	Indicator 2: Connections with family	Indicator 3: Principles of living	Indicator 4: Environmental philosophy
Community	Revered local sites; ceremonies	Historical events	Harmonious relationship with landscape	Existence involves cycles of land, sea change
Community culture and artefacts	Photographs; stories from Elders	Newspaper articles; role of family in community	Experience country at all times; songs, stories	Everything connected with everything else
Ideas and knowledge	Behaviour of animals as weather change	Understanding of plants, animals	Only take what is necessary; walk softly	Indigenous peoples always present at location
Reflection	Discussion with family, teachers	Discussion with community groups, elders	Interview with local newspaper, identities	Memories, discussion with Elders
Making public	Parent–teacher nights, newsletters	Exhibitions, displays at school	Articles in newspapers, social media	Choir, dance groups for local community
Links to school curriculum	Integrated projects	Observing weather; local crops and animals	Charting changes and impact on local conditions	Principles and critique of evolution
Implications for school curriculum; mathematics, science, technology	Environment major ongoing principle of curriculum, learning	Incorporates social media, timelines, relationships	Raises categories of values, themes, conflicts, customs	Dialogue, narrative, teamwork, themes, patterns, meaning, environment

Brief definitions of each index practice (column 2) can be adapted to meet local circumstances, including current approaches and curriculum planning being implemented by teachers, although the problem of knowledge relativism must be borne in mind. The interface practice index applies to knowledge exemplars and therefore enables curriculum evaluation rather than for assessment purposes regarding individual students. Using the index makes it possible to chart progress year by year, or to moderate curriculum development and improvement across different schools, if required. Table 6.3 has been designed for the environment knowledge exemplar above.

The interface practice index is constructed so that the separate indices provide an increasing gradation of complexity from left to right. A more detailed gradation could be arranged through the provision of additional columns and

Table 6.3 Interface practice index for Knowledge Exemplar 2: Environment

Practice	Definition	Index 1	Index 2	Index 3
Continuity	Dialectic between abstract, concrete knowledge; anti-dualism	Establishes projects that feature practice, reflection, environment	Encourages links between outcomes and perspectives	Supports creative thinking about new ideas, cause, effect
Inquiry	Open-ended, based on personal interest	Investigates own practice for improvement	Participates as team member	Incorporates local and global studies into practice
Praxis	Cycles of ethically-framed action for change and public good	Implements description, explanation, reflection and change of practice	Develops curriculum and cross-curriculum praxis approaches to learning	Constructs learning environments of ethically-informed action for the public good
Dialogue	Democratic, open discussions for consensus	Compiles, discusses environmental artefacts of personal learning over time	Participates with environmental artefact, knowledge that show meanings of practice	Engages discourses that clarify practice and illuminate the reflection of practice in practice
Habitus	Human dispositions and structures that relate to activity	Identifies family, personal viewpoints of environment	Reflects on reasons for personal views	Considers other views based on personal practice
Fields	Human activities that relate to habitus	Recognises family, personal learning from immersion in personal practice re environment	Supports communities of practice for improved learning environments	Critique of practice for changed conditions to formulate new practice
Capitals	Cultural, economic, social features of human influence	Identifies features of family, cultural, economic background	Considers range of cultural, economic, factors	Critique of culture, economic factors for new practice
Reflexivity	Relationship between habitus and field	Activates, connects with families, local communities	Integrates family, community culture and knowledge into curriculum	Participates with community groups to investigate local history, knowledge, language
Internal goods	Set of practice properties that enable human knowledge, virtue	Incorporates language, family interest, activity throughout practice	Develops awareness of language and other practice properties	Encourages enhanced use of practice properties
Knowledge	Defensible human understanding arising from inquiry and reflection	Participates in discussion of project artefacts, outcomes	Considers different reasons for project results	Compiles ideas for continuing studies based on agreed project conclusions

more particulars in each cell. The items included above refer to the curriculum for middle years projects, but they have general applicability across more junior and more senior subjects and year levels. This is a matter of professional judgement and interpretation for the teachers concerned. A point has been reached therefore where curriculum design incorporating a combination of integrated studies, content and philosophy workshops, knowledge exemplars and the interface practice index has provided a progressive and pragmatic epistemological paradigm in which to locate a more appropriate understanding and practice of literacy, numeracy and student assessment for all children.

7   Creative knowledge formation in the humanities and arts

Happiness a state of being
constructed throughout the ages
with permanence for everyone
to grasp and wonder eternally
regardless of social consciousness
restricting a buoyancy of mind
useless against the cries of suffering.

Why is it that some ideas take hold in the mind while others do not, or take hold at particular times for particular people? The filing cabinet view of mind would probably suggest that there are plenty of gaps that need to be filled because of the child's background, inadequate teaching or insufficient effort. The neural network model of mind would probably comment that the range of experience has not been extensive or intensive enough to allow connections to be made between current and new ideas. From a structuralist standpoint, there may be a structure in the brain that considers all spiders to be scary and dangerous. No matter how often the child is told that this is not so (information placed in the 's' file), the view remains fixed. It may be however that, at some point, due to a new experience in relation to the evolving combined experience of the child, a new structure is formed whereby spiders are considered as more acceptable and less frightening. Exactly how one understanding (structure A) is transformed into another new understanding (structure B) is unknown and will vary for each person, or indeed how a principle or more abstract idea (all spiders are scary) is changed by direct practical experience. Piaget talked about 'appearances' and how the child's 'reason' cannot change how phenomena 'seem to be'. What does seem clear is that learning occurs when a new relationship is established between the subject (child) and object (spider) when each acts on the other in a dialectical manner. It is difficult to see how this new relationship can occur, be worked upon, be refined and emerge if the prospects for action are limited, such as when the only opportunity for personal experience involves a small rectangular sheet of white paper on a desk top.

Dewey's integrated view of learning involved aesthetics, the incorporation of expression and form, the relationship between subject matter and interpretation, the nature of art and the relationship between the different branches of art. In describing the difference between art and aesthetics, he wrote (Dewey, 1958, p. 356):

> On one hand, there is action that deals with materials and energies outside the body, assembling, refining, combining, manipulating them until their new state yields a satisfaction not afforded by their crude condition – a formula that applies to fine and useful art alike. On the other hand, there is the delight that attends vision and hearing, an enhancement of the receptive appreciation and assimilation of objects irrespective of participation in the operation of production.

In this regard, Dewey was noting the difference between art and aesthetics as being concerned with materials and objects and their role in human experience. He integrated his notion of aesthetics as the act of experience into a theory of experience that went even further, where a democratic society seeks the liberation of experience for the continuing development of meaning and value for all citizens. This is a difficult task for society, let alone for schools, but sets a broad direction that can be established across the entire curriculum for all schools. Dewey also contended that objects and events (like spiders and brushing past a web) have both place and origin in a perceived and broader world as part of lived experience. We attend to these events when there is a personal reason, as objects of inquiry. When these structures are formed in the mind they enable new structures and ideas to be created in relation to others. If this is the general model of knowing then it applies in all cases, to all knowledge and understanding. Prospects for acting on the area of triangles or the use of doing words need to be available for understanding and meaning. A new structure such as 'hippopotamus' won't make a lot of sense if it exists only in the mind of the teacher or as squiggles on a page and not in the mind of the learner. When there is a settled relationship between the combination of present structures and the new, the learner will come to know the new concept. Understanding the relationship between two sides of a triangle and the included angle is difficult until such time as experience has enabled this relationship to be practised, to be tasted, to be seen and heard, to be experimented. There is a reverse (or continuing integrated) process as well: the more we come to know an object, the more we discover its relationship with other objects and fields of inquiry, the deeper meaning in general becomes. Walking to the park and discussing the different birds we see connects us more with the idea of category, quantity and the decimal point.

This accumulating body of experience, including art, enables us to reconsider what was previously overlooked. According to Dewey, art exposes the hidden expression of experience and takes us to new places of delight and surprise. In this aesthetic process, the objects of experience take on these new qualities and change in our understanding of them. A painting or poem regarding the landscape may invoke new feelings and impressions not present before, creating new, unusual cognitive structures and new perceptions of the objects (bush) themselves. Not only are we changed by new understandings of tree, dust, cold and colour, but the trees themselves take on new meaning and are changed. The ghost gum with its green leaves illuminated by the midday sun is now different to what it was before. A new relationship with the concept of circle is established as we explore the distance around the outside and across its centre, a new relationship is established between the describing word and its object as we explore labels such as 'ghost' and 'green', 'outside' and 'centre' used in different ways at different times. As we become closer to meaning through experience, inquiry and imagination, it becomes possible to go beyond the immediate and see the properties of objects in many situations. Playing on the seesaw enables experience with the notion of equality. Again, this must require the combination and interaction of a wide variety of structures for such transformations to occur, leading ultimately to what we have called 'abstract' thought, thought that not only expresses view such as 'I like the rain', but can discuss and critique that view in an informed way. It is here that the aesthetic is active and imaginative, going beyond the meanings and values of the immediate into the constant practice of expression.

Locating the humanities

A significant proportion of schooling is usually allocated to the humanities, involving studies of people and society, history, politics and geography. Like other subjects, the purpose of the humanities is to consider truth, beauty and goodness, major questions and values being confronted both nationally and internationally and to provide an informed knowledge base for productive citizenship. Subject content can be dealt with separately, or be integrated across traditional boundaries and, as has been mentioned previously, will always be a selection from that which is available. Well known for his concept of 'multiple intelligences', Gardner (1999) suggests three topics that he considers important for all children to encounter in school: Darwin's theory of evolution, Mozart's music and the Holocaust. While these may be included separately in science, the arts and history, they can all fall within the humanities curriculum as well. Metaphorically, Gardner considers each of these topics and many others presented to students as large knowledge and intellectual icebergs, with each revealing only a small amount of its massive profile and complexity at first glance. He suggests that application of multiple intelligences can enhance access to such knowledge icebergs in three ways (pp. 186–187):

1   by providing powerful points of entry
2   by offering apt analogies
3   by providing multiple representations of the central or core ideas.

Such an approach links closely with Dewey's notion of continuity and inquiry, Freire's emphasis on culture and community and Bernstein's knowledge structures. Gardner notes that it is characteristic of all seminal ideas that they can be studied and thought about in more than one way and that they can all be 'represented' or 'embodied' in what he calls 'model languages'. He describes the diagrammatic 'branching tree' of Darwin's evolution and comments that 'Geometry will capture shape, film will capture motion, logic will isolate causative factors' and that it is the person who is able to consider all such languages and the different perspectives they provide who will assemble 'the most versatile, flexible and desirable understanding' (p. 206). Clearly, the humanities offer a wonderful opportunity for bringing to bear multiple perspectival model languages or epistemologies drawing on local cultures and meaning that all students bring to class.

Recognised as a knowledge discipline, history is a contested area of the school curriculum and often excites conservative criticism. It can be defined in terms of a succession of events and dates that has laid the moral and political foundation of a country and which should be known to all children. Whether or not studies of religion should be included here is one of the most heated aspects of the debate, including where the controversy between evolution and creationism fits historically. Rather than a somewhat passive and neutral time-line of events and dates, the study of history can be defined as analysis and critique of key ideas and contradictions that have been dominant aspects of social life at particular times and the type of change that has consequently occurred. This tension within the school curriculum has swayed pendulum-like between arguments for a strongly controlled curriculum by state or national governments and a more flexible framework of guidelines for professional and school-based curriculum development.

There is an interesting problem here for neoliberals who would prefer to minimise central control, but who have a vested interest in historical interpretation and propagation. Pearl and Knight (1999, pp. 88–90) are strong advocates of democratic schooling and quote extensively from the 1989 Bradley Commission in the United States which argued that the study of history is important for the two foremost aims of US education, that of 'personal integrity' and 'preparation for public life as democratic citizens', as well as 'preparation for work'. They note particular recommendations of the Bradley Commission that the study of history should be compulsory and embrace more than the mere attainment of useful information:

> To develop judgement and perspective, historical study must often focus upon broad, significant themes and questions, rather than the short-lived memorisation of facts without context. In doing so, historical study should provide context for facts and training in critical judgement based upon evidence, including original sources, and should cultivate the perspective arising from a chronological view of the past down to the present day.

Postmodernists and poststructuralists are particularly concerned with opposition to the 'grand narratives' or threads of history and do not want to see them at the centre of historical studies in schools and universities. Instead, they prefer local narratives disconnected from general themes and influences. In their support for the grand narrative of democratic schooling, Pearl and Knight argue cogently for democratic curriculum and student voice in schools and for sturdy connections between schools and citizenship. There is a careful line that must be trod here for all democratic educators regarding the developing student mind as independent historical investigator. Students need to be immersed in what it means to be a historian, capable of marshalling and analysing the evidence without fear or favour and how sensitive and controversial issues are presented. Issues such as the bombing of Dresden during World War II, the bombing of Hanoi during the Vietnam War and violence during the Eureka Rebellion in Australia continue to be emotional, moral questions that are difficult to confront: history is not neutral. Citizenship is also a complicated matter necessitating a critical and independent stance without expecting students of any age to accept passively current and traditional social mores and habits. Groups that have been discriminated against, who experience poverty and hardship and who have articulated values that constitute a different worldview have a democratic right to propose their own concept and practice of citizenship in opposition to those of the nation state.

The humanities will also be a part of what Kalantzis and Cope (2008) call 'new learning', a view of education that does not simply reproduce past practices, but is built upon intricate contemporary issues for more appropriate and participatory student learning. Incorporating their approach to 'multiliteracies', they outline four principles that form the basis of new learning: diversity, acting as a counter to the 'one-size-fits-all' approach to education and teaching; deep knowledge, or grounding learning in epistemologies of possibility, origins, nature and extent of human knowledge; design, or providing a systematic focus on learning experiences and tracking learning processes; global content and aspirations, or regarding changing technologies, cultures and economies around the world.

Kalantzis and Cope then envisage a new approach to civics that builds on the modern past, but extends beyond neoliberal constructs to involve considerations such as multiple layers of self-governing communities, social entitlements and fairness concerns and multiple aspects of citizenship in many divergent communities. Civic pluralism in their minds entails community rights and responsibilities and the negotiation of processes as communities change composition and outlook. The humanities are therefore looked upon by conservative and progressive political and educational perspectives as being crucial to the purpose of schooling, more so than the sciences and mathematics. They are subject to continuing pressure as the social conditions alter and schools are increasingly expected to take account of – if not resolve – many community issues. Together with language, studies of history and of society are perhaps the fulcrum of schooling discontent.

Establishing arts as a form of knowing

In his early work first translated into English, Bourdieu (1971, p.175) described the intellectual field within which creative works are produced. He spoke of the many forces involved that, when considered in existence, combination and opposition, determine the positioning of each work and artist in relation to all others. He commented that, at any given time, not all cultural forces, for example, theatrical performances, sporting spectacles, recitals of songs, poetry or chamber music, operetta and operas, are equal in value and that 'the various systems of expression from theatre to television are objectively organised according to a hierarchy of independent opinions, that defines cultural legitimacy and its degrees'.

As shown in Table 7.1, Bourdieu compiled a list of artistic pursuits and relationships in terms of the potency of legitimation and legitimating authorities, ranging from what might be called 'high' or bourgeois art to 'low' or popular and common activities. His list remains reasonably accurate today, although it may need to include popular dance as a form separate from theatre and music, film and media generally and computer-based technologies, with stronger cultural forces perhaps being added to the middle column, involving large music video concerts, large sporting events and the cult of national and international celebrity. It is interesting to note that the 'sphere of the arbitrary' is still accurate, but all items now have an enthusiastic television presence with large audiences worldwide.

After more than 40 years, Bourdieu's table still reflects the class nature of society and how the 'sphere of legitimacy claiming universality' continues to separate bourgeois art from the lives of ordinary working people. Bourdieu was of course writing from a French perspective, but this could be seen as being similar to other wealthy countries then and now. As the standard of living in these countries has risen since World War II, access to bourgeois art has correspondingly increased, including the various genres of theatre, productions and exhibitions that originate in one country travelling across borders to defray their high costs. The question then becomes the nature of art itself and exactly how its ideological motives are promulgated through schools and other organisations.

Table 7.1 Relationship amongst arts

The sphere of legitimacy claiming universality	The sphere of what is in process of legitimation	The sphere of the arbitrary as regards legitimacy (or the sphere of sectional legitimacy)	
Music	Photography	Dress design	Cookery
Painting	Jazz	Cosmetics	
Sculpture		Interior	Other daily
Literature		Decoration	aesthetic
Theatre		Furnishing	choices, e.g. sports
Legitimate legitimation authorities (universities, academies)	Legitimation authorities in competition with each other and claiming legitimacy (critics, clubs)	Non-legitimate legitimation authorities (haute couture designers, advertising)	

Source: Bourdieu (1971), p. 174.

Dewey considered art as a specialised experience of human experience generally. According to Hickman (1990, p.79), Dewey considered that science is about the significance of objects, whereas art is about the expression of objects, or 'Science leads to an experience, art constitutes one.' Hickman then comments that Dewey saw education in the arts as 'a matter of communication and participation in values of life by means of the imagination and works of art are the most intimate and energetic means of aiding individuals to share in the arts of living'. The artistic producer and consumer are changed by the experience regarding new understandings, attitudes and the like, while the object of art itself takes on new meanings; the stone is not merely a stone any more, but part of a sculpture that depicts an ancient ruin; the word is not a few marks on paper any more, but part of a provocative legend. Connections between art production, appreciation and interpretation are indicated in Table 7.2, where the 'internal goods' of a poem and painting are intimated:

If art in general can be considered as social practice and experience, with poetry and painting constituting the concise expression of ideas in different

Table 7.2 Internal goods (draft) of artistic products

Poem	Painting
Western District	
Layers of dazzling green carpet the land incongruous amidst the pain of drought but characteristic of an aged landscape where species struggle for existence enmeshed by time and distance in contest. Clouds of grey and white churn and eddy pushed by violent winds from the west expectant with continuity and nourishment at least for the moment, until such time as the atmosphere mutates into hostility. But today, illuminated by Bohr's theory of photons and quanta streaming earthward the land is tranquil extending in all directions attended by verdant stands of gum and cypress; in a nearby paddock moisture silently screams.	
Internal goods	*Figure 7.1* Image of a lily pond
Language	**Experience traits**
Knowledge	
Action	Completeness
Thought	Uniqueness
Interest	Unifying emotion

formats, then, as referenced previously, the 'internal goods' of practice suggested by MacIntyre (1983) should be able to be discerned. Five internal goods or properties of practice, also noted previously, are listed under the poem and each can be considered from the point of view of the artist and of the viewer. Readers of the poem will act in using their own language, thoughts and background knowledge in connecting with the writing and in their search for meaning. They will draw on their own interest and social practice in how they wonder about certain words and phrases and ruminate on options regarding what the artist had in mind. The artist will go through a similar process, from original idea, to experimenting with certain arrangements of materials, to evaluating drafts as they appear.

In his discussion of Dewey's approach to art, Jackson (1998) explains the traits of experience that the arts embrace and intensify. Dewey describes having an experience as complete 'when the material experienced runs its course to fulfilment' (p. 7), not separated from, but integrated with, all other experience. The second trait raised by Dewey is that of uniqueness, or 'a single quality that pervades the entire experience in spite of the variation of its constituent parts' (p. 8). This point has also been noted previously in regard to the different influence that each internal good of practice will have with different practices or experiences. The painting may relate strongly to the viewer's knowledge of the garden at the home of an ill friend where they sit and talk, rather than interest in the species of flower.

Dewey comments on this issue for the third trait of unifying emotion when he writes, 'Experience is emotional, but there are no separate things called emotions in it' (p. 10). Emotion such as satisfaction, fear and wonder are contextual, having been established by previous experience and act as a filter for current and new experience. Completeness, uniqueness and unifying emotion as the traits of artistic experience can be used to consider both the painting and poem and be brought into relationship with the draft internal goods for the same purpose.

Bringing authentic artistic experience into the school curriculum requires commitment to the principle of 'student as artist' in the same way as 'student as historian' denoted changed roles for teaching and learning. It is usually the case that not many teachers are practising historians, authors, poets, geographers or sociologists, although some teachers will be practising artists holding public exhibitions, concerts and workshops. This makes it difficult for teachers to encourage students to participate with them in creating new artistic works, in thinking like a practitioner and in experiencing deep understanding of artistic production, appreciation and interpretation. The argument applies equally to the teacher in not grasping fully the process of learning being undertaken by students and the multiple problems and misrepresentations being encountered. Assessment of artistic progress is also difficult, given that the learning environment will consist of a network of social and educational practices that involve internal goods, properties or traits that will be experienced differently by different students.

This is a clear example of where the superficial assessment of students rather than a sophisticated evaluation of curriculum practice distorts learning and demeans capabilities in a major area of knowledge. Considering the arts as enabling a form of learning that clarifies, refines, intensifies and textures experience as the basis of knowledge supports the learner in making more complete sense of the world. Perspectives of the saxophonist and dancer have much to offer the lab technician and statistician. Rather than forcing the arts into a conservative instructional mode, the arts should challenge the traditional curriculum to make all practices accessible and knowledgeable.

Key idea: sociology, epistemology, aesthetics

As has been argued previously, there is little emphasis on an explicit philosophy of education and schooling today given the prevailing neoliberal view. Dominance of market economics has ensured that the role of the school in 'living well' has been severely refurbished to mean individual and private benefit rather than the public good. The neoliberal has little time for aesthetic life for, as Dewey (McDermott, 1981, p. 573) indicated with such pellucid clarity and grandeur:

> An object is peculiarly and dominantly aesthetic, yielding the enjoyment characteristic of aesthetic perception, when the factors that determine anything which can be called *an* experience, are lifted high above the threshold of experience and made manifest for their own sake (original emphasis).

What schools can do however in 'lifting high above the threshold of experience' for all children of diverse social standing is to reconstruct the curriculum and approaches to teaching and learning so that the influence of conservative ideology can be combated as much as possible. In analysing the humanities and arts as creative forms of knowledge at the interface of practice between sociology and epistemology, it is possible to respect the socio-economic background of all students and to fashion experience so that artistic capabilities are recognised. What might be called 'art-centred experience' can then form the basis of 'aesthetic practice', or the interpretations and meanings that arise from artistic works and experience. Aesthetics can be incorporated into epistemology as further experience and practice that aid learning and therefore become an important practice at the interface of sociological and epistemological practice. For Dewey, the formal conditions of aesthetic form were continuity, cumulation, conservation, tension and anticipation (Jackson, 1998, p. 45). Continuity involves connections between abstract and applied knowledge, but is broader, involving habits of mind and intellectual growth. Past and present, materials and thoughts are forever interacting to construct new meaning. The term cumulation refers to the build-up of emotion, tension and understanding as the endeavour proceeds for both producer and consumer. Dewey describes conservation as the mix of energies and forces that are active in experience and which 'push and pull' as the experience continues. Conservation also involves meaning, as the experience demands that what has gone before is reconsidered in relation to what might follow. The concept of tension refers to the compression or release of the energies of practice, especially if the appreciator has spent time with the work and has found it challenging, confusing, puzzling, up-lifting. Finally, Dewey draws a distinction between anticipation that occurs before an artistic experience and anticipation that occurs during the experience. Anticipation is difficult to describe in advance, although it involves the thrill of what might occur, unexpected connections throughout and the possibility of reaching new heights of perception. Interestingly, in relation to aesthetic practice, Jackson (1998, p. 52) quotes the poet Wallace Stevens, who preferred to not offer explanation of his poems:

> Things that have their origin in the imagination or in the emotions very often take on a form that is ambiguous or uncertain. It is not possible to attach a single, rational meaning to such things without destroying the imaginative or emotional ambiguity or uncertainty that is inherent in them and that is why poets do not like to explain.

Views such as this show an unmistakable differentiation between how science on the one hand and arts on the other are conceived, not only by the general public but by the various professions as well. There is probably an emblematic image of science in the minds of many involving a vague, self-possessed person in a white coat working with complicated equipment on complicated ideas. This has probably been cemented in schools by science and mathematics subjects that are dislocated from the life of students and which culminate in binding formalisms. On the other hand, there are fervent artists who speak from the heart without necessarily justifying their stance with evidence taking into account the recognised views and informed criticisms of others.

Unlike science, arts subjects in schools may also contain these features that link to some extent with local culture and respect personal affiliations. We are reminded here of the knowledge structures of Bernstein involving vertical and horizontal arrangements. However there are no epistemological reasons to assume that the nature of the knowledge and ideas of science, mathematics, humanities and arts is fundamentally different in complexity and density, depending on how they are organised and encountered. If school subjects are arranged as social practices with integrated projects and defined internal goods, properties or traits then the degrees of difficulty associated with each practice will be similar or the same. Redefinitions of knowledge can occur across groups of year levels such as the early, middle and senior years. Specialist subjects in the senior years, or indeed content workshops at all other levels, will take up specific issues in more depth. For example, setting up and loading the potter's kiln could be similar to the setting up of distillation equipment in the chemist's lab. Finetuning the piano and violin will raise similar concepts to using a cathode ray machine. Analysing the meaning of a poem may be similar to puzzling over a paragraph in a journal paper. Using a graphical calculator can inform activities in sport, the composition of paint mixtures, adjustments of a car engine and the level of blood alcohol content. Those who support experience, inquiry and reflection as learning accept that learning means learning about something (process and content) and there is great respect for mathematical and scientific knowledge, but the rigid imposition of knowledge structures and formalisms from outside school on children in school can make learning almost impossible.

Integrated project

This is the third curriculum chapter that suggests how general principles regarding key areas of knowledge practice can be incorporated across the curriculum. Discussion of integrated projects and knowledge exemplars therefore will be similar across the curriculum Chapters 5–7. Arising from consideration of humanities, arts and aesthetics, a further fundamental change for schooling – indeed, for society – has been suggested above; that is, a strengthening of Dewey's notion of learning as experience and inquiry associated with the conceptual reconstruction of Bernstein's discourses. Linking humanities and arts should be straightforward given their similarities. Rather than the concept of vertical and horizontal relationships amongst knowledge, all school subjects are now seen as a network of knowledge discourses that are engaged when necessary by students to pursue their learning, scaffolded as social practices in classrooms and in the process of thinking itself. Some discourses may be essentially vertical or horizontal at a specific point for specific children, but at other points for other children the discourses may be much more interactive. It is not necessary to discard the terms humanities and arts but, in keeping with the 'network of discourses' proposal, reconceptualisation (which can occur to a greater or lesser extent) does mean that the domains are seen as broadly integrated, holistic and connected, drawing a clear line of distinction with current designs. Forms of assessment will not rely on the recall of propositions and rules, but would expose progress with meaning. It may be that if the new fields are accepted as being primarily concerned with learning, experiment, play and thinking rather than specified content, then formal assessment will not be required. Identified content could be included in other subject domains as a practice rather than being organised as a separate entity. As discussed in Chapters 5 and 6, specific workshops to consider particular humanities and arts content could be arranged during the week or semester, resulting in an integrated curriculum model, as shown in Figure 5.3. The essential feature of this approach is epistemological, where students are participating in an explicit and defensible paradigm of experiential or pragmatic knowledge and learning.

With a small number of integrated studies being the preferred epistemological model, there will be less subject content involved compared with traditional curriculum designs. The amount of content included is always a selection from what is available, with less content demonstrating the intention of delving deeper into meaning rather than skimming across the surface of knowledge. This will be reflected strongly in the philosophy workshops that will investigate understanding of humanities and arts concepts, their origins and use. For example, a range of issues can be informally raised to encourage students to think and propose creatively about their worlds: 'How do playwrights *think* of plots?' 'Why didn't the generals just sit down and *make* peace?' 'What *impact* did silent films have on the audience compared with the impact films have on audiences today?' Their comments are not wrong and are not assessed, but form the basis of their expanding knowledge base. As dialogue and experiment proceed, the adult can introduce other ways of thinking about experience perhaps through creative, descriptive, dramatic and aesthetic means: 'What are the differences between *entertainment* and teaching?' 'Was it *right* for the atomic bomb to be dropped?' 'How would you change scene 2 so it is more *evocative*?' 'How did Picasso express his ideas in painting *Guernica*?' These questions can be approached philosophically, historically, artistically through discussion and related to other accepted information and conventions from teachers, granddad, books, posters or the Internet. Philosophy workshops and content workshops arise from the integrated studies, with Table 7.3 showing a draft outline of an integrated project that emphasises humanities and the arts.

Table 7.3 Overview of Integrated Project 3: *Alice in Wonderland*

Level	*Middle years 5–9*
Topic	*Alice in Wonderland*
Interface practices	Humanities knowledge
	Arts knowledge
Focus issues	What ideas and attitudes do the characters exhibit?
	How is imagination stimulated by plays?
	What is the history of *Alice in Wonderland* and the history of local productions?
Activities 1 (weeks 1–2)	Attend or participate in performance
	Formation of project teams; general discussion and clarification of focus issues; collation of background materials; critical reviews; initial contact with theatrical groups
Activities 2 (weeks 3–4)	View and discuss video
	Collect data from interviews with actors, audience, newspapers, reports; initial documentation of ideas, issues arising
Activities 3 (weeks 5–6)	Identification and categorising of issues regarding *Alice in Wonderland*
	Drafts circulated to local theatrical groups for feedback
Progress outcomes (week 7) (for assessment)	Public exhibition and discussion of findings
	Contribution to blog, social media
	Communication with theatrical groups, actors
Ongoing studies (week 8)	Investigation of the main ideas in productions that appeal to different audiences
	Analyse different genre of plays developed in different countries and why
	Contact with actors in different countries regarding trends in theatre

This integrated study of climate change enables mathematics, science and technologies to be underscored throughout and for particular aspects of these practices to be consolidated in the separate philosophy workshops. Focus questions will generate issues around the climate change argument, how science is being used or misused in support of a particular viewpoint, the nature of appropriate evidence and the social values that are generally agreed as being important. Small groups or project teams of students will investigate these questions under the guidance of teachers but will be as independent as possible. Obviously, the role of the teacher is crucial, participating with students as a team member and offering advice and avenues to pursue within the overall epistemological framework of the study. Arranging issues, ideas, conflicts and the like will require careful tabulation and community checking for accuracy. Outcomes from the project are available for assessment and include public performance, exhibition and discussion of findings as well as Internet communication for comment and feedback. Other aspects of the study can be identified for ongoing work depending on progress made and the time available. As integrated projects of this type accumulate across each year level and across schools in general, it will become possible to consider 'exemplars of knowledge' as the basis of the curriculum, generated locally rather than from the textbook.

Knowledge exemplars

As integrated projects are completed, parents (through community meetings or learning-circle discussions), teachers and students can begin to reflect on their composition and any themes or features they see emerging. These themes can then be detailed on a matrix involving key aspects as agreed by participants. Indicators of each aspect can then be suggested so that there is a clear display of the nature and quality of the work undertaken. Table 7.4 shows a matrix or 'knowledge exemplar' (for a more extensive discussion, see Hooley, 2009) arising from the *Alice in Wonderland* integrated project and concerns the issue of 'theatre arts' that could be identified as being central to the study.

Four indicators are provided for each feature of the knowledge exemplar. For example, with the 'community culture and artefacts' feature, there can be seen a strong influence of local connections with theatrical events and local people, resulting in respect for community culture and knowledge. The final two rows of the knowledge exemplar show how links can be made to the regular school curriculum. That is, beginning with the local knowledge of students around negotiated key issues of importance to them and their community, a process of investigation ensures connections with school subjects and, for this exemplar, the incorporation of reconceptualised literacy/numeracy as arts/humanities, or better still, philosophy. As mentioned above, the accumulation of integrated projects and knowledge exemplars over time could form the basis of the regular curriculum, thereby shifting the intellectual centre of gravity from the general to the local, at least in the initial stages of investigation.

Table 7.4 Overview of *Knowledge* Exemplar 3: Theatre Arts

	Indicator 1: Connections with local community	Indicator 2: Connections with family	Indicator 3: Principles of living	Indicator 4: Humanities, arts philosophy
Community	Local themes, issues, sites, ceremonies	Historical events	Personal enjoyment through experience of arts	Concise ideas for clarity, intensity, expression
Community culture and artefacts	Photographs; stories from Elders	Newspaper articles; role of family in community	Respect for local songs, stories, plays	Culture, artefacts as basis of community, understanding
Ideas and knowledge	History of local theatre, festivals, public arts events	Reading, arts always important to all members	Ideas connect, refine ideas from other domains	Important for a balanced, informed life
Reflection	Discussion with family, teachers, artists	Discussion with community groups, Elders, artists	Interview with local newspaper, identities	Memories, discussion with Elders, artists
Making public	Performances, parent–teacher nights, newsletters	Performances, exhibitions, displays at school	Reviews for comment, articles in newspapers, social media	Performances, choir, dance groups for local community
Links to school curriculum	Integrated projects	Incorporate views, criticisms from family	Social justice issues re access, resources	Principles and critique of arts, humanities
Implications for school curriculum; humanities, arts	Artistic experience major ongoing principle of curriculum, learning	Incorporates social media, timelines, relationships	Raises categories of values, themes, conflicts, customs	Dialogue, narrative, teamwork, themes, patterns, meaning

As a final step in the process, ongoing monitoring of teaching and learning progress and quality can be undertaken by application of an interface practice index (Table 7.5) for each knowledge exemplar. Brief definitions of each index practice (column 2) can be adapted to meet local circumstances, including current approaches and curriculum planning being implemented by teachers, although the problem of knowledge relativism must be borne in mind. The interface practice index applies to knowledge exemplars and therefore enables curriculum evaluation rather than for assessment purposes regarding individual

Table 7.5 Interface practice index for Knowledge Exemplar 3: Theatre Arts

Practice	Definition	Index 1	Index 2	Index 3
Continuity	Dialectic between abstract, concrete knowledge; antidualism	Establishes projects that feature artistic practice, reflection	Encourages links between outcomes and perspectives	Supports creative thinking about new ideas, cause, effect
Inquiry	Open-ended, based on personal interest	Investigates own practice for improvement	Participates as team member	Incorporates local and global studies into practice
Praxis	Cycles of ethically framed action for change and public good	Implements description, explanation, reflection and change of practice	Develops curriculum and cross-curriculum praxis approaches to learning	Constructs learning environments of ethically informed action for the public good
Dialogue	Democratic, open discussions for consensus	Compiles, discusses artistic artefacts of personal learning over time	Participates with artistic artefact, knowledge that show meanings of practice	Engages discourses that clarify practice and illuminate the reflection of practice in practice
Habitus	Human dispositions and structures that relate to activity	Identifies family, personal viewpoints of culture, arts	Reflects on reasons for personal views	Considers other views based on personal practice
Fields	Human activities that relate to habitus	Recognises family, personal learning from immersion in artistic personal practice	Supports communities of practice for improved learning environments	Critique of practice for changed conditions to formulate new practice
Capitals	Cultural, economic, social features of human influence	Identifies features of family cultural, artistic background	Considers range of cultural, artistic, factors	Critique of culture, artistic factors for new practice
Reflexivity	Relationship between habitus and field	Activates, connects with families, local communities	Integrates family, community culture and knowledge into curriculum	Participates with community groups to investigate local history, knowledge, language
Internal goods	Set of practice properties that enable human knowledge, virtue	Incorporates language, family interest, activity throughout practice	Develops awareness of language, family artistic, other practice properties	Encourages enhanced use of practice properties
Knowledge	Defensible human understanding arising from inquiry and reflection	Participates in discussion of project artefacts, outcomes	Considers different reasons for project results	Compiles ideas for continuing studies based on agreed project conclusions

students. Using the index makes it possible to chart progress year by year, or to moderate curriculum development and improvement across different schools if required.

Table 7.5 has been designed for the theatre arts knowledge exemplar above. The interface practice index is constructed so that the separate indices provide an increasing gradation of complexity from left to right. A more detailed gradation could be arranged through the provision of additional columns and more particulars in each cell.

There is a similarity of proposals regarding curriculum outline and detail discussed in Chapters 5–7. This was intended and is to be expected when the main idea of learning is based on the anti-dualism philosophy of Dewey and the pragmatic process of experience, inquiry and reflection resulting in integrated projects and knowledge exemplars across the curriculum. Figure 5.3 shows a third area of study that has not been detailed in the previous chapters, consisting in general terms of sports, technologies, excursions and eclectic cultural studies. Time needs to be available during the week for activities of this type, to enable students to learn musical instruments, participate in clubs and societies, to join school and interschool sporting programs, to attend camps and excursions and to undertake studies in various craft and trade workshops. Such 'practical' activities relate to the purpose of Dewey in establishing the Laboratory School (Durst, 2010) at the University of Chicago in 1896. The curriculum involved in part gardening, cooking, textile and material workshops so that students became familiar with 'occupations' or the embodiment of ideas in action. In these activities, the effect of ideas could be felt and imbibed not so much as preparation for life outside school, but for the authentic experience of life itself. Dewey was working through these curriculum practices over a century ago and it would be interesting to see his preferred curriculum today with the teaching, resource and technological base available. A colleague of Dewey at Columbia University, Kilpatrick advocated the project model for implementing the experiential approach to learning so that students would become 'better citizens, alert, able to think and act, too intelligently critical to be easily hoodwinked by politicians or patent-medicines, self-reliant, ready of adaptation to the new social conditions that impend' (Kilpatrick, 1918, p. 334, quoted in Pring, 2007, p. 108).

The integrated project curriculum model of Figure 5.3 envisages on average integrated studies being conducted during four mornings of the week, content and philosophical workshops being undertaken during the afternoons and practical studies and activities being spread over the equivalent of one day. On this model, four sessions would be available during the week for integrated studies of mathematics and science and another four sessions would focus on humanities and arts. As noted previously, the integrated model allows for less time on specific content compared with current traditional knowledge or content arrays, but the process of experience, inquiry and reflection together with access to online materials will encourage greater depth of thought, action and understanding. Pedagogical approaches appropriate to integrated inquiry learning are discussed in Chapter 10. In the end, both traditional/conservative and progressive/radical epistemologies have little substantial evidence to support their positions, even after a century of contest. Traditional education continues to assess content outcomes superficially and progressive education has still not consolidated programs to the extent that progressive forms of assessment have been introduced, trialled and validated over time. World wars, economic depression, political interference, poverty and discrimination and the current dominance of neoliberalism have distracted and redirected the education profession from epistemological progress. But this is no excuse.

8 Indigenous learning and culture

Rebounding between the large and small
thought refuses to be constrained
irrespective of outer prejudice and command
seeking to falsify resolute deliberation
demanding explanation of nature's way
interests of compassionate humanity prevail.

It is not easy to grasp the notion of Indigeneity, or what it means to be Indigenous, the worldview and perspective of Indigenous peoples. This is so whether of Indigenous or non-Indigenous origin. Similar questions of being and existence have confronted all peoples across the centuries, involving many unresolved issues in the minds of many, such as creation; land and country; morality and values; truth, knowledge and learning; law and justice; politics, history and culture; community and language; identity, family and kinship. In broad terms, these issues can be considered in three categories. First and in addition to being the original inhabitants, there is the concept of human being itself and of being from the land, related to all aspects of country. Second is the issue of community, where different groups of people have different histories, language, song, ceremony and artefact that bring community members together with similar understandings, experiences and aspirations. Third, there is the matter of Indigenous identity and recognition which, according to the United Nations, involves self-identification, community acceptance and historical connections with pre-settler societies (UN, 2013). These three components of existence, community and identity interrelate to form a consciousness of Indigeneity that distinguishes Indigenous peoples but which at the same time establishes a basis for connection with the non-Indigenous and often dominant worlds. However, imperialism, racism and the formation of nation states have made the continuation and strengthening of Indigenous perspectives almost impossible, especially in Fourth-World countries (dispossessed Indigenous nations within colonised societies), where oppressed and marginalised viewpoints are, by definition, disregarded by the powerful and privileged.

In rejecting the non-Indigenous perspective, some Indigenous communities may seek to live quite separately from non-Indigenous people, either in a separate nation state of their own, or in a separate community within a nation state. If the former, a strong commitment of purpose and realisable approaches to a range of social and political issues are required, such as style of government, economic development (production, trade, employment, taxation), legal systems, relationship with other states, including military, public health, housing, transport, education and the like. If the latter, then a set of procedures will be required to frame and regulate contact between Indigenous and non-Indigenous peoples on a daily basis, whether formal or informal. Such procedures will include living alongside non-Indigenous neighbours and participation in the social and political events of the dominant society.

The issue at stake here is whether such arrangements will automatically weaken or destroy Indigenous history, language and worldview, or whether strength of purpose will enable 'two-way' (Hooley, 2009; see below) approaches to eventuate. That is, a coming together and respect for Indigenous and non-Indigenous ways of living that allow different understandings and cultures to co-exist. Experience suggests that the 'two-way' approach is extremely difficult to achieve because of the very strong persistence of colonial, racist and discriminatory features of the dominant society. Under these powerful socio-economic circumstances, finding appropriate circuit breakers that can unite rather than divide requires tolerant and imaginative proposals that enable the participation of all citizens. At a local level, working side by side every day, sporting events, celebrations and festivals, daily encounters in shopping centres and other places of business, membership of neighbourhood groups such as environmental and historical societies all contribute to deeper understanding through community activity. At a more general level, participation in government and electoral issues, administration of public hospitals and schools, development of housing precincts and employment opportunities bring community members together to resolve problems for community interest. The assumption here is that such work at the 'cultural interface' (Nakata, 2007) will assist mutual ideological change at the same time as allowing cultural preservation.

Combating the pernicious features of imperialism, colonialism and racism demands broadness of mind and strength of will that do not falter as prejudice, bias and narrow ideological preconceptions emerge. Rather than (understandable) anger or frustration at the lack of progress in developing shared understanding, two analytical considerations need to be taken into account. Personal experience is a powerful and determining factor in how we view the world and is usually not overcome – or indeed challenged – merely by logical thought or discussion. As mentioned above, some type of action or circuit breaker is generally required to impact on deeply held views that have been formed over many years. A fear of water, of spiders, or of heights will not be overcome by thinking or discussion alone, but will require personal, intimate contact with each. In other words, each expression of life needs to be lived rather than exist abstractly, in the mind only. A deep-seated fear of or anxiety towards other people because of perceived difference will not be resolved until such time as people of difference can live and act together for reciprocal benefit. Whether or not activity and problem solving will succeed in strengthening links rather than division will depend on persons of practical wisdom who can identify major problems or issues that will gain from community attention, significant persons who can offer advice and suggest ways of proceeding, patient and calm persons who show the necessary qualities of persistence and diligence and persons who live the virtues of relationship and friendship, especially during difficult times. These are tough requirements when the surrounding ideology tends to the opposite. They are tough requirements for those who have a long history of being exploited, of being dispossessed and dismissed. When this has happened, the prospects of finding or creating situations that meet the requirements of mutuality, practical wisdom, advice, patience, calmness and persistence are limited.

Culture, ways of knowing

In a series of commentaries arising from interviews with Noam Chomsky regarding ongoing resistance by Indigenous peoples in the Americas to the globalisation and homogenisation of their cultures, the concept of *comunalidad* was described. In brief, the concept is understood as 'the principle and practices of communal life and the source of Indigenous identity and resistance' (Meyer, 2010, pp. 30–31). Going beyond the more restricted meaning of 'community' alone, the term *comunalidad* refers to Indigenous understanding of life that is 'permeated with spirituality, symbolism and a greater integration with nature. It is one way of understanding that human beings are not the centre, but simply a part of this great natural world' (Luna, 2010, pp. 93–94). So defined, *comunalidad* contributes to Indigenous epistemology and pedagogy of knowledge that respect the dialectic between humans and land such that each is part of the other and each depends on the other. This establishes the notion of relationship and connectedness as central to all life on Earth and the role of humans as custodians of land for future generations.

For non-Indigenous people, the idea of *comunalidad* will most likely be difficult to understand and accept but, if brought to the table of mutual activity described above by persons of practical wisdom, will provide an avenue for discussion and application. In a similar way, non-Indigenous participants may raise the philosophical and scientific issue of evolution and how plant and animal species have adapted over the years to meet environmental concerns. Here, both groups are demonstrating a profound relationship and connection with the land on which life itself depends and which brings both peoples together with strong attachment. Both groups can recognise that their identity and social purpose have similar precursors and that there is mutual human interest and reciprocity (collective rather than individual) in coming to a clearer understanding of each other's viewpoint. This of course is an idealised version of overcoming cultural and political suspicion and fear, but it contains the key ingredients of how social activity for shared advantage can impact prejudice and jaundiced predisposition.

Similar to *comunalidad* for Indigenous peoples of the Americas, Macfarlane *et al.* (2008, p. 107) report the Maori concepts of *whānau* (extended family) and *whakawhanaungatanga* (building family-like relationships) from New Zealand. These concepts 'indicate both a sense of *belonging to* and a sense of *relating to others* within a context of collective identity and responsibility' (original emphasis) and are necessary supports of learning. Before the European invasion of North America, Native American children were also taught how to survive through hunting, fishing, child rearing and the like and responsibilities to their extended family and tribe (Reyhner, 2008) Unfortunately, rather than education systems seeking out and incorporating social and community philosophies such as these as key features of curriculum, learning has become increasingly institutionalised and formalised over recent years as globalised economies have demanded compliance with standardised marketised imperatives. Accordingly (and begrudgingly), larger proportions of national budgets have been allocated to education in response to increased school-leaving ages, smaller class sizes, increased teacher salaries and improved facilities. As mentioned earlier, the dominance of neoliberalism has ensured that other crucial factors that impact education and learning have been given scant attention, such as the nature of knowledge itself, how learning occurs, the place of daily experience in learning and the significance of culture and values. In terms of culture, Raymond Williams (1989, p. 4) wrote that:

> A culture has two aspects: the known meanings and directions, which its members are trained to; the new observations and meanings, which are offered and tested. These are the ordinary processes of human societies and human minds and we see through them the nature of a culture: that it is always both traditional and creative; that it is both the most ordinary common meanings and the finest individual meanings.

Williams emphasises the notion of culture as meaning and the connections between what has gone before and contemporary happenings. In this way he indicates a high regard for the experiences of ordinary people and their role in cultural formation, rather than seeing culture as the exclusive preserve of the wealthy and privileged. Indigenous culture can be seen in the same light, drawing on the history, language and interpretations of families and communities as new situations and events interact with current understandings. Knowledge and learning shape the basis of meaning, with culture being dynamic and supple as the traditional and creative interweave. There is however a major cultural problem for Indigenous communities around the world as globalisation continues, languages disappear and connection with the old ways becomes more difficult. This is particularly challenging and worrying for Indigenous people who live in close proximity to non-Indigenous neighbours and who share many aspects of modern life, including compulsory school and non-Indigenous knowledge.

Indigenous knowledge that is shared and community-based rather than individual and competitive poses a number of intricate issues for non-Indigenous law, science and educational practices. This is sometimes seen as a problem to be solved, rather than the possibility for democratic engagement. According to the Native American Battiste (2008, pp. 89–90), 'To effect reform, educators need to make a conscious decision to nurture Indigenous Knowledge, its dignity, identity and integrity by making a direct change in school philosophy, policy, pedagogy and practice.' Indigenous communities around the world have regularly reported a small set of principles by which they see learning and knowledge occurring. Confirmed by Australian studies (Hughes, 2000; Hughes *et al.*, 2004), these include learning from the land, proceeding from community interest, the respectful participation of Elders, holistic connections between knowledge, forms of observation and practical inquiry, longer time spans and the place of culture involving language, ceremony and communication.

In discussing his work on the connections between digital applications and Aboriginal knowledge in Australia, Christie (2005) makes a number of significant ontological and epistemological comments. He is interested in how digital environments such as the database can assist 'collective memory-making which is fundamental to renewing traditional knowledge in each new generation' (p. 62) and how digital systems can support this process:

> When Aboriginal elders are inducting their young people into their ancient knowledge traditions, they are not so much interested in teaching them the content of their knowledge, but the shared background which make truth claims and performances possible and assessable, the practices of intuition which derive axioms from theorems, the modes of performance through which truth claims and performances can be made and the complex ethical and aesthetic work which is done in validating and privileging some particular performances rather than others (p. 66).

The fact that the regular curriculum in the major economies has found it incredibly difficult to incorporate and work with these principles indicates either a lack of ontological and epistemological sophistication, or the continuing influence of prejudice and bias regarding diversity. What is striking however when reading the literature is the close correspondence between ways of knowing and the approaches of integrated inquiry learning outlined by pragmatic philosophers such as Dewey (1958, 1966). As mentioned previously, schooling has struggled to implement a truly integrated and inquiry curriculum and still maintains a system that is heavily characterised by behaviourism. This may be due to the strong cultural, yet essentially unexamined and uncritiqued, framework that has grown up around a particular subject, as with school mathematics, or the power relations that are maintained by privileged forms of knowledge through strict regimes of assessment. These features of culture and power that determine curriculum design and pedagogical practice make it extremely difficult for Indigenous considerations to be heard, let alone impact substantially on daily classroom life.

Taking the concept of Williams above regarding culture as meaning and the proposition that schools are primarily concerned with meaning making for all students, it should be possible to design an approach towards learning that is culturally inclusive for all students. While it is not unusual to come across such comments in the literature, it is more difficult on the ground to redirect a curriculum that is based on the spread of predetermined knowledge regardless of cultural and community context. For Indigenous students, the curriculum at all levels must involve a set of key principles that recognise culture, community and environment and which encourage genuine participation by community members in the life of the school. A list that could begin discussion at the school level could include:

- learning based on personal and community interest for meaning making
- personal and community learning that draws on all aspects of local culture through the enhancement of ideas, curiosity and imagination
- harmonious, respectful relationship with the natural environment
- learning that is generated locally and tempered by global issues
- processes of holistic inquiry with thinking, doing and reflection combined in all learning
- negotiated, integrated project-based learning in all areas of curriculum
- community partnerships and participation in schooling, especially by Elders as mentors, facilitators and advisors in residence
- democratic decision making with parents, teachers, students on major curriculum matters.

These are considered as epistemological features of culture rather than sociological. That is, they constitute an approach towards knowledge and learning that links with the cultural context of local communities and which provides a realistic framework for culturally inclusive pedagogy in the classroom. It is most likely that mainstream schools and teachers will need to begin from the beginning in establishing respectful relationships with local Indigenous communities, a process that takes considerable time and patience for conviction and trust to be confirmed. In effect, a process of curriculum change of this magnitude is equivalent to a change of schooling itself, to an approach that sees the purpose of schooling as independent meaning making for all students as they grow and experience life and develop their own emerging theories of the world. It is a view of schooling that, while located within and modified by hegemonic knowledge, respects and enables the epistemologies of students to flourish in their own right.

Learning together: language and literacy

Reading has always been considered central to learning – indeed, central to what it means to be a cultured and educated citizen. For those working people of the World War II generation, who left school often with a primary school education to go to work in the factories, shops, mines and farms, reading and writing were important aspects of life involving newspapers and magazines, books from the local library, all manner of forms regarding employment, mortgage and rent notices, community news, health documents and the like. Letter and card writing was also a main way of keeping in contact with family members, with mothers and grandmothers usually being responsible for keeping a record of birthdays, celebrations, family events, embarrassing relations and associated scandals. It is understandable then that reading and writing were major concerns of schooling and were subjects that were intimately understood by parents and the community generally. Following World War II and the rapid expansion of secondary schooling in the major economies, the curriculum became somewhat more abstract, although as the school-leaving age increased, many students of working families left as soon as they were legally able to do so to take up apprenticeships and other forms of employment. Only a small proportion of students continued on to university-level studies during this time, meaning that the increasingly 'academic' curriculum of secondary schools was not always congruent with the life experience of students remaining at school. Of course, it is the responsibility of schools to introduce students to ideas and experiences they would not otherwise encounter, but if the gap between new and old understandings becomes too great, barriers to comprehension begin to emerge.

Indigenous families are instantly embroiled in the language and learning debate when their children attend regular schooling. From the discussion above, language and culture are strongly connected and the lack of opportunity to utilise their language at school is a major impediment for most Indigenous children. The issue then arises as to how Indigenous children can access and engage a second language both at school and in the dominant society for purposes of formal and informal social participation. This may be a different question for second-language learners who come from a country where a different language is spoken but where cultural practices and values are similar.

Indigenous people are quick to point out that multiculturalism is different to the inclusion of Indigenous groups that usually have a quite different worldview, including that of knowledge and learning. Hughes (2000) above noted the general characteristics of Indigenous culture, including country, community and holistic knowledge and the role of language and ceremony. Thus, language has an obligatory connection to all aspects of community life – connections that, if severed by school, distort the very nature of language and learning themselves. Some key principles of curriculum were also noted above that are required to support Indigenous culture, including learning based on personal and community interest for meaning making, learning that draws on all aspects of local culture through the enhancement of ideas and negotiated, integrated project-based learning in all areas of curriculum. Active language making is central here, with a silent or language-depressed classroom being an exclusionary and frustrating environment for all children, including Indigenous. Participating in curriculum matters is an extremely difficult task for all parents (and in many cases professional teachers as well) depending on the school structures that are available, but raising provocative questions of community, culture and language must be attempted if the literacy of the dominant society is to become a possibility of liberation for all marginalised children.

In discussing the stages of Indigenous education in the United States, Gregory Cajete, a Tewa Indian from New Mexico, suggests that they form an interrelated 'life way' on the path to becoming 'more fully human' (Cajete, 2012, p. 152). He goes on to explain:

> Indigenous education traditionally recognised each of the most important interrelationships through formal and informal learning situations, rites of passage and initiations. Since the highest goal of Indigenous education was to help each person to 'find life' and thereby realise a level of completeness in their life, the exploration of many different vehicles and approaches to learning was encouraged. This was done with the understanding that individuals would find their own best approach in their own time.

There is a stark difference being expressed here between the philosophies of Indigenous and non-Indigenous learning. Indigenous learning is directly related to coming into harmony with the natural world and an understanding of life experiences through story, ceremony, ritual, song, dance and works of art. In broad terms, the notion of *Mitakuye Oyasin* or 'we are all related' (Cajete, 2012, p. 150) also expresses a similar view for the Lakota people of North America. On the other hand, non-Indigenous learning through formal education concentrates on a separation of life and knowledge, privileging instead more intangible knowing such as principle, generalisation and theory of subject content. Under these conditions, the difficulties faced by minority Indigenous populations in majority mainstream schools are paramount, if not insurmountable. Such difficulties are magnified when assessment procedures fall into the same dominant and conservative ideology, ensuring failure by measurement.

From an Australian Indigenous perspective, Martin (2009, p. 72) affirms this view when she comments that ways of knowing require a person to know 'who your people are' and 'where you come from.' She continues that this means 'to know one's Stories of relatedness to your Ancestors, your Country and its elements of past, present and future'. Again, the issue of relatedness between humans and the physical environment of land, plants, animals, sky and waterways takes priority for living and therefore of learning. This is the basis of the major philosophical contradiction that exists between Indigenous and non-Indigenous learning that places an enormous burden on regular schools locked into more conservative pedagogies.

Snyder (2008, pp. 216–217) proposes that the history of literacy is an important component of thinking about and constructing a productive literacy for the twenty-first century. She comments that:

> Literacy is inextricable from the changes that have taken place in communities, societies, nation states and the global domain, both in recent times and over the centuries. Literacy is also ever-evolving. Today, as much as in any other historical period, new literacy practices are emerging and the concept of literacy continues to change as it has always done.

This intelligence has important application for Indigenous peoples and their relationship with regular curriculum. It means that, at any particular time, non-Indigenous schooling does not have all the answers and that there is always scope for innovation and contestation. There is a very strong literature on the different approaches to literacy and many examples of progressive practices that can be used to challenge conservative and static programs. As discussed elsewhere, the notion of multiliteracies offers new ways of conceptualising literacy from a cultural and therefore Indigenous perspective. Incorporating electronic social media and other electronic platforms can provide new avenues into language, communication and literacy for Indigenous students, bridging current and emerging strategies.

Another example from the African American experience, although more sociological than epistemological, is the story of High School X (Prendergast, 2003), that documents long-term efforts to relate literacy and racial justice. The school has adopted policies of engagement for students who are uncomfortable at other schools, who have not achieved academically, who are looking for a multicultural curriculum of respect or who may have suffered harassment of various types. Named after the African American activist Malcolm X, the school's 'entire curriculum reflects its community building efforts through study of historically disenfranchised groups and critique of American domestic and foreign policy' (p. 126). Courses include the juvenile justice system, Native American history and women's studies, arising as a result of having as much student participation in their design and presentation as possible. High School X may still be a case of mainly 'teaching about' (sociological) issues as distinct from 'learning with' (epistemological) practices, although students and teachers would no doubt argue that they do live the dilemmas covered every day.

Community and epistemologies

It is incumbent on regular schools to find appropriate ways of including Indigenous students and other students at the educational periphery in all learning. Incorporating Dewey's philosophy of pragmatism, as discussed earlier, and the associated notion of practice-based learning, the proposal for 'two-way inquiry learning' (Hooley, 2009) has been developed as a means of establishing a democratic epistemological framework for cultural inclusivity. The dimensions of two-way inquiry learning, as shown in Table 8.1, have been reworked since originally published and are now grouped within two categories of identity and community and schooling and epistemologies. These categories draw attention first to the essential connections between learners, communities and the natural world and second to the incorporation of appropriate structures and epistemologies by schools that enable rather than restrict participation.

The concept of 'two-way' or 'both-way' schooling is reasonably familiar in the literature (Harris, 1990), but has been criticised on the grounds that, in an inequitable society, the dominant will always dominate, the exploited will always be exploited. In schools, this means that recognised and privileged

Table 8.1 Dimensions of two-way inquiry learning

Dimension	Description
	Identity and community
Dimension 1	Holistic views of life and learning where knowledge arises from and returns to social and cultural environments for the betterment of communities of interest and where formal systems of education must be connected with the major debates and philosophies within communities to ground their purpose and meaning
Dimension 2	Continuity of society, experience and nature as the basis of all learning and of formal learning programs
Dimension 3	Recognition that the expression of learning occurs in different ways for different children based on their cultural and socio-economic background, but that a set of similar factors may exist in all cultures that emphasise construction of new knowledge rather than instruction in old content. This demands a respect for the knowledge and culture that all children bring to school and an acceptance that learning occurs actively from this identity
	Schooling and epistemologies
Dimension 4	Integrated educational practice and theorising of practice incorporating respect for and learning with the local community and natural environment
Dimension 5	Long-term systematic processes of inquiry, reflection on experience, reflexive experience and story telling
Dimension 6	Validation of children's learning, knowledge and experience based upon long-term consensual and democratic dialogue amongst participants on what is generally considered as being acceptable, credible and trustworthy
Dimension 7	Teaching and learning that enables a framework of:

- holistic, integrated and constructed knowledge
- emphasis on knowing by doing and experimental work
- collaborative interaction in real-life situations
- negotiated decisions on directions and purposes
- strategies of trial, error and critique
- multiple pathways for entry and inquiry
- open-ended learning for teachers and students
- applying context-specific and general ideas
- utilising respected local and expert advice as required
- encouragement of personal, group and community interests
- being challenged by local and global events

knowledge will always be given preference, even if some consideration is given to minority understandings. The key ideas of science, mathematics, language, literature and history, for example, will remain unaltered by other perspectives, especially as far as formal assessment procedures are concerned. Two-way *inquiry learning* – as distinct from two-way *schooling* – attempts to deal with this problem by focusing on Dewey's inquiry approaches to learning across the curriculum and establishing recognition of different epistemologies present in any and all classrooms. This approach also means that all students regardless of background are included in similar cultural and practice-based learning so that different groups of students are not considered as having different 'learning styles' that can sometimes be stereotypically labelled 'deficient' or 'superior'.

Two-way inquiry learning has two major characteristics that contrast manifestly with the neoliberal world. First, in respecting and recognising the culture and background of every community member and student, it counters the view that human society and individuals are determined solely by the capitalist market and that life's purpose centres on individual advantage and economic prosperity. Second, in supporting a view of learning and schooling that positions knowledge and comprehension firmly in the social and natural worlds, it responds to the conservative belief that learning is a one-way transmission of what is correctly known and authorised from expert to novice. In both cases, two-way inquiry learning enables strategies that draw upon and strengthen personal and community epistemologies and the development of forms of social organisation for all citizens, Indigenous and non-Indigenous, that are inherently democratic and collegial. Two-way inquiry learning is based upon a dialectic of knowledge, where consciousness and knowledge emergent and present are seen to be in relationship with all other consciousness and knowledge, where such networks and connections are crucial for meaning and can be altered for new meaning. All learners will have certain elements of understanding that have been formed indelibly from educative and miseducative experience and which remain unchanged for long periods of time. Attempting to grasp the structure of a molecule, or the causes of a historical event, may be difficult for the young student for this reason. It is however feasible for many ideas to exist in formation interacting with each other so that new perspectives can be supported over time. Inserting aspects of two-way inquiry learning into Indigenous and non-Indigenous community and schooling traditions and rigidities can open up possibility and options that may otherwise be inconceivable.

Coming to grips with Indigeneity

At the beginning of this chapter the question of Indigeneity was raised as a central question of inclusion and exclusion. The concept of Indigeneity is used here in its global context and is taken to denote a consciousness or worldview or set of perspectives that are distinctively Indigenous. It has been mentioned previously that Indigenous philosophy involves in part an interconnected view of the world, belonging to the land, kinship relationships, family and community story telling and oral conventions of knowledge and learning by Elders and other community members. The lack of an articulated and shared understanding of an Indigenous worldview is perhaps the major problem and barrier to insight if productive and shared work at the 'cultural interface' is to proceed for collaborative research and other projects in schools and other organisations. In considering Indigeneity in terms of worldview, perspective and what it means to be Indigenous, philosophical ideas that emphasise community, culture and identity have been encountered, such as *comunalidad* from North, South and Central America, *whānau* and *whakawhanaungatanga* from New Zealand and *Mitakuye Oyasin* from the Lakota Native Americans. These concepts all relate existence and humanity to the natural world and provide a basis for the production of knowledge, harmony and wisdom.

An issue that may cause some discussion with non-Indigenous approaches to education is whether or not knowledge as conceptualised here is predetermined and essentially unchanging and is known by Elders for passing on to the next generation. This view is contrary to the notion of culture as dynamic, transformed and transforming processes of meaning making, in accord with the suggestions of Williams above 'that it is always both traditional and creative; that it is both the most ordinary common meanings and the finest individual meanings'. Knowledge as a central aspect of culture is evolving and expanding all the time as human experience grows and new conceptions form. Many people now consider the Earth to be spherical rather than flat, the atom to be mainly empty space rather than solid and light to have both particle and wave functions. Ideas such as these impact on our understanding of human existence and unsettle taken-for-granted suppositions.

There are certain risks in attempting to provide some brief overview comments regarding the complex issue of Indigeneity, especially those involving Indigenous and non-Indigenous peoples living and working together within organizational procedure and regulation of the dominant society. A misunderstanding of viewpoint can cause tensions to develop. Dodson (2003, p. 32), for example, has pointed out that 'For Indigenous peoples, there is no doubt that self-determination and self-identification are their inherent and inalienable rights. In both this country and internationally, the principle of self-identification has been enshrined in the law.' However for those citizens who have a deep commitment to social justice and educational equity there is no choice but to express thoughts and proposals as clearly as possible for discussion and response. For non-Indigenous scholars and activists, the task of looking deep within personal understanding and recognising elements of racism and colonialism to decolonise accepted methodologies and practices (Smith, 1999) is immense. The comment by Wilson (2008, p. 69), for example, can be taken as a guide, that for Indigenous people, 'research is a ceremony'. This indicates that the development of knowledge and culture needs to respectfully involve the participation of all those who are concerned and the bringing together of appropriate combined experience and understandings for consideration.

Bridging the concept and practice of Indigenous identity with the reality of schools and the formal curriculum can be guided by an Australian proposal of '8Ways' (2012), whereby 'Teaching through Aboriginal processes and protocols, not just Aboriginal content, validates and teaches *through* Aboriginal culture and may enhance the learning for *all* students.' In addition, the ontological and epistemological ways of being, knowing, valuing and doing, listed earlier, can be investigated across the 'common ground between mainstream and Aboriginal pedagogies':

- learning through narrative
- planning and visualising explicit processes
- working non-verbally, with self-reflective, hands-on methods
- learning through images, symbols and metaphors
- learning through place-responsive, environmental practice
- using indirect, innovative and interdisciplinary approaches
- modelling and scaffolding by working from wholes to parts
- connecting learning to local values, needs and knowledge.

As the above points indicate, incorporating Indigenous identity into the school curriculum is not the same as seeking to Indigenise the school curriculum. Rather, it involves a specific approach towards knowledge and learning that builds upon local culture and experience and which can be applied in all subject areas. As such, it constitutes an approach to literacy and to schooling engagement that is essentially epistemological in character but which may generate some tensions with current pedagogies. For example, more experiential 'modelling and scaffolding by working from wholes to parts' may not be regular practice in either literacy or numeracy, where more inductive and step-wise techniques may be preferred, including the use of information and communication technologies stratagems. Learning needs to involve the whole child, family and cultural connections such that holistic meaning becomes available to enhance identity. Under these conditions, it may be possible to begin with small projects or pilot studies that provide experience for teachers and students in 'mind-sized' bites and from which progress with learning can be evaluated. Such work may not result in an immediate epistemological 'paradigm shift', but it may mean that taken-for-granted non-Indigenous approaches will be challenged to some extent, making greater participation and inclusion possible.

Related to personal experience of 'cultural interface' and 'two-way inquiry learning', the anthropologist Turner (1967) explained the concept of 'liminality' as the encountering of different experience and rituals whereby identity, values and understanding become ambiguous and confusing, until such time as new thinking emerges. It is possible that new thinking will not come forward if current ideas are too strong or intransigent, or the 'liminal' experience is not sufficiently collegial.

Similarly, in their discussion of language, learning and the impact of digital technology, Gee and Hayes (2011) detail what they call 'three social formations' (pp. 121–131). They suggest that the 'oral social formation' allows for interpretation that is 'dialogic, interactive and flexible'. Next, the 'literate social formation' enabled records of previous exchanges to be kept and to provide reference points for future proposals. Such records are often decontextualised (across time) and are considered differently than in the ebb and flow of conversation. Gee and Hayes then describe the 'digital social formation' that allows the oral and the literate to be combined and negotiated by users.

It is these features that begin to break down the roles of authority and institution and which potentially at least can return citizens who may have been excluded to more respected and participatory positions. A 'digital iden-tity' emerges. However, as processes of globalisation and technologising have continued, the strength of the public sphere and relationships within the public have become eroded, with greater emphasis on the individual and the local. It may be however that digital and social media will tend to recover notions of community and public as the channels of communication and expression are recouped by the citizenry. For Indigenous communities, this possibility is significant, as less formal, more conversational and culturally inclusive literacy is accepted, contact with family and community often dispersed is maintained and connections with the dominant society can be explored in ways not feasible before. In this fluid context that is still being worked through, Gee and Hayes ask prophetically whether 'modern social media [is] giving rise to new global publics' (p. 131) or to new forms of separation and isolation. For Indigenous communities and families, this question applies to the 'public sphere' of school and to the public practice of literacy.

Attempting to understand the meaning and implications of Indigeneity for society raises multifaceted issues of the meaning and implications of non-Indi-geneity for society, or, in essence, what it means to be human. Enabling differ-ent worldviews to co-exist around the big ideas and contestations of the day is a major contribution to social progress that formal education pursues and one that must include Indigenous culture and knowledge. Significant and challeng-ing ideas need to be included in this search to assist comprehension of all par-ticipants, such as Indigenous ideas of being from different communities noted above, together with other epistemological possibilities of 'cultural interface', 'two-way inquiry learning', 'digital identity' and 'liminality'.

Looked at in this way, Indigeneity involving Indigenous consciousness, community and culture becomes a crucial factor in encountering and compre-hending the modern world and creative knowledge production. While there may be differences between worldviews in conceptualising time, space and origins, these do not prevent opposing views entering perhaps tentatively into a harmonious or semi-harmonious relationship and establishing the basis of new knowledge, values and satisfaction. Rather than being an added ingredi-ent, Indigeneity should be considered as a reconciling democratic construct of learning and 'systems of meaning' for all citizens, regardless of social class, cultural background or creed.

Part III

Critical theorising and research

Questions of knowledge need to be constantly interrogated, theorised and applied across all areas of education by the practitioners concerned. This can be undertaken within regular democratic and equity frames of reference or from more radical and far-reaching perspectives involving ideology critique, socio-political analysis and critical consciousness. A critical approach to knowledge, teaching, learning and research will involve all participants reflecting on the appropriateness of different paradigms of knowledge, how participation in learning was encouraged and the methodologies used for research. Part III discusses a critical view of knowledge in relation to research, teaching and learning and the education profession generally. There is recognition that a neoliberal worldview is antagonistic to a critical stance and that implementing significant aspects of criticality across all stanza of education will be difficult. The final chapter therefore begins discussion of a new reflexive sociology of knowledge to guide educational discourse and action such that connections can be made between progressive sociology and epistemology in the interests of all children. By this designation, reflexivity is taken to mean the application of ideology critique, socio-political analysis and critical consciousness not only to knowledge produced but to the perspectives and methodologies of sociology and epistemology themselves. Without such critical rigour and intellectual guidance, systems of education based on social class will continue to discriminate atrociously against the tolerated majority in the interests of the privileged minority.

9   Research as bricolage

A small cottage appears amongst the bush
tired weatherboards a witness to change
did thirsty cattle drovers find refuge there
visiting newborn when the herd was fenced?
then, a hill glimpsed between swaying trees
connecting with landscape across the years
our journey constantly making us anew.

All people have a human and democratic right to the best knowledge that each
and every society has to offer. In this case, the word 'best' refers to knowledge
that has credible outcomes, is in accord with social experience and scientific
experiment and has been subject to consensus over time. The word 'scientific'
involves the use of a broad range of exploratory techniques and principles of
science that have arisen throughout the modern era, as well as an extensive
range of investigatory practices used by ordinary citizens as they engage their
realities every day. Emerging from the historical and socio-political conditions
that exist, knowledge, or those general frames of understanding regarding the
social and physical worlds, goes beyond the vagaries of personal experience and
knowing and provides guidance for human activity and community. Whether
or not knowledge exists as 'truth' that holds throughout the universe, or is forever relative, changing as conditions alter, remains a great philosophical question as humans search for meaning and significance. Some 'truth' is accepted
for long periods of time before new observations, contestations and theorising
form new 'truths', especially regarding the nature of existence. Placing the
Earth at the centre of the universe was a previously held 'truth' and currently,
the debate between Newtonian and quantum physics continues unabated.
Whether the atoms on one planet are the same as the atoms on another has yet
to be determined. At the local level, country people may have a closer relationship with the natural environment than city people, providing different insights
into connections between all living species and the land. If society is based on
social class, then knowledge will also have a social class basis and bias that can
inform, relate to or dispute knowledge from other classes.

In many industrial societies, knowledge has a formal connotation of objective, neutral and generalised principle and is seen to result from a specific process of research. On the other hand, Appadurai (2006, p. 167) puts forward the view that research involves 'a generalised capacity, the capacity to make disciplined enquires into those things we need to know, but do not know yet'. He goes on to comment that 'All human beings are, in this sense, researchers, since all human beings make decisions that require them to make systematic forays beyond their current knowledge horizons.' Two competing worldviews are at work here: one that sees the vast bulk of humanity receiving knowledge and truth after it has been discovered and verified by experts in their different fields and the other that recognises the role that ordinary people have in constructing their own knowledge from their (incomplete, subjective) personal lives.

Of course, it is not expected that every citizen will be involved in the generation of all knowledge, that each person will conduct medical research in the morning and work on the production line in the afternoon. But it is contended both philosophically and practically that all citizens are capable of engaging in knowledge production, whether formally or informally, and in fact this is a pressing necessity as the problems and dilemmas of daily life challenge and accumulate. An understanding of fluids and density is vital as the experienced motor mechanic works on the hydraulics of an expensive limousine and theorises various solutions to a spongy brake system. While the motor mechanic may have little direct understanding of the problems and methodologies of medical research, the medical researcher may have little understanding of hydraulic principles of the company vehicle. Stenhouse (2012, p. 128) was in broad agreement with this approach when he wrote:

> Research may be broadly defined as systematic inquiry made public. The inquiry should, I think, be rooted in acutely felt curiosity and research suffers when it is not. Such inquiry becomes systematic when it is structured over time by continuities lodged in the intellectual biography of the researcher and co-ordinated with the work of others through the cumulative capacity of the organisation of the discipline or the subject.

As is to be expected in a class society, neoliberalism appropriates much of the above research discourse for its own purpose. That is, in general terms, research and knowledge must suit the interests of the bourgeoisie and the broad directions of the market and economy. This explains the huge expenditure that supports military and technological research together with the gathering of espionage data around the world, even though it is somewhat contradictory with the central role of the individual, small government and the supposed liberal notion that 'anything goes'.

Neoliberalism also concentrates and therefore distorts research in another important way. Connell (2009) proposes what she calls 'Southern Theory', whereby the dominance of Europe and North America regarding orthodox knowledge in the social sciences is at least counterbalanced by ideas, theories and texts from the unorthodox southern hemisphere. Connell suggests that a new meaning for 'grounded theory' is required, where theory is linked 'to the ground on which the theorist's boots are planted' (p. 206). She argues for a strong connection between the local and the global so that, rather than the application of 'pure general theory', what she calls 'dirty theory' emerges, or 'theorising that is mixed up with specific situations. The goal of dirty theory is not to subsume, but to clarify; not to classify from outside, but to illuminate a situation in its concreteness' (p. 207). This approach to research that respects the understanding of local practitioners, especially in relation to their local problems and imperatives, directly challenges the authority of research philosophies and methodologies imposed from the other or outside worlds, but instead takes generalisation as a means of reworking local situations. The boiling point of water may be generally around 100 degrees Celsius at sea level, but pollution of the river may change this imperceptibly and give rise to new insights about sickness in the township.

It is difficult to discuss research as a totality, as assuredly it is not. Knowledge and research are riven by philosophical and socio-political differences based on social class, race and gender, economic and political purpose, authority and geography, knowledge disciplines in the social and physical sciences and differences in methodology. As a specific instance, qualitative methods are also undergoing constant change as new approaches are sought that are seen as being more appropriate and more detailed for new social conditions. For these reasons, according to Denzin and Lincoln (2003, p. 6), there is somewhat of a crisis of purpose in the social sciences that has forced some researchers to question 'whether social science as conventionally configured' is really explicating and improving the human condition as it should. Denzin and Lincoln continue that such questioning has spawned 'more radical forms of ethnographic and interpretive work, derived from the theoretical and praxis-oriented philosophies of critical theory, action research and participatory action research'. Like Connell and Stenhouse above, they suggest that these approaches position the 'issues of respondents' as the central concerns of research.

It may be thought that matters like these are peculiar to the social sciences, but they are very similar in the physical sciences as well. Pharmaceutical research, for example, exhibits all of these characteristics, beginning with funding decisions on the basis of human need or company profit, the appropriate methodologies to be employed, the cost and accuracy of available instrumentation, extent of trialling, the techniques used for validation of results and the interpretation of meaning. All of these involve human debate and decision at every point where different debate and decision will produce different outcomes. What this means is that research is open to disputation in the same way as all other aspects of uncertain human adventure and that the approaches adopted at any particular time will depend on how hierarchical, ideological and cultural relations are worked out amongst participants.

Confronting the bricolage

From the above discussion, a central question of constructing knowledge and research paradigms that primarily benefit the excluded and deprived must be contemplated. Connell's view of being respectful of, but not dominated by, powerful, affluent and metropolitan stances must also be taken seriously, or at least to begin with local concerns, so that they are then 'clarified' and 'illuminated' from outside. New approaches are required that break through ossified thinking and practices and that genuinely conceptualise knowledge and research as being initiated by culturally inclusive conventions. For instance, in his studies of the culture, language and mythologies of native peoples of South America, the anthropologist Claude Lévi-Strauss discussed the notion of 'prior science' and 'science' societies. He suggested that the French concept of 'bricolage' might be useful here in understanding how myths and legends are used to help explain the physical and social worlds. Lévi-Strauss was beginning with local issues and then inserting broader concepts from the metropolis for analytical purposes. He pointed out that a 'bricoleur' is like a traveller who does odd jobs and who works with what is at hand in pursuing and solving a wide range of problems. The bricoleur 'uses devious means compared to those of a craftsman' (Lévi-Strauss, 1966, pp. 16–17) and further:

> The characteristic feature of mythical thought is that it expresses itself by means of a heterogeneous repertoire which, even if extensive, is nevertheless limited. It has to use this repertoire however whatever the task in hand because it has nothing else at its disposal. Mythical thought is therefore a kind of intellectual bricolage, which explains the relation which can be perceived between the two.

Lévi-Strauss appears to be saying here that mythical thought involves a set of events and experiences that are brought to bear on particular issues, regardless of the nature of those issues, to assist the participants in relating to them. This could be similar to using whatever tools are available in the toolbox regardless of their application, for instance using a screwdriver to hammer in a nail. This may be a 'devious' means, but the craftperson would be aware of other solutions.

An advantage for the bricoleur is that non-traditional approaches can be used to tackle specific problems and that the rules and regulations that may have been raised around such issues do not constrain practical activity. These insights of Lévi-Strauss are suggesting that 'prior science' and 'science' societies can be grappling with similar questions, but that the myths and legends of the former constitute the only toolbox that is available, uninformed by the theories and generalisations of the latter. The notion of bricolage as an organisational and epistemological concept has been further developed by Kincheloe (2001) as a means of destabilising mainstream educational structures and establishing practices more in alignment with the lives of ordinary people.

Kincheloe identified the concept of 'bricolage' as a philosophical approach to learning, knowledge and research and a means by which the various features of human life and scholarship impact on knowing, the features of history, economics and the like, noted above. Drawing on the work of Lévi-Strauss (1966) and Denzin and Lincoln (2000), Kincheloe argued for the conception of teacher and researcher as 'bricoleur' such that diverse methodologies and understandings are brought together in the act of inquiry and research. He recognised that the complexity of knowing well a range of knowledge disciplines required a 'life time commitment to study, clarify, sophisticate and add to the bricolage' (Kincheloe, 2011a, p. 179) and later 'in the deep interdisciplinarity of the bricolage, researchers learn to engage in a form of boundary work' (p. 186). This is no easy task and will probably require teams of practitioners bringing to bear their combined disciplinary know-how, philosophies and experience on difficult problems and ideas. One lifetime is not enough. A critique of both quantitative and qualitative methods in the social sciences and humanities would reveal issues of bias, accuracy, consistency and authentication as well as the lack of relationship between the objective and subjective that raise many troubling issues regarding the stability and trustworthiness of research generally. Kincheloe's commitment to establishing a new comprehensive, cultural, respectful, inclusive approach of knowing, of rigorous interpretation of experience and of theorising through the bricolage opened up a new vision of learning and schooling for teachers and students alike:

> Thus, bricolage is concerned not only with multiple methods of inquiry but with diverse theoretical and philosophical notions of the various elements encountered in the research act. Bricoleurs understand that the way these dynamics are addressed – whether overtly or tacitly – exerts profound influence on the nature of the knowledge produced by researchers.
>
> (Kincheloe, 2011a, p. 180)

In this discussion, the concept of bricolage is used for epistemological purposes, but it can also be used in terms of families bringing together all their resources for mutual benefit. Low income, for example, may mean that all family members undertake a range of economic activity, part-time work and odd jobs to support overall finances and may involve early school leaving. It may mean enrolling in a number of short-term job-training programs that enable a number of positions to be taken up when available.

Such activity is an important aspect of the epistemological bricolage, but for schooling purposes there must be a shift beyond sociological concerns only to the structures, discourses and cultures that interact and influence schooling and learning. This is a necessary shift to explain and combat the notion of 'deficit' associated unfairly and unfortunately with low income and marginalised groups of children. The epistemology that is being described here does not refer to a psychologised version of the child, but to an epistemology of structures and discourses that constantly interrelate and correlate as learning and experience proceeds. Learning thus resides within or is constituted by a series of social, epistemic and objectifying relations between the learner, society and knowledge. This enables the capabilities and knowledge or cultural capital of children to be respected as the basis of learning and the notion of 'deficit' to correspondingly apply to the lack of structural and organisational capability to support the learning of all children. Use of the term 'surplus' regarding culture and capability could perhaps turn this discussion into its opposite.

Viewing the researcher (including teacher, student, citizen) as bricoleur sees knowledge production and meaning making as taking place within complex social environments, the elements of which cannot be ignored. Kincheloe (2004, p. 23) points out that 'Bricoleurs understand a basic flaw within the nature and production of monological knowledge: unilateral perspectives on the world fail to account for the complex relationship between material reality and human perception.' Accepting different ways of looking at the world and of analysing experience as being valid or truthful enables researchers to critique their own understandings and to interrogate their methodologies with enhanced rigour.

An inability to proceed in this way may help to explain why progress with Indigenous issues, for example, around the world is so frustratingly slow, especially when non-Indigenous approaches to knowledge and learning are imposed (see below). At its heart, recognising complex research and knowledge environments as bricolage encourages researchers and learners to ask themselves a series of questions that are often overlooked in traditional research. These questions are essentially epistemological and include how community understandings develop concerning the nature of knowledge within the socio-political context being investigated, how participants relate to knowledge generally and to culturally inclusive knowledge of their location, how meaning is constructed and agreed from experience, how knowledge and meaning are refined and altered over time and how knowledge, learning and meaning contribute to personal and social identity. These are extremely difficult questions, but at some point in a research study, researchers will attempt a tentative 'creative leap' of resolution regarding them based on the combined data at hand. All research in the social and physical sciences finds itself in this position of cautious interpretation with various detail and uncertainty available at the time presented for discussion and further study. For example, first-draft simplified outcomes may be expressed as:

- Four weeks before the election, 62% of voters sampled supported the Prime Minister while 35% supported the Leader of the Opposition.
- Higher-performing students in the middle years of schooling are progressing at a slower rate in reading than higher-performing students in comparable countries.
- After 6 weeks of intravenous application, no increase in tumour size was observed.
- Students of Chinese background achieved substantially higher test results in senior mathematics than students from locally born working-class families.
- National unemployment rates across the country fell by 0.1% for the second quarter of the year compared with the previous year.

In each of these cases, many subsequent questions need to be considered before any definite conclusions can be made. Of course, the purpose of such enquiries may be limited, to provide preliminary analysis only, but epistemological (and sociological) questions similar to those mentioned above will become immediately apparent. Definition of terms, the purpose of each study, background of participants, appropriateness of methodologies, accuracy and degree of error and relationship to other similar studies all come into play. Research as bricolage and researcher as bricoleur is one attempt at recognising the complexity of research and knowledge formation and, rather than denying the 'messiness' of research, embraces its historicity, incongruities and confusions.

In Table 9.1, different philosophical approaches to research are shown that either complement or collide with bricolage understanding. Within the table three major perspectives of knowledge are outlined, namely positivist, a suite of experiential approaches with similar characteristics and Indigenous. Indigenous philosophy is included because it provides a fundamentally different way of viewing the world to dominant standpoints, especially neoliberal, and thereby challenges many current economic, political and cultural conditions. Such perspective and challenge supports critique and rigour of knowledge production. Having already positioned bricolage as a major conceptual research orientation,

Table 9.1 Paradigms of research

	Philosophy	*Methodology*	*Validation*	*Authority*
Positivist	Verified, sense perceptions	Empirical measurement	Agreed rules	External
Experiential	Outcomes of activity	Description, empirical	Consensus, judgements	Community, internal, external
Mixed	Perceptions, outcomes	Qualitative, quantitative	Consensus, judgements	Community, internal, external
Bricolage	Negotiated interaction with research objects	Negotiated, constructed, varied	Consensus, judgements	Community, internal, external
Action	Self-reflective inquiry for improvement	Qualitative, quantitative	Consensus, judgements	Community, internal, external
Practitioner	Self-monitoring of practical situations	Qualitative, quantitative	Consensus, judgements	Community, internal, external
Indigenous	Continuing integrated themes, relationships, customs	Holistic, storied, ceremony, experienced	Elders, community, family	Elders, community, family, internal, external

some other approaches will be briefly considered below, with implications drawn for social justice and equity purposes.

Practitioner and action research

In many respects, formal education as known in the modern era is still an under-developed field of learning and inquiry. Most countries of the world do not have mass systems of primary and secondary education, whether or not education is a distinct discipline in its own right is uncertain and there continues to be intense debate regarding the purpose, direction and funding of education for all citizens regardless of background. The education profession around the world is decidedly worried about the economic and political impact of national and international neoliberalism on education and resists to some extent, but policy makers have in the main succumbed. If the field of education is under-developed and under political stress, then it follows that the same applies to education research as well. Education is a diverse field involving history, economics, sociology, philosophy, psychology, comparative international studies, teacher education, higher education and vocational education as well as the structures of schooling, curriculum, pedagogy and assessment. Given the range of philosophies indicated in Table 9.1 added to this mix, it is understandable that education research, while being an extremely active field, has not as yet established a strong and comprehensive research, theoretical and literature base in every aspect. This is particularly so for epistemological theorising and practice. In addition to these considerations, it must be remembered that the exploration of research methodologies appropriate to education also proceeds vigorously, especially in the qualitative area, a difficult journey when education remains essentially a derived and patchwork field drawing on the traditions of other knowledge domains. This indicates that education is not an established discipline in its own right with its distinctive epistemologies, practice procedures, knowledge claims and validation processes.

In the middle of the twentieth century, political and economic events of unequalled magnitude and hostility, such as the Great Depression, the rise of fascism and World War II, changed human history forever. For those who survived, a new world order was necessary to try and ensure that such momentous and horrendous mistakes would not occur again. Rather than the vehement and aggressive hand of authoritarianism and dictatorship, a more autonomous, democratic and egalitarian life was sought – one where ordinary people were responsible for making their own decisions at work and in society generally. Accordingly, post-war reconstruction saw a new emphasis on education for everyone, so that the children of all families would have access to important knowledge, to productive citizenship and hopefully, to a brighter future than their parents.

For educational research, a (new) principle of 'action' aligned with Dewey's pragmatism and the structuralism of Piaget emerged, whereby knowledge was actively constructed by humans interacting with objects of knowledge and reflecting on the outcomes of such interaction for new action and thinking. Kurt Lewin is generally attributed with coining the phrase 'action research' at this time – the notion of action research as combined thinking and action, 'a form of self-reflective inquiry undertaken by participants in social situations in order to improve the rationality and justice of their own practices, their understanding of these practices and the situations in which these practices are carried out' (Carr and Kemmis, 1986, p. 162).

By 1971, the Centre for Applied Research in Education had been established by Lawrence Stenhouse and colleagues at East Anglia University, United Kingdom and Stenhouse in particular became well known for, amongst other educational principles, his advocacy of 'teacher as researcher' and the 'process model' of curriculum, teaching and learning. In 1986, *The Action Research Planner* (Kemmis and McTaggart, 1986) was published, containing the spiral of 'plan, act, observe, reflect' that greatly influenced educational research around the world. Whether or not action research has been successful in strengthening educational research and in persuading new understandings and compositions of human practice and existence can be debated.

There are various forms of action research. At one end of the spectrum is research that is pursued to improve current practice with little other intent in mind, a process of 'technical rationality'. This could involve a teacher experimenting with different-sized groups in class and observing whether students appear to be settled with fewer or more partners. As well as improving practice, action research can have an explicit proper or ethical benefit for participants. For example, a teacher at specific times of a lesson could set up girl-only discussion groups to see if this provided added personal and cultural support for the involvement of girls with mathematics.

Finally, action research can set about changing practice to the extent that new reflections, understandings and arrangements of practice are conceivable and can be acted upon, opening up new options of knowledge production and attitudes towards living. In this case, a group of teachers may work together on a science curriculum that begins with community events and then incorporates recognised science ideas so that students see science in daily experience, for their own construction, not dominated by the textbook.

Action research involves both action and research, but not all projects that ensue under its name necessarily involve both at all times with new knowledge or insights as the desired outcome. Therefore what is known as practitioner research is not the same as action research, although those engaged in action research are generally undertaking practitioner research controlled by themselves.

Practitioner research intends that practitioners conduct their own research using a range of techniques, but they do not necessarily proceed with cycles of action and reflection; they are not necessarily seeking to reconstruct personal understanding of their own practice, or impact and change their conditions of practice. A group of teachers, for example, may administer an algebra test, discussing and noting pass and failure rates across classes and recording the results before moving on to the next topic without any change of teaching practice at all. In their documentation of the principles and practice of practitioner research, Cochran-Smith and Lytle (2009, pp. 15–16) note the important role of students and contribute that the positioning of them as researchers can disrupt arrangements where teachers are merely seen 'as the transmitters of others' knowledge and students the recipients'. Practitioner research is therefore an important step in breaking the conservative ideology of research being always imposed and conducted by 'experts' so that practitioners have the authority and respect to investigate their own practice for improvement.

Participatory action research takes the concept of action research further and has been developed with an explicitly emancipatory purpose. Expressing a strong South American focus of resisting social oppression and improving society for the majority, Fals-Borda (1991, p. 4) describes participatory action research as linked to the ideas of the Spanish philosopher, José Ortega y Gasset, such that, 'Through the actual experience of something, we intuitively apprehend its essence; we feel, enjoy and understand it as reality and we thereby place our own being in a wider, more fulfilling context.' Fals-Borda then introduces the Spanish idea of *vivencia,* meaning the combination of experience and commitment in the service of the subjugated. Here again, a number of philosophical concepts are brought together that envisage knowledge and learning as involving personal and social action, preferably in groups of like-minded participants, reflecting and thinking intensely about the outcomes of action and then how such revised thinking can be enacted for continuing change and advancement of social practice.

Carr and Kemmis (2005) however detect a problem with this outlook and with the development of action research generally. In reflecting on the 20th anniversary of the publication of their influential book, *Becoming Critical,* they note the global changes that have occurred during this time and whether their initial and subsequent writing and theorising have responded adequately to new challenges. In particular, they refer to the challenge of postmodernism and poststructuralism and whether the modern, emancipatory aspiration has become a product of a bygone era. Additionally, the power and pressure of neoliberalism have dominated the period of *Becoming Critical,* making it extremely difficult for any progressive counter-hegemonic ideology to endure. Carr and Kemmis (2005, p. 355) conclude that they do not see critical (discussed elsewhere in this volume) action research as 'method or technique', indicated above as 'technical rationality', and go on to comment:

> Instead we would continue to portray critical action research as an *idea* that, as it passes from one historical context to another, has to be reinterpreted and reconstructed so that it can continue to offer practical and realistic ways of realising emancipatory aspirations through critical reflection and transformative action.

It is not obvious from the literature that action research in its various concatenations has smote the fire-breathing dragon of aggression, ignorance and irrationality, but there is little evidence that others have been more successful. It does not appear that action research has formulated new theories and principles of education and educational knowledge that have constituted original understandings or perspectives in the modern age. The weakening throughout sociology of a detailed social class analysis also means that the nature and hope of social and educational emancipation are fragile and that social class needs to be reintroduced into research discourse as a major factor of doing and thinking.

Education research

It is reasonably common for teachers to pronounce that they are not overly enthusiastic supporters of education research. This may be because of a disconnect between the topics of academic research and the issues that teachers consider important, or education research that is still in a juvenile stage of development and does not have appropriate methodologies to impact strongly on schools and classrooms. It may also be the case that the nature of teachers' work is seen more as a craft or art that does not rely on theorised professional knowledge; teachers are born, not made and, after all, parents look after children every day without preparation or qualifications. These possibilities may reflect the view that the paradigm of schooling, teaching and learning that still dominates the teaching profession centres on the idea that significant knowledge for children is decided by adults and is already known (often defined outside of schools by policy makers, academics, consultants, curriculum designers and textbook writers), with the role of schools being to pass facts and information on to students and to measure compliance. The British philosopher Richard Pring (2004, p. 220) comments on this situation as follows:

> A criticism of educational research is that it does not create a body of knowledge upon which policy-makers and professionals can rely. First, a lot of research is small-scale and fragmented and there is no cumulative growth of such knowledge. Second, educational discourse seems to be full of people criticising others' research such that there is nothing conclusively verified – no *knowledge*. Research conclusions seem more like transient beliefs than well-established knowledge.

The first point made by Pring concerns how education research conducted mainly by universities is actually funded and approved. Application for large, prestigious research grants involves an extended process of discussion amongst the research team regarding research questions and methodologies to be followed, drafting and redrafting the application and then submitting for approval. High-esteem grants of this type are often awarded to a small number of universities and it is difficult for researchers in other institutions to obtain significant funding. This means that longitudinal studies that include provision for the employment of research assistants are often in the minority of grants awarded, inducing the phenomenon of small-scale projects and the non-accumulation of outcomes. Pring then raises the point of educational and political argument regarding schooling and research creating the impression that little substantial knowledge is available and that verifiability is doubtful. It is most unfortunate when serious questions of education become subject to constant public political disputation that demeans the quality of the debate and indeed can deliberately mask the difficult and perhaps ideological underlying issues and concerns.

It should not be implied that only long-term, large-scale research projects are capable of generating theoretical knowledge for education. Short-term, small-scale studies (that may include action research and practitioner research) have an important role in this regard, although there is the difficulty of follow-up and connecting with other such studies and their results that contribute to a larger picture. This is a consideration made by Bridges (2003, p. 21) when he notes that research is often assumed to be 'scientific', involving hypothesis testing, expensive equipment, trials conducted over long periods of time as well as publishing in recognised international journals. He also makes interesting comment regarding the connections between philosophy and research, a point of particular significance given that such linkages are very seldom made in the literature. Educational philosophy is not a strong field at present. Bridges (p. 21) describes *philosophising about educational research,* where the epistemological and ethical characteristics of research are scrutinised, *philosophy as a form of educational research,* where philosophy becomes a methodology in its own right and finally, *philosophising in educational research,* as a continuing means of clarifying and explicating the questions, concepts and problems being studied. Proceeding without an acknowledged philosophical framework or methodology explains to some extent the lack of emphasis on epistemological research and therefore the lack of knowledge outcomes that relate closely to classrooms and teaching. There remains the problem of how research results are made known to practising teachers. It could be argued that all teachers should be reading a wide range of research journals, but this may be unrealistic. Other strategies are obviously required, involving professional learning strategies conducted at school level, professional associations, blogs and websites generally (see Chapter 11).

Ethical principles must also structure educational research projects not only to protect all participants against disrespect and exploitation but in terms of an ethical approach to knowledge itself; that is, how knowledge is regarded, produced, accepted and utilised by humans for public good. While observing the similarities of purposes, values and methodologies between teaching and research, Saunders (2007) remarks that there may be conceptual differences as well that impact on how each is viewed by teachers and researchers alike. Of particular interest is her proposed comparison of teaching and research shown in Table 9.2.1. (Saunders, 2007, p. 69) that demonstrates the different views of knowledge and professional practice possibly held by practitioners of each.

In accepting her division of teaching as 'activism' and research as 'scepticism' in relation to knowledge production, Saunders provides a useful means of understanding why teachers may see little practical application for research outcomes and why researchers may have little contact with the daily tasks of

Table 9.2.1 Some ideal typological contrasts between teaching and research in relation to knowledge

Teaching as 'activism'	Research as 'scepticism'
Social-relational	Epistemological-scientific
Vested interest	Neutrality
Priority question: 'What use is this work?'	Priority question: 'How valid is this work?'
Looking for confirmation	Looking for refutation
Concerned to identify extent of applicability	Concerned to identify type/extent of error
Insights for action	Insights for understanding
Priority outcome: 'How will this knowledge enable me/my colleagues to take action/s and/or make decision/s?'	Priority outcome: 'How does this research enable new theory and/or knowledge to emerge?'
Management issues concerned with implementation	Management issues concerned with quality assurance

Table 9.2.2 Expanded notions of 'activism' and 'scepticism'

Teaching as 'activism'	Research as 'scepticism'
Democratic, collegial forms of organisation	Expert, detached forms of organisation

schools. Stenhouse, of course, found a way of eliminating this division through his 'teacher as researcher' approach and the 'process model' of curriculum that relied on both teachers and students becoming researchers, investigating and constructing knowledge together. Again, there is a conservative model of knowledge and of schooling that promotes the division with research that may in fact be correct if that is the philosophy held by those who control and fund schooling. On the other hand, progressive philosophy of knowledge that connects personal and community experience with knowing and learning will have a specific interest in uniting teaching and research at each level of schooling to liberate the creative capabilities of all practitioners. In this respect, perhaps an additional row could be added to Table 9.2.1 to cover this point of difference (Table 9.2.2).

Since release of the No Child Left Behind (US Department of Education, 2013) legislation in the United States, the question of 'evidence-based' research has become central to education debate. Researchers have had to meet somewhat intense criticisms that their work does not involve a scientific methodological 'gold standard' of randomised trials and does not focus on a purely 'what works' approach. A number of issues arise for education, including what counts as evidence, how professional decisions are made and what is the process of continuing professional action. The evidence-based approach seems to accept only the scientific research paradigm, while discounting other forms of evidence such as practice-based. It assumes that the generalised result can be applied exactly to specific instances without variation. It also assumes the integrity and accuracy of the studies being referred.

In education, practitioners draw upon a wide range of research applicable to specific situations. Evidence-based accounts seem to portray direct application of scientific results only, whereas, in practice, there is usually a combination of local expertise with the best available external research. In education, practitioners draw upon a wide range of research applicable to specific situations to make decisions regarding specific classes and specific students. Finally, evidence-based research seems to imply that, once scientific results are administered, solutions will follow. It does not draw implications for when the results from one application fail and how this evidence is taken into account to decide the next response. In education, practitioners are constantly reviewing evidence from practice and designing new strategies for learning from specific situations.

Researching Indigenous knowledge

Considering the specific characteristics of Indigenous knowledge and research enables other methodologies to be strengthened through evaluation and critique from the perspective of a different worldview (see Chapter 8). In their major analysis of Indigenous knowledge, Semali and Kincheloe (1999) use the provocative term 'subjugated knowledge' to describe the relationship between Indigenous knowledge and dominant 'epistemological and curricular power' (p. 31). They argue that, rather than Indigenous knowledge becoming a new body of subject content for inclusion in the curriculum, it can be 'employed as a constellation of concepts that challenge the invisible cultural assumptions embedded in all aspects of schooling and knowledge production' (p. 32). This approach enables teachers to move past the conservative technique of merely adding new content for meek acceptance to the curriculum, to encouraging students to use a different philosophical lens to analyse and probe ideas and propositions. Indigenous explanations regarding the medicinal use of various plants, or how to navigate the seas without maps and compass, or how to interpret the stories of a painting can all be considered in a non-judgemental way alongside scientific accounts to enrich understanding. Semali and Kincheloe (pp. 33–39) discuss in some detail what they see as the benefits of Indigenous and subjugated knowledge being utilised as a philosophical point of departure in mainstream education:

• promotes a rethinking of our purposes as educators
• focuses attention on the ways knowledge is produced and legitimated
• encourages the construction of most just and inclusive academic spheres
• produces new levels of insight
• demands that educators at all academic levels become researchers.

A key aspect of Indigenous research that exemplifies the above points is oral history. It may be difficult for some researchers to accept the oral traditions of Indigenous peoples as being accurate and therefore the inclusion of personal, family and community voice and story may be ignored. Indigenous oral history is deeply philosophical and needs to be considered from different points of view depending on the actual issue being studied. A historian may be speaking with an Elder regarding events that occurred many years before. In answering a specific question, the Elder may agree that the events happened at a certain time, but in the Elder's mind this may be a wide range of years in accord with a cyclical rather than linear understanding of time. In this case, it may be difficult for the Elder's view to corroborate a historical event exactly, or to be more specific when giving evidence in a court of law, for example.

Story telling is also a part of oral history but stories do not necessarily have to be told in exactly the same way each time for the meaning and purpose of the story to be conveyed. The purpose or moral of the story may be to indicate how humans should behave in relation to nearby tribes, rather than the exact reason why a particular bird has certain colouring. Non-Indigenous researchers need to be aware of such nuance if they are involved with oral reports and include their comments and interpretations carefully and with courtesy.

Building on the notion of orality and story telling, Hooley (2009) has developed narrative inquiry as a democratic means of qualitative Indigenous research. Clandinin and Connelly (2000) in their prominent work have also noted that the storied lives of individuals and communities support the practice of narrative inquiry as a means of understanding. Similarly, Beattie (2009, p. 36), as an ardent supporter of narrative and the imagination, comments that 'We need poetry, myth, metaphor, story, music, art and nature to nurture all aspects of ourselves.' When using narrative methodologies, the researcher, as in the case of the historian, is always working with interpretations. Preferably and from a bricolage point of view, this means considering the data over long periods of time, gathering additional and alternative records and versions and constructing a matrix of possible explanations, conclusions and theories. In his approach to taking all such matters into account for research purposes, Hooley (2009, pp. 177–194) has proposed an integrated three-dimensional concept of narrative inquiry involving sociological, epistemological and ontological practices:

- sociological: looking backwards (where I have been: history, events, records); looking forwards (where I am going: challenges, conditions, hopes, change)
- epistemological: looking inwards (who I am: identity, culture, current knowledge); looking outwards (who I can become: new people, experiences, capabilities, new knowledge)
- ontological: looking below (my connections and origins: being, Mother Earth, natural environment); looking above (my visions: aspiration, rituals, traditions).

Inspired by Clandinin and Connelly (1994), this approach enables Indigenous narrative inquiry to transition from field experience (data such as letters, reports, notes, interviews) to field texts (formal and informal narrative constructions), from field texts to research texts (themes, arguments, principles) and then from research texts to research accounts (possibility, explanation, generalisation).

Under these arrangements, questions of validation involve community learn-ing circles of Elders, community and family members and research participants reaching consensus that the data and comments made at each stage of the research are appropriate, accurate and credible.

Research should involve as many cycles of narrative formation as possible (written, oral, graphical, technological), so that observation, ideas and state-ments can be refined as much as possible and brought into correlation with the collective view. Attempting to assemble culturally inclusive research in this way for Indigenous or non-Indigenous purposes suggests that participants, including researchers, do not remain inert but are changed through their par-ticipation and interaction with others. This is a significant epistemological and practical point, as it means that not only do researchers reposition themselves in relation to the issues being studied, but the general social field within which the research is located also changes. For example, during a conversation or interview, an Elder may mention that a certain ancestor witnessed acts of vio-lence being committed against an Indigenous community by colonial settlers. This detail may not have been revealed before but, once spoken, changes both the understanding of those present and the history and culture of the local community and therefore changes the research. Positivist and strictly empirical research does not consider matters of this type.

Following the guidance of Semali and Kincheloe above has indicated how the incorporation of principles of Indigenous research into research considera-tions generally provides for greater rigour and intelligibility of the research pro-cess. Additionally, as Lomawaima (2008, p. 194) highlights, academic freedom is preciously guarded by university researchers, but this does not ensure that 'tribal concerns and perspectives' are respected. She raises the thorny issue of whether academic professionals, even of Indigenous background, can represent tribal communities appropriately, although this a question of representation that all communities must face. She states the issue powerfully in the following passage:

> Power is at the crux of the matter, after all. In Indian America, power means sovereignty and sovereignty means self-government, self-determination and self-education. Today – and in the future – sovereignty means that tribes should and will make the rules that researchers must respect and follow. I believe that tribal review does not necessarily mean that high quality research will be eviscerated, obliterated, impaired, or infringed upon. Instead tribal review can easily motivate better research, research that will be meaningful and useful to tribal communities.

Lomawaima makes the case for Indigenous people to be in charge of their own lives and of their own knowledge and research. She rejects the view that tribal people (urban, regional, remote) cannot undertake reviews of quality when in their own interest. This philosophy can be extended to the capabilities of ordinary people everywhere.

10 Reflexive teaching and learning

Looking across blue fields of igneous rock
created by molten flows and errant disruptions
eons ago as the earth sought clarity of form
worn smooth by the eternal passage of energy
frenetic torrents of water leap from the precipice
to destroy themselves metres below momentarily
before continuing their dash to the distant mouth
united in a selfless determination of perpetuity.

All humans are interested in the decimal point, the hexagon and the sunset. It would be strange indeed to say that they are not, or that personal interest in such matters depends on social background, whether proletarian or bourgeois. To say that knowledge is a social practice and is socially constructed does not lock human learning into a predetermined or static social position, but it does demand that human thought and understanding can move backwards and forwards between intellectual and practical modes. Conversely, a deficit theory of knowledge and of humanity demands that certain social groups are precisely confined to particular social trajectories from which there is no escape. Perhaps there are occasional intellectual molecules that can break through the barriers of surface tension. The conservative epistemological view sees phenomena as essentially isolated, stationary and one-sided where change can only occur in terms of quantity or place. In contrast, the progressive and dialectical world-view sees the internal contradictoriness of phenomena as the basis of change in quality and external factors as the conditions of change. An egg may hatch into a chicken, but a stone cannot, no matter the surrounding temperature. At very high temperatures, the stone may become liquefied and change its form, but will still not hatch a chicken.

In regard to the nature of change, Heraclitus (535–475 BC) proposed that change is a fundamental property of the universe, including the 'unity of opposites'. He suggested that all phenomena comprise opposite characteristics such that 'the path up and down are one and the same'. At a later time, this principle was adopted by Marxists so that the struggle between internal opposites is responsible for pushing development forward: without up there is no down, without heat there is no cold, without night there is no dawn. The unity of opposites does not deny that certain features of existence are present at certain times, but proposes that there is always constant motion between them, with motion and transformation being dominant rather than immobility and stagnation. In terms of learning, the external conditions can change from city to beach, or indeed from home to school, or from biology to history, while the learner makes sense of environmental change from the internal basis of adjustment that arises from a totality of evolutionary cultural and social experience.

A progressive view of learning supports the idea that knowledge is in a constant state of movement as the unity of opposites plays itself out. At one point in the process understanding is difficult and frustrated, but at another point, as the conditions alter, knowledge changes and becomes more connected with experience; to make the internal conditions operative, the external conditions need to change. From this it follows that, if the formal school curriculum demands that knowledge is motionless and must be accepted as ordained, then the internal characteristics of children at that particular time may not allow relationships with that knowledge to be formed. This is a function of adult curriculum, not of the child. At this point, rather than denying the community, language, history, experience and interest of the child, these properties need to be utilised even further to enable new ideas to be considered and constructed. Thus we have the central flaw in the argument that 'teacher quality' means 'better' teacher procedure, keeping both knowledge and child invariable. Improved teaching needs to focus on changing the external conditions of learning and doing so that the internal conditions of thought and knowing can coalesce. If intellectual status or equilibrium rather than movement and expedition dominates, then the epistemological paradigm of learning is incorrect and distorted practice becomes extremely aggravated and problematic.

Emphasising a progressive 'unity of opposites' regarding knowledge demolishes the concept of 'deficit' learning. There is no reason why every child regardless of background cannot savour encounters with the equation, gerund or sodium chloride molecule provided that the conditions of learning enable this to happen. Knowledge however must be located in the experience and culture of the child and pathways of wonderment must be available. When a combination of experience does not generate new understandings, then new combinations are required. While we still operate at the level of broad descriptive models of learning, it can be hypothesised that the external properties and relationships of learning are similar to internal properties. From a conservative viewpoint, this means that memorisation and repetition result in stronger memorisation within the brain. From a progressive viewpoint, processes of active inquiry result in a strengthening of inquiry understanding in the brain.

Members of the working class encounter a wide range of knowledge every day and observe the outcomes of experience and application. Over time, this process ensures that the pipes carry water, the engine begins and the potato grows. When it becomes too hot, a window is opened, when the path is dark, a candle is lit and when the ants scurry to their holes, rain can be expected in the near future. Humans of all backgrounds create and evaluate their learning in this way, dealing with opposites on an hourly basis and changing conditions to suit their purpose. Why modern schooling does otherwise is difficult to fathom.

All subjects in the formal school curriculum could easily adopt a philosophical investigation into knowledge as their main direction, focusing on a comprehensive pedagogy of the unity of opposites. Within the epistemological context of community, language, history and interest, all ideas are considered awkward and open to interpretation. How accurate is the boiling point of water, the time of day, the size of the moon and the speed of light? How many molecules are there in a certain volume of solution? Why did the war begin and was it right? Are people different and why do warriors die? Surely the dense mathematics textbook can be cut in half to allow such philosophical and open-ended investigations to occur. Those who argue that 'deficit' learning is the natural order for certain groups of people, including those of low income, different nationalities and who have been dispossessed, are obligated to show why this is so in epistemological rather than sociological terms. A dogmatic view of so-called deficiency cannot explain movement from knowledge of individual events to knowledge in general, or the relationship between external and internal causes, or the connections between understanding and socio-cultural experience.

In schooling, the narrow view of stagnation sees truths as emerging from mid-air in purely abstract terms to be imposed on unsuspecting minds. There is no connection between the particular and the general, the local and the distant and between knowing and doing. The principle of movement indicates that changing the conditions of learning can change non-knowing into knowing at any time and that the capability of all children to learn cannot be underestimated or disrespected. This is why all children are interested in the decimal point, the hexagon and the sunset. These are all aspects of social life and, like breathing, learning is essential for social life to continue.

Bourdieu and habitus–field reflexivity

Before considering the nature of pedagogical practices for experiential and progressive learning, the concept of unity of opposites will be connected with Bourdieu's notion of reflexivity. Following the defeat of fascism and the end of World War II, sociology, like most human activity, was concerned with finding peace and harmony and a better understanding of society and meaning. While social class remained a major factor of analysis withn Marxism, its dominance could be viewed with some suspicion because of its inevitable pathway to class antagonism. Marxism also emphasised the economic base of society that saw major social trends being dictated by economic imperatives.

The post-war years demanded new, perhaps trending idealistic, models of society that were not economistic or deterministic in nature but would allow for greater human agency. Bourdieu's approach was to maintain a relation between economic and socio-cultural factors and to analyse the position and positioning of participants in 'social space' as a consequence of their totality of personal and political characteristics. He therefore mediated the question of social class through the reflexivity of the habitus-field relationship. In this way, participants would not be manipulated or dominated by socio-economic factors so that social and cultural capitals as well as material resources are recognised. In discussing Bourdieu's approach to 'epistemic reflexivity,' Maton (2003), for example, notes how knowledge claims are influenced by the changing relation between objects of study and the structures of a field of inquiry, such that, 'The aim is not to uncover the individual researcher's biases but the collective scientific unconscious embedded in intellectual practices by the field's objectifying relations' (p. 58). This shows that Bourdieu was aware of the problem that reflexivity could be criticised as repetition of individual and superficial self-reflection that was trapped within its own preconceptions and partiality. Instead, he proposed a collective endeavour of rigorously analysing the properties of a field and clarifying the relation between participants, the objects of study and knowledge already known.

Bourdieu proposed a number of theoretical features that enable a continuing two-way interaction between subject and object, between theory and action, or between question and participant. How does Bourdieu inform analysis of social and political issues and how do social and political agents interact with Bourdieu, bringing their own understandings and interpretations into play? Bourdieu is a structuralist in the sense that he recognised and analysed the place that objective structures such as customs, ideas and bureaucratic regulations have on human will formation. On the other hand, he did not support a structural determinism, where people have little choice but to reproduce the policies and discourses of their societies, but are able to impact and change. There is thus a relation between what people know and other objects within the environment in which they live. In this way, Bourdieu was attempting to break with the idea that citizens are mere putty in the hands of social imperatives and ideologies, particularly the economic, and provide a means of conceptualising human initiative and inventiveness. His concepts of habitus, field, and various forms of capital such as the cultural and symbolic are central to his thought and method on these points.

It now becomes necessary to account in more detail for human improvisation, creativity and personal agency, so that a break with dominant conservative ideologies can be made – a rupture with our own thinking and identity, in fact. Bourdieu accomplishes this task through the epistemological concepts of practical sense and reflexivity. Practical sense or doxa, in Bourdieuian terms, involves our understanding of a particular field of action, its rules and procedures and how progress is made within acceptable boundaries. Reflexivity and its historical and structural location assumes a deeper understanding of the field and its knowledges so that initiatives can be taken as the circumstances alter to benefit a particular social actor. These two notions enable learning to be constructed as experience is gained, but it is learning that occurs within the framework of the habitus and in relation to it.

A problem arises here in being able to theorise how a major turnaround in thinking occurs in opposition to the habitus. Bourdieu however makes quite an astounding claim on this point:

> Early experiences have particular weight because the habitus tends to assume its own constancy and its defence against change through the selection it makes within new information by rejecting information capable of calling into question its accumulated information if exposed to it accidentally, or by force and especially by avoiding exposure to such information.
>
> (Bourdieu, 1990b, p. 61)

The notion of differentiated experience and the process of reflexivity enable the habitus to adapt and adopt new ideas without necessarily being dominated by them. On this basis, a person with a particular cultural and economic experience can maintain that view while incorporating views to the contrary.

In formulating his ideas of habitus, field and cultural capital, amongst others, Bourdieu has certainly identified himself as a structuralist. Margolis (1999, p. 67), for example, offers a critique, commenting that 'the habitus is never really segregated (in Bourdieu's mind) from this universal generative structuralism' and that 'it applies empirically, only piecemeal, to strongly traditionalist and preliterate societies'. His descriptive theory may be incomplete in terms of a more evidence-based explanation, but proposing structures to oppose structures at this time may require that not all detail is provided or is necessary. If all experience from field activity impacts on habitus, then both enhancement and attenuation will occur. This means that the relationship between habitus and field should be as sensitive to touch as possible, so that all experience can be considered on its merits without some experiences necessarily dominating others. This is the argument for learning having a broad base of experience from which new perspectives can be appraised. As noted previously, a theory is a guide to action and provides scope within itself for change and variation, if not negation. Bourdieu and Wacquant (1992, pp. 89–90) recognises this when they state:

> The very notion of field implies that we transcend the conventional opposition between structure and history, conservation and transformation, for the relations of power which form the structure provide the underpinnings of both resistance to domination and resistance to subversion, as we can clearly see in May 1968.

Here Bourdieu is saying that it is possible to transcend the duality of structure–history where one may dominate the other and that the 'relations' of power can generate resistance and subversion. The question that arises is how social agents set up different relations so that different outcomes are possible and where the relation between habitus and field has also been changed. This is of central concern for people working across cultural settings who, for example, need to be able to resist their own predispositions of racism and other forms of prejudice. Teaching staff in schools and universities need to be able to design curricula that are culturally inclusive regardless of their own cultural back-grounds and understandings.

Habitus-field analysis

Taking the analytical notions of Bourdieu regarding habitus, field, cultural capital and reflexivity as a guide, it is possible to develop a habitus-field analysis to assist teaching, learning and curriculum design, the relationship between who we are and what we do (Hooley, 2013). The suggested approach is to introduce praxis inquiry or critical praxis protocols into teaching as a means of organising units of study, but then encourage a habitus-field analysis with teachers and/or students to provide the detail lying behind each protocol (see Chapter 11). For example, a class may reflect on a particular activity in terms of each of the columns of the habitus-field analysis grid, as shown in Table 10.1. Detail provided here is based on a teacher's actual background, or on a sum-mary of the collective experience of a class of students. The discussion could begin with brief consideration of habitus, with an example from the activity and with brief entries or comments from teachers and/or students inserted in each column. Table 10.1 shows some generalised comments that could fall under each heading as a result.

To theorise the process being undertaken here, teachers can develop a reflexive study of their own practice to appreciate learning better and become more informed regarding possible course and pedagogical change. In this way, investigation of the 'socio-transcendental conditions of knowledge' will con-solidate and intensify and consequently teachers will hopefully engage a greater understanding of the note by Grenfell (2008, p. 12) that, 'Bourdieu talked about the way his work was a kind of "auto-socio analysis", as a way of making sense of the social forces that had shaped his life trajectory.' It can be concluded from Bourdieu that a critical approach to teaching and research will involve a meticulous self-analysis of habitus, field and the relationship between them. For each student project undertaken it will be necessary to consider the social field, the education field and the field of knowledge and in particular the posi-tion and positioning of researchers within each. This will be difficult to achieve honestly and accurately and will require the assistance of colleagues. It will be difficult to achieve for individual projects undertaken on a short-term basis, as personal learnings and changes to habitus occur under the influence of lifelong processes, folding and refolding in and on each other.

After a first draft of Table 10.1, it becomes necessary to explore each field of action in relation to Bourdieu's concepts of power, institution and indi-vidual to enable a more detailed analysis regarding the relationship between dominant groups in society (wealth, influence) and their impact on fields, regarding the interrelationships between dominant institutions and individu-als and regarding the relationship between individuals of the field themselves.

Table 10.1 Habitus–field analysis grid (for specific teacher)

Habitus	Current social field	Current education field (employment)	Current knowledge field (personal beliefs)
Working-class family Irish connections Dominance of mother Country town Coastal environment Centre politics Some unionism Little religion Importance of reading Little ongoing schooling No university aspirations	Permanent employment Modest income Working-class aspirations Left/ish politics Union background Iraq, Vietnam war No religion Major large city Dominance of education Marriage, two children Divorce	Equity, democracy Schools, universities Teaching, research Mathematics, science, language Writing Unions	Equity, democracy Integrated, inquiry Learning by doing and reflection Personal constructed knowledge Access to privileged knowledge
Habitus-position (what is)	*Social field-position*	*Education field-position*	*Knowledge field- position*
Remain essentially as above, lifelong	Aspiration is to retain position and values as above – modest, working class, progressive	Remain as above – equity approach to education for all	Remain as above – inquiry learning across all knowledge
Habitus-positioning (what could be)	*Social field-positioning*	*Education field-positioning*	*Knowledge field-positioning*
Remain+ as above	No formal repositioning, but increased recognition of views as experience gained	Remain as above	Strong, consistent epistemological positioning, in support of equity, democracy

This analysis should result in a description of social life that involves both objective conditions (field structures, power connections) and subjective conditions (characteristics, dispositions) as the basis of developing critical understanding. As an example, the education field has been begun to be detailed in Table 10.2.[1]

Table 10.2 Relations within education field (for specific teacher)

Education field	Power	Institution	Individual
Equity	Wealthy class Unions People's movements	Top 100 companies Business groups Governments Think tanks Armed forces Legal system Media	Global networks Social capital networks
Democracy	Wealthy class Unions People's movements	Top 100 companies Business groups Governments Think tanks Armed forces Legal system Media	Global networks Social capital networks
Schools	Wealthy class	Top 100 companies Business groups Governments Think tanks	Global networks Social capital networks
Universities	Wealthy class	Top 100 companies Business groups Governments Think tanks	Practitioners Writers Theorists Advisors, consultants
Teaching	Practitioners Theorists Wealthy class Governments Writers	Top 100 companies Business groups Governments Think tanks Regulators	Practitioners Writers Theorists Advisors, consultants
Research	Funding bodies Researchers Theorists Governments	Top 100 companies Business groups Governments Think tanks Regulators	Practitioners Writers Theorists Respected practitioners
Knowledge	Practitioners Writers Researchers	Researchers Professional groups Governments Funding bodies	Practitioners Writers Theorists Respected practitioners
Writing	Authors	Funding bodies	Authors
Unions	Members	National groups	Officers Social capital connections

There is a strong philosophical connection between the epistemological ideas of reflexivity and unity of opposites. Reflexivity is concerned with the relationship between habitus and field as experience is gained and each impacts on the other; neither dominates necessarily and without one there is no other. Unity of opposites denotes the relationship between different aspects of a phenomenon and how external conditions act on internal causes for change to occur. Both reflexivity and unity of opposites emphasise movement rather than stasis and both counter predetermination and deficit ideologies. It is unclear exactly why particular experience is educative or miseducative, or why some experience opens up new ideas and other experience blocks new thinking. For example, some children will be attracted to the view from a tall building, while others will not be enticed to walk across a low bridge. Some children will readily adopt the political or religious views of their parents, while others will reject such views entirely. Some children will be entranced by the steps involved in a brief mathematical proof, while others will be confused and embarrassed. What this seems to suggest is that particular children at a particular point in their learning do not yet have the internal structures that allow connections to be made with other structures and that further experience is required so that new links can be formed. The dominance of educative experience (beauty of the moon through a telescope) versus the dominance of miseducative experience (fear of heights after falling down a hill) indicates that strong structures are formed that are difficult to alter without appropriate new experience. A non-idealistic stance needs to be adopted here, in recognition that strong previous experience will be difficult to adjust, regardless of the priorities of parents and teachers. Families who have lost relatives in battle will have durable views on war, either for or against. Learning then becomes the democratic responsibility of the adult/teacher, not the deficiency of the child. Pedagogies chosen by teachers can either encourage the possibility of often messy, noisy, reflexive practice for all students across all knowledge, or the isolation of opposites into the individual arbitrary of stationary acceptance.

Pedagogy, reflexivity and unity of opposites

In his famous essay *The Practical: A Language for Curriculum*, Joseph Schwab (1978, p. 287) began in this way:

> I shall have three points. The first is this: The field of curriculum is moribund. It is unable, by its present methods and principles, to continue its work and contribute significantly to the advancement of education. It requires new principles which will generate a new view of the character and variety of its problems. It requires new methods appropriate to the new budget of problems.

Long before the current thrust of neoliberalism, Schwab denounced the unthinking imposition of theory generally from outside education to schools and classrooms. He argued for the practical, not inductive or deductive, but deliberative, where learners make decisions to guide action. Decisions are never true or indeed trustworthy but are judged in comparison with alternatives and consequences. Decisions are specific rather than general, apply to the concrete and are liable to unexpected alterations.

Schwab suggested that the problem with theory in education is that it tended to fasten problems and approaches for children, it makes presuppositions in line with accepted thinking and that it demarcates issues in an abstract, separated way. The practical on the other hand is always related to personal affairs based on need that requires changing. In a significant comment, Schwab pointed out that practical situations can be changed by considering either end points or starting points, that is, human personal necessity. In his critique of American schooling over 30 years ago and his determination not to be consumed by the external theoretic, Schwab may not have paid enough attention to how new ideas are created from the familiar, or how children can theorise their own culture and practice to enter new fields of challenge. On every issue raised in the classroom, some children will have more direct experience and thereby can begin to engage a new idea, while others will have less direct experience and will require more specific advice, guidance or signposts. Some may have seen the Crab Nebula or the Southern Cross in a photograph, but never marvelled at constellations of stars in the night sky. Merely posing or imposing the abstract can be extremely counter-productive. At this point then, we attempt a brief summary of the key features of pedagogy that will bring together the theoretical principles raised throughout previous chapters with the reality of classroom teaching:

- negotiated projects that focus on the interests of participants
- cycles of practice, reflection, change with unexpected outcomes
- legitimate problem posing/solving as the basis of investigation
- emphasis on the active use of language and dialogue in all its forms
- integrated knowledge arising from philosophy, mathematics/sciences, humanities/arts and broad cultural studies
- culturally inclusive, community-based framework for all projects.

To illustrate, some brief examples of pedagogy are given in Table 10.3 regarding each of the integrated projects discussed in curriculum Chapters 5–7.

It can be seen that the suggested approaches to teaching and learning are spread across the six general principles noted above and can be used in each of the curriculum domains. That is, the approaches all concentrate language and dialogue as a form of communication, knowing and expression; they all involve small-group work over continuing cycles of practice and reflection; there is minimal difference between the approaches for different studies, bearing in mind that specific content workshops are held; and there is utmost respect and recognition for the cultural backgrounds of students as they negotiate their interests and pursue meaning. It may be that different results are obtained for the boiling point of water at different places in the science lab or around the school, but such results are taken as legitimate subject to debate and explanation rather than rejection.

Table 10.3 Integrated projects and pedagogies

Integrated project	Pedagogies
Philosophy	Small-group discussion to prioritise issues
People and cultures	Gathering of census data regarding populations
	Compiling photographic evidence of conflicting views
Mathematics/sciences	Conducting small-scale experiments on local weather
Climate change	Graphing long-term trends of national climate
	Assisting projects with local environmental groups
Humanities/arts	Interviewing artists involved in production
Alice in Wonderland	Redesigning scenes to express different ideas
	Writing reviews for local newspaper
Cultural studies	Composing new lyrics for songs of local events
Sports, technologies, instrumental music, camps and excursions, craft and workshop	Reporting to parents regarding international trip
	Designing/making toys for children in hospital

How is it possible to measure boiling point accurately in different places at school with the equipment that is available? Would it be possible to take a series of measurements, graph the results and send to a scientific organisation for comment and suggestions for further experiment? Two authentic cases that arise from the integrated studies approach are outlined below.

Case 1: Wall newspaper

I was exhausted. It must have shown on my face as I sat down dejectedly at the staff room table. My friend Mike from the English Department looked up from his sandwich and stated the obvious: 'Another rough session?' 'I've tried everything. I thought today that the problem sheet I had prepared on finding the area of irregular shapes would interest them – but apparently not.' Mike contemplated the remaining tomato and lettuce slices in front of him for a second or two before saying quietly, 'You know, if we could arrange it, I could take them for an English session to see how they respond; they might be different.' I jumped at the chance. Mike was still a fairly new teacher like myself and was recognised as getting on well with students.

In due course, I was sitting in the mathematics office wondering how my Year 7 class was going with Mike. I had to have a look. Walking down the corridor, I hesitantly put my head around the door. Students seemed to be everywhere, in small groups, sitting on the floor, perched on tables. Every so often, a group would go and show Mike the large sheet of paper they had been working on. After a few words, they would then stick their sheet up on the wall, next to other sheets that were placed there. As I watched, the wall newspaper grew before my very eyes: big headings, colour, blocks of text, diagrams, all concerning the sports camp they had been on recently. There was a hum of activity as the newspaper gradually encircled the room. Out of the corner of his eye Mike saw me – and smiled.

Case 2: Calculating the difference

Being young and wanting to change the world, I was up for anything. But I should have known better. The principal had just reported to the staff meeting that he was concerned that a group of students in Year 9 were constantly in trouble and were in danger of being expelled from school; nothing seemed to work for them. Was anyone interested in taking them as a special group this year to try and keep them attending as much as possible? I immediately volunteered although, according to Chris later, there was a general consensus in the room of 'Better him than me!' and 'Won't he ever learn?'

Things did not go as I had planned; the group was impossible to engage and my imagination was severely strained. Heading off to class with a sigh of resignation, I picked up the set of maths textbooks on the table and, for some unknown, unplanned reason, the box of calculators that had also been left there from another teacher. As soon as I walked into class and placed my bundle of materials on the front desk, there seemed to be a collective 'Oh, calculators' from the students who, without any word from myself, came out to the front, took a calculator and problem sheet and began working through the questions. My whole life flashed before my eyes – could this actually be happening? Could the group be transformed at the speed of light after so many years of trouble at school? Could it be that they had barriers to their mathematics learning that had built up over the years that had never been resolved, but suddenly, the calculator enabled them to move forward? As I watched incredulously, I wondered how I had been so stupid, why no one had ever advised me to always 'put the learning first'!

These genuine cases of classroom practice demonstrate the integrated character of learning regardless of the particular domain of school knowledge. In each case, participants are involved with ideas that have been initially decided by teachers, but over which they then take some form of personal control. They are able to construct a wall newspaper of their own design about their own direct experiences, rather than be told what problems to attend from the teacher. This goes to the question of negotiation. They are able to move past intellectual blockages so that they can discuss issues with non-judgemental open-ended alternatives, rather than try to seek correct answers with procedures they don't understand. This enables cycles of practice to be established as they edge closer to personal revelation. Experiments can be conducted that are bona fide not only in their capacity to investigate questions of interest for students, but in their various results that raise a number of possible explanations and avenues for ongoing study. This goes to the issue of authority as students confront the unexpected products of investigation and inquiry and let their minds run free to consider the aesthetics and properties of beauty and truthfulness. Shakespeare experimented with language and created new sayings, meanings and imaginings that have become commonplace. Einstein conducted thought experiments that challenged how humans understood themselves and their place in the cosmos. Hawking proposes new ideas about black holes and then raises serious doubts about his own thinking. If the experimentation, reflection, public discourse and reflexive contestation process of knowledge production and unity of opposites are good enough for Shakespeare, Einstein and Hawking, then they are good enough for the nation's classrooms.

Learning stories

In her Presidential Address to the 2012 Annual Conference of the American Educational Research Association, Ball (2012) developed what she called the 'zone of generativity' to take account of the knowledge–practice gap in educational research. By this, she means the difficulty of translating research outcomes into practice due to the inaccessibility of research reports, the lack of communication between researchers, practitioners and policy makers and the often unfortunate use of research to justify current policy rather than to establish new directions.

Ball described generativity as the 'stage in which we strive to create or nurture things that will outlast us; to strive to contribute to positive changes that benefit others' (p. 287). According to Ball, the zone of generativity consists of four stages of reflection, introspection, critique and personal voice so that 'knowledge becomes powerful as we conduct research that serves to make the world a better place' (p. 289). She refers to the work of Vygotsky (1978) and the zone of proximal development where 'there is no wrong place to enter the zone – you enter the zone of generativity *where you are*, at your current level of knowing and you measure your development against your own progress' (p. 289, original emphasis).

While Ball's comments concern educational research, there is strong resonance with learning generally and the range of processes encountered earlier. Teachers could easily introduce students in all subjects to cycles of reflection, introspection, critique and personal voice in relation to the production, communication and evaluation of their own knowledge as it forms in relation to other knowledge. Gardner's work on leadership has a number of interesting features that link with Ball's approach, again for our purposes, to be viewed in epistemological terms for schools and teaching. Gardner (1995, pp. 290–295) identifies six constants of leadership as follows:

1 The story: a central message that relates to the groups concerned, that provides sense of identity, background, possible future options and is inclusive of most participants.
2 The audience: a complex relationship between the story teller and the audience that is ready to respond, depending on the history of the groups involved and whether the story needs to take new directions or strengthen current positions.
3 The organisation: a demand that requires support from institutional or organisational backing without which progress with the story is difficult. Features of the story are taken up by various organisational factions that can continue independently.
4 The embodiment: a defining characteristic of the story teller that s/he lives the story so that his or her 'actions speak louder than words'. The authentic story teller is non-hypocritical with the exemplary life appreciated by others.

5   Direct and indirect leadership: a pursuit of influence through direct speaking or symbolic products for their specific domain, or indirectly by working through broader and related forms of organisation that already exist.
6   The issue of expertise: a need to achieve credibility through expertise in a particular area, but the concomitant difficulty of maintaining that position over time as other requirements begin to take precedence.

Teachers of mathematics/science and humanities/arts, let alone all other subjects, can relate to these constants. There are innumerable stories to be told about the structure of DNA, the discovery of X-rays, the life of Marie Curie, Ernest Hemingway and Oscar Wilde. The story of science and the human quest to understand more comprehensively the nature of the universe unfolds around us every day and includes students. As Gardner notes, the task of the story teller is to judge the readiness of the audience to respond in the way that the politician must judge the mood of the electorate. A teacher needs to embody the stories of knowledge, the enthusiasm for knowing and the morality of teaching if students are to consider rather than dismiss what is being told. Teachers can chose to directly intervene or interfere in the learning of students, to constantly instruct in correctness, or to be there, to assist and advise when required as projects continue. To successfully accomplish the latter, they must have a firm grounding in the knowledge of their domains so that the learning moment can be grasped when questions are raised. In summary, what might be called 'narrative' or the capability to contextualise and 'narrate' the story of knowledge for students, or to enable students to construct their own knowledge narratives, is often unfortunately lacking in curriculum and particular knowledge domains.

What is the epistemological explanation for the power of story and narrative? In families and workplaces everywhere, people relate through the stories they tell, whether these concern the reasons for a failed experiment, when a particular child suddenly started walking, the antics of cousin Jake, or the amazing day when the championship was won. Stories and narratives have both descriptive and explanatory effect that provide accounts of experience from different perspectives, as well as propose why certain experience has influence on the thinking of participants. It is not known how the experience of story and narrative exactly interacts with the brain, given that only very general models of cognition are available for discussion. As a theorist interested in these matters, Wilson (1998, p. 6) has developed his theory of 'consilience' which, similar to the notion of 'coherence', is defined as the bringing together 'of knowledge by the linking of facts and fact-based theory across disciplines to create a common groundwork of explanation'. He suggests in a manner most congruent with the compass bearing of this book that:

> The greatest enterprise of the mind has always been and always will be the attempted linkages of the sciences and humanities. The ongoing fragmentation of knowledge and resulting chaos in philosophy are not reflections of the real world but artifacts of scholarship.

There is little agreement on the nature of mind as distinct from the physiology of the brain and how human experience is actually converted into subjective feeling, or learning. How do humans *know* the colour purple, the sense of loss when a parent dies, the thrill of an impending night at the theatre? How do humans *appreciate* the pattern of a tiger's coat, the properties of an isosceles triangle, the sparkle of quartz rock? Wilson grapples with these questions of mind and consciousness, but must resort to descriptive and therefore contested terms. From a biological perspective, he describes the nature of consciousness as the processing of huge numbers of 'coding networks' that 'create scenarios that flow realistically back and forth through time' (p. 120). He contends that there is no monitoring device in the brain to supervise its infinite activity and connections, leading to the proposition that:

> There is no single stream of consciousness in which all information is brought together by an executive ego. There are instead multiple streams of activity, some of which contribute momentarily to conscious thought and then phase out. Consciousness is the massive coupled aggregates of such participating circuits. The mind is a self-organising republic of scenarios that individually germinate, grow, evolve, disappear and occasionally linger to spawn additional thought and physical activity (p. 120).

On this basis, some 'scenarios' must be stronger than others; for example, the impact of moonlight on the water is greater than the impact of rain falling on a tin roof. In some way, clumps or circuits of neurons in the brain must be able to connect with other clumps or circuits of neurons to create the feeling of knowing and learning – or alternatively, the feeling of ignorance and frustration. Neuronal assemblies are thought to contain coalitions of up to 100 million brain cells. If structures or scenarios phase and phase out based on the type of experience gained and the live connections that can be made with other structures and scenarios, it follows that the broader the base of experience, the broader the capability of structure and scenario building. If there is no evidence of an overall controlling mechanism, as noted by Wilson, and there is no need to propose some type of additional neural mechanism to account for the concept of 'mind', then the neural network theory of brain and mind provides a coherent and holistic model of learning and of humanity. If the brain causes a reaction to experience such as 'anxiety' when a child is late home from school, then the brain can also cause a reaction to experience of 'knowing' when the teacher asks the child a question. If the organic human feels 'hope' when the telephone rings, then the organic child can embody a feeling of 'understanding' when reading a poem.

Pedagogies of discussion, experiment, inquiry, reflection and the like would seem to support the creation and strengthening of neural networks and provide greater opportunity for selection amongst schema and scenarios for decision making and meaning making. However this is speculation and, as was mentioned previously regarding artificial intelligence, there is much complicated work that remains for human learning to be fully comprehended. Brain imaging techniques and theories of brain 'plasticity' are still relatively unsophisticated but are providing some data for analysis in relation to how the brain works (Boleyn-Fitzgerald, 2010). Ethical questions must be confronted regarding the extent to which research should probe the mysteries of human consciousness, if there are prospects of changing consciousness itself.

Note

1 Material in the above sections regarding Bourdieu, reflexivity and habitus-field analysis, is based on unpublished and published work by Arnold *et al.* (2012).

11 Constructing professionalism

Sometimes exposed sometimes submerged
co-existing for innumerable centuries
rock pools enabling and sustaining life
hidden species found in unique consortia
visited by stormy petrels and sea dragons
dependent on atmospheric ebb and flow.

Education in Finland has received a great deal of attention over the past decade since international test results have rated it extremely highly (Tryggvason, 2009; Sahlberg, 2011). Somewhat ironically, after being evaluated by traditional test procedures, the Finnish system itself has not been dominated by market forces and does not feature a competitive examination regime. Funding for education remains adequate, although is not overly generous in relation to OECD countries. Other features include policies that focus on educational equity and high regard for teachers built on exacting selection procedures into teaching and continuing professional learning. All teachers are required to have a Masters degree, a qualification that is gradually being introduced in a number of other countries. Debate continues worldwide on this requirement regarding its efficacy, the extent and nature of its research component and whether the degree should be a more broadly based Master of Education (MEd), or more practically based Master of Teaching (MT). In regard to teacher preparation, Sahlberg (2011, p 73) reports that 'Due to the popularity of teaching and becoming a teacher, only Finland's best and most committed are able to realise those professional dreams'. He goes on to state that competition for teaching places is therefore intense, meaning that 'Annually, only about 1 of every 10 applicants will be accepted to prepare to become a teacher in Finnish primary schools. The total annual Finnish applicants in all five categories of teacher education programs number about 20,000.' This is a significant difference with most other countries. Finland is relatively small geographically with a small, essentially monocultural (yet changing) population, making the social and educational issues faced quite different to those in large, multicultural countries. Finnish history and aspiration for national identity help to explain its dedicated community support for education, literacy and self-development.

What constitutes good schooling and teaching changes over the years and must be seen in relation to the economic and political system that exists. Connell (2009, p. 214), for example, outlines 'three competing discourses in contemporary England: a "competent craftsperson" model, preferred by government; a "reflective practitioner" model, widespread in universities and a "charismatic" model of the teacher circulating in popular culture, Hollywood movies etc.'. She points out that other approaches are adopted beyond the English-speaking world, including the Confucian tradition of moral authority and the Zen Buddhist tradition of 'cognitive revolutionary', who seeks breakthroughs in student perception.

Political pressure to move away from the 'reflective practitioner' model that has been present for some time comes with the neoliberal territory, but there is resistance to reverting to the conservative 'teacher as technician' model, passing on and assessing set content. From a social class point of view, the role of the school and teacher is to support the dominant ideology of the day, whether this is done directly or indirectly. This does not prevent the teacher introducing students to a range of philosophies on a day-to-day basis, but overall, students are submerged in a sea of dominant knowledge, pedagogies and procedures that establish authority. While education remains an under-developed and under-researched profession, there is a weak knowledge base available to teachers that has the effect of reproducing what is, allowing at the same time, political and bureaucratic interference. In supporting a much more progressive educational ideology, Kincheloe (2011b, p. 257) brought an unequalled intellect to bear on his understanding of knowledge and research and pushed the concept of bricolage (see Chapter 9) to its limits. His insights are exceedingly valuable regarding schooling and teaching:

> As bricoleurs plan their escape from the limitations of monological knowledge, they envision forms of research that transcend reductionism. In this context, they understand that complexity sets the stage for the need for the bricolage, the necessity of new ways to understand the complications of social, cultural, psychological and educational life. Once again, the complexity principle gets in our face: knowledge production is a far more complex process than we originally thought; there are more obstacles to the act of making sense of the world than researchers had anticipated.

In laying down the challenge of 'teacher as bricoleur' (which can be taken as a specific extension of Stenhouse's 'teacher as researcher'), Kincheloe transforms the role of teacher from that of mere conservative purveyor of knowledge to collaborative producer of knowledge, alongside students and within the complexity of the socio-cultural environment of every classroom. As mentioned previously, the notion of complexity is both ontological and epistemological, referring to the nature of being human, as well as the way that learning proceeds. Rather than working within classrooms that are predetermined by the curriculum, teachers establish flexible areas of possibility, where students bring their complex cultural backgrounds to bear on interesting and difficult problems for investigation and continuing construction of new ideas and perspectives. This is at the heart of the question of student 'engagement' across the curriculum. That is, either students are enabled to activate their experiential, inquiry processes of learning, or they are not; either they are encouraged to cross their own threshold of complex understanding into zones of possibility and generativity, or they are constrained forever in the monotonous tedium of compliance. Thus, there are diverse conservative, progressive and critical competing notions of professionalism, how the role of the teacher is viewed and how the democratic obligation of schooling is to be pursued.

There are three defining features of a profession. First, members of a profession recognise the well-being of the people they serve as their top priority and ensure a confidential relationship at all times. Second, members of a profession are appropriately qualified, have an extensive experience and knowledge base and contribute to extending not only the knowledge of the profession, but its reputation as well. Third, members of a profession have independent status in terms of their governance and viewpoints and reject interference from outside individuals and groups. Professional bodies are often powerful in their own right with, for example, legal, engineering, medical and education organisations taking strong stands in pursuit of their own interests. In some areas, professional groups and industrial unions co-exist, while in other areas, groups can have both professional and industrial concerns. For some professions, self-regulation occurs through a registration process, whereas it is also possible in other cases for government legislation to control registration and entry to the profession. Government bodies need to be careful in setting registration and employment conditions as these will inevitably impinge on professional activity and rights that should be decided and monitored by members themselves.

A particularly sensitive area is that of reprimand and possible dismissal from a profession when members transgress accepted behaviour. A 'code of conduct' has usually been developed by members over time to guide such situations and is usually discussed and refined through professional learning sessions to take account of experience and changing circumstances. Darling-Hammond (2012) has outlined a set of principles for a quality system of teacher evaluation that is supportive of the teaching profession and will assist ongoing development, especially for new entrants. Her principles involve common statewide standards, performance-based assessments, local evaluation systems, support structures and aligned professional learning. While Darling-Hammond is attempting to provide a framework for the profession in the United States during the neoliberal period, it is important that any proposals are worked through and decided by the education profession itself and not imposed by outside pressure.

Signature pedagogies epitomise professional education

While President of the Carnegie Foundation in the United States from 1997 to 2008, Professor Lee Shulman embarked on a ten-year program to research how people are prepared for a range of professions involving law, engineering, teaching, nursing, medicine and the clergy. He was looking for distinctive forms of teaching and learning that enable members of each calling to think professionally, act professionally and to be professional. Shulman (2005) called these features 'signature pedagogies', or defining characteristics that go to the heart of professional knowledge and practice (Gurung *et al.*, 2009). In addition to a profound understanding of the field, Shulman accepted that professional education comprises grounding in accomplished and responsible practice for the good of others. In broad terms, signature pedagogies have surface, deep and implicit structures. Respectively, these involve the techniques that are used in teaching, assumptions about how best to participate with and learn specific knowledge and a moral dimension regarding values and attitudes.

Signature pedagogies are also characteristic of particular professions, are pervasive throughout a curriculum, are habitual and routine and they socialise new entrants into the general mode of conduct of professional life. Shulman noted that signature pedagogies involve uncertainty of practice and decision making, the engagement and responsiveness of students and the formation of disposition and identity. It may be tempting to remain at the surface level when considering possible signature pedagogies of teacher education, that is, the techniques and procedures that are apparent in classrooms. Such techniques could involve beginning with real-world problems, developing arguments, analysing texts, co-operative group work and observation and discussion of practice. This could however lead to superficial understanding. Interestingly, it was not Shulman's intention to distinguish a particular model of professional education that could then be utilised by all professions. It is obviously inappropriate to take a clinical model from medicine, for example, and attempt to impose this on engineering. Rather, Shulman set out to explore professional principles that could inform and be adapted by all professions based on their own experience and warrants.

In a recent study of site-based pre-service teacher education conducted by Victoria University (2011) in Melbourne, five research findings were identified that could form the basis of investigating non-superficial signature pedagogies in education. Victoria University is well suited to this task as it has a long background in constructing teacher education that emphasises partnership in learning, immersion in professional practice and a praxis inquiry approach towards active learning. Site-based approaches to teacher education at Victoria University involve around 20 pre-service teachers being placed in a partnership school to work with mentor teachers and university staff on classroom teaching, curriculum development and the theorising of teaching and educational practice throughout the year. In this way, the dilemmas of practice can be immediately discussed, investigated and reconfigured as they occur. In the *Vision Unlimited* project, a theorised understanding of site-based education that emerged involved the features of inspiring practice, transforming educational discourse, challenging culture and pedagogy, investigating recursive processes of learning and enabling ethical knowledge for teachers and students. The

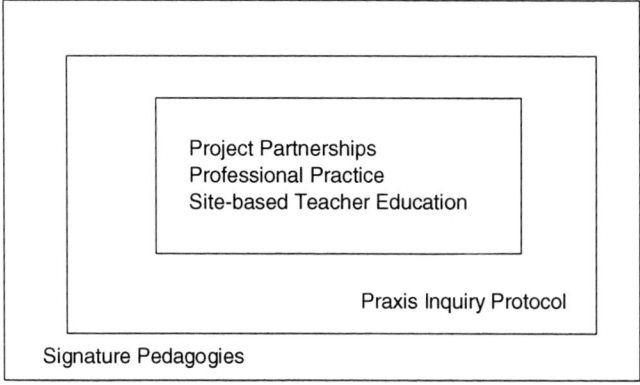

Figure 11.1 Attributes of site-based teacher education

Source: Vision Unlimited, School of Education, Victoria University, Melbourne (2011)

project suggested that the complex relationship between the key attributes of site-based teacher education could be shown as in Figure 11.1.

The notion of praxis being incorporated here fits nicely with Shulman's concept of signature pedagogies regarding professional practice in the service of others. Aristotle, for example, drew a distinction between the human virtues of techne or technique, episteme or knowledge and phronesis/praxis or ethically informed action for the social good (Kemmis, 2012). In supporting praxis inquiry as ethical practice that is described, explained, theorised and changed to improve teaching and learning, teacher education of this type involves practitioners in the deep and implicit values of professional conduct. Whether or not the five research outcomes noted above establish an accurate platform for ongoing investigation of signature pedagogies in initial teacher education remains to be seen. They do however clearly demarcate a praxis form of thinking, acting and being grounded in practice from a clinical approach imported artificially from outside education. In fact, it could be argued that many teachers and educators already adopt a praxis approach depending on the conditions they face as they construct ethical action in the interests of students every day. Shulman's concept of signature pedagogies and shared conventions of teaching and learning pose significant challenges for teacher education. Rather than being a list of rules to follow perhaps developed elsewhere, they create a framework of ethical professional practice within which professional understandings and actions are collaboratively constructed. Learning from all professions will persuade the signature pedagogies of education to be identified and enacted.

How does a particular approach to teacher education confront issues of social justice, cultural diversity and economic context? Such matters remain substantially unresolved around the world and could be ignored by teacher education if not considered important in favour of subject content, teacher proficiency and the like. Conversely, an approach that views learning as arising from engagement with the 'internal goods' of social practice could identify a number of 'signature pedagogies' that broadly characterise the social and epistemological disposition of teacher education. This model attempts to emphasise the links between how humans come to understand their worlds and how structures, organisation and cultures are both formed and reformed in the process. Under this arrangement, society and the diverse lifeworlds of learners cannot be ignored. Accordingly and based on the work, research, publications and presentations of the School of Education at Victoria University over many years and its principles of practice, partnership, praxis and a series of draft signature pedagogies for teacher education can be proposed for ongoing research and debate:

- professional practice
- teacher as researcher
- case conferencing
- community partnership
- portfolio dialogue
- praxis learning
- participatory action research.

These distinctive signature pedagogies for teacher education are non-hierarchical, as groups of practitioners consider important issues, plan and implement strategies for improvement and evaluate outcomes for continuing investigation. They incorporate the reflexive relationship between personal and professional habitus and fields of practice which must of necessity draw upon the social background of participants. In this way, issues of social justice and equity infuse and inform the carriage of projects as participants explore and develop epistemologies of knowledge and learning.

Case pedagogy as pedagogy of teacher education

This section proposes case pedagogy as a distinctive and progressive pedagogy of teacher education. Primarily, they build on the experience of incorporating cases into teacher education and pre-service teacher education at Victoria University, Melbourne. They also draw upon the use of cases from elsewhere and for different purposes, such as Harvard Law and Business Schools. The specific rationale for case teaching outlined here is the identification and development of teachers' knowledge from the experience of teachers themselves. A collaborative case conference is described and suggested as the overall concept and mechanism for the articulation of teachers' knowledge from the extended practice of case and commentary writing.

In a very broad sense, formal education sanctioned by the nation state is pursued to first support the interests of the nation state regarding worthy and productive citizens and second to support the general development of the individual. Different philosophical traditions have emerged over the centuries that have related these aspects in different ways, particularly as the economic and political character of different societies has changed. From this position, schooling and therefore teaching are both situated in the social milieu of their times, although each will be contested from conservative and progressive perspectives. A conservative approach to schooling and teaching identifies valued knowledge and culture as being known and accepted ready for diffusion. A progressive approach to schooling and teaching encourages participation in the active construction of knowledge and culture by all students, drawing on their social background and culture. Learning is seen to be a dynamic process where ideas and understandings emerge from social inquiry in relation to the views and perspectives of others. A point between these two outlooks describes education as initiation into worthwhile modes of activity and thought concerned essentially with forms of recognised knowledge. Each philosophy envisages a very different role for schools and for teachers, students and parents.

During the welfare state post-war period (1945–1980) and the expansion of secondary schools in the wealthy countries, schooling was or became biased towards a student-centred approach (Plowden Report in UK, Karmel Report and school-based curriculum in Australia), whereas during the neo-liberal era (1980–2012) schooling became biased towards the measurement of student performance determined by the state (No Child Left Behind in the United States, NAPLAN in Australia, standards and accountability procedures, national curriculum). Teacher education has generally followed economic and social tendencies.

Harvard Law and Business Schools are well known for the case method of teaching. Use of cases at Harvard Law School dates from 1853, but we are told vigorous interrogation of them and students by professors can be a very exacting experience. Since 1921, case methods have also been a core aspect of the Harvard Business School curriculum. It is suggested that 'every Harvard Business School classroom becomes a crucible for participant-centred learning' and that, as well as relying on cases rather than lectures and readings, students are engaged through teaching themselves. The process may involve students being provided with a variety of materials regarding a particular issue, such as the history and financial details of a company, which small groups of students then discuss and analyse (over time). As a total group, the professor may then raise a series of problems, issues and questions regarding the case of that company.

At Harvard Law School, cases as precedent written by judges become the object of detailed discussion and cross-examination of options. For a different purpose and writing in the 1970s, Stenhouse advocated the use of case study and case records in educational research as a means of compiling evidence and of making it available to researchers, readers and learners, for public scrutiny. This was associated with his advocacy of practitioner research as the basis for teaching or the 'teacher as researcher' concept of teaching. In addition, Shulman (2005) has pointed out that in all forms of professional education there is an underlying intention of attempting to think and act like a professional that involves continuing engagement with practice. In encouraging students to connect with the authentic problems and dilemmas of the profession through cases, 'thinking like' becomes possible as the untidy and complex nature of practice is uncovered. This then needs to be followed by prospects of 'acting like' in authentic situations.

Experience with cases in teacher education at Victoria University (1997) was initiated in 1995 following seminars by Judith Shulman conducted at Monash University. Subsequently, Lee Shulman also gave a lecture at Monash, where he argued for 'depth of understanding' around the key structures of knowledge rather than 'surface' learning. The approach adopted at Victoria University was not the same as in the United States, with 'teaching cases'. Rather, cases were written by participants (teachers, pre-service teachers) as a form of data gathering concerning their experience, knowledge and learning. A case was a brief piece of informal participant writing of approximately one page that described an incident of practice, whether a problem or interesting event that had occurred in a classroom, school or home. As description is the main purpose in order to establish a clear view of practice, author reflection is not usually included, although some brief reflective comment may be difficult to exclude. More reflective cases may be a further step with a different purpose to descriptive cases. This means that a case does not follow a question-and-answer format, where a situation is not only constructed but responses are provided post hoc to resolve the matter.

Brief case commentaries can also be offered by colleagues. A commentary is similar to a professional conversation, where non-judgemental comments are provided to continue dialogue around practice. They are not intended to provide verdicts on what the case describes and do not attempt to interpret cases correctly. Written comments may be around a paragraph (12 lines) in length and extend issues raised in the case. A collection of cases and commentaries compiled by participants involved in a particular program or project makes available a wide range of data for analysis of practice. At Victoria University, cases have been used extensively as data collection when working on research studies or professional learning activities with teachers and have been incorporated into many academic units of pre-service courses. Professional portfolios for graduating teachers usually contain a number of cases as evidence of progress.

Case (Teacher 1): War in the Pacific

'What's happening today, Deb, another song?' Deb looked up from unpacking her bag and a smile lit up her face: 'No, not today, but I thought we could try some Japanese air raids instead. I've asked Michelle if we can use the props room as there are no drama classes today.' I suspect that for the next few moments both our minds returned to yesterday's class and the range of activities that Deb had planned for her Year 10 class to focus on 'War in the Pacific,' a common theme in humanities. This was good timing, as it was coming close to Anzac Day, the commemoration of Australia and New Zealand in World War I, the war to end all wars: newspaper reports on the screen, cartoons regarding prisoner of war camps, maps and small plastic soldiers, original film of the bombing of Darwin and paper planes whizzing across the room to simulate distances between Japan, Singapore and Australia. When Deb gave out a sheet and asked the class to follow the words and listen to a song from 1942 regarding how Australians saw the American soldiers based here, they read and listened intently. Perhaps Gardner was on to something with the role of music in learning – evidence of multiple intelligence.

'How will you organise it?' 'Well, I've got a video of an air raid and the props room can be a shelter,' Deb explained, 'but I'll have to keep the noise down to not annoy Anita next door; she was a bit grumpy last week.' For some reason I was immediately filled with confidence that this new teacher would not be intimidated by the restrictions of the curriculum at her first school next year. She was thoughtfully planning lessons to connect with students and was persisting with creative activities. In the debrief yesterday, I had spoken of the stories my mother had told me about the Americans in Australia and how the lesson had brought back many personal memories for me. Sometimes it seems clear that my words are not striking home, but on this occasion our shared experiences of life and lesson were definitely linked; her eyes said so. 'It took me six hours to prepare that lesson, but it was well worth it.'

Commentary (Teacher 2): War in the Pacific

Great idea, Deb. When I've tried war themes they have usually responded, although we have to be careful in not repeating what they've done before. I like to have a discussion in class beforehand, especially about any family connections. Someone will have been involved and there are many emotional issues that crop up. Parents may have been involved in the Vietnam conflict, for example, and that is still very raw. In our location, there will probably be people from other countries who had war experience, from Iraq, Afghanistan, or Syria, for example. I like your plan for air raid simulations and will probably give that a go in my classes as well. Perhaps we could find an air raid siren somewhere – although old Principal Jack won't be too pleased with that. Your combination of activity and discussion seems good and should help students get a better understanding of war situations, but let's hope that's as close as they get. Chat soon.

Case conference

A means of analysing case and commentary data as developed at Victoria University is the case conference. A case conference is a professional learning strategy designed to identify a series of key themes and issues that have arisen from professional practice and on which practitioners reach consensus regarding accuracy and significance. Such key themes and issues (teachers' knowledge) are then available for practitioners to reflect upon and incorporate in their future work for improvement. Organisation of the case conference which proceeds over 4–5 hours is as follows:

Session 1

Step 1

Form groups of three to four practitioners each (3 minutes).

Step 2: case reading – 15 minutes × 4 cases = 60 minutes

To begin, one member of the group distributes copies and reads their first case. Following the reading, the remaining members discuss the case, while the author remains silent. That is, the intention is that the author does not explain the case, or answer questions, but allows the group to come to their own understanding. In the mind of the author, the group's interpretation could be different to what was intended. The discussion begins by the group asking the following questions of itself: What is the case about? Is the case about one or a number of issues? What further information is required to help our understanding?

Step 3: commentary writing – 5 minutes × 4 cases = 20 minutes

Each person writes a brief commentary to the author of each case. A commentary is a professional conversation where a colleague makes some helpful comments about what has been written. A commentary does not make judgements about what is considered to be right or wrong in the case, but continues a dialogue about the issues raised by the case. For our purposes, a commentary is about 6–10 lines long.

Session 2

Step 4: case reading and commentary writing (75 minutes)

Repeat steps 2 and 3 for case 2.

Session 3

Step 5: bundling and analysis (75 minutes)

5 minutes × 4-6 cases = 30 minutes.

 Each member of the group writes one issue/theme/comment on a sticky label and continues until all comments have been identified for each case.

Session 4

Step 6: concept map

All group members then negotiate and arrange all sticky labels under appropriate headings according to the issues on each label. This should result in a small number of lists on a table or wall of sticky labels that show key issues. Arrange the issues in a concept map, showing the links between main issues (20 minutes).

Session 5

Step 7: reflections and projections

General discussion amongst entire group regarding validity of lists and nature of concept maps (10 minutes). Photographs of concept maps for inclusion in portfolios. General discussion amongst entire group regarding implications of each issue and how each issue can be further incorporated or investigated in their classrooms. What are the implications of the issues identified for 2011, 2012? (20 minutes)[1]

The history of case and commentary writing together with the case conference process outlined above makes a strong claim for case pedagogy as a distinctive signature pedagogy of teacher education. If so, there are imperatives to expand this work to include case records and public evidence (as advocated by Stenhouse), casebooks that provide access to case examples for participants and the implementation and documentation of case methods that delineate different approaches to working with cases (that may or may not include the Harvard Business and Law School techniques). The excitement and satisfaction generated by the case conference for graduating teachers and current teachers are palpable when they work through cases of their own practice and produce explicit concept maps of their own knowledge as beginning or experienced teachers. Case pedagogy has a strong literature and experiential base and is a distinctive signature pedagogy of the praxis model of teacher education.

Professional learning and research

In early writing from a major centre of action research at Deakin University, Australia, McTaggart (1991, p. 26) noted that the influential work of Carr and Kemmis (1986) was concerned with redressing the balance between theory and practice in favour of the action research practitioner. It is important to quote McTaggart at length on this point, to indicate one of the main features of the philosophy of action research that has been present from the beginning of the field:

> The goal of Carr and Kemmis was not to specify the conditions which would make action research possible. And they wanted to do more than to establish an epistemological basis which would give action research a place as *one* legitimate form of educational enquiry. Through the critique of other forms of educational enquiry, they aimed to show that action research was the *only* legitimate option for educational researchers. Part of the argument embraced the fundamental tenet of the critical approach – that the correctness of their views could only be worked out through the self-reflective practice of action research. Similarly, to specify the optimum conditions for active research in advance would have violated the same principle. The institutional conditions for action research could only be worked out through efforts to make it a cohesive, critically informed practice (original emphasis).

That action research could be proposed as 'the *only* legitimate option for educational researchers' is a remarkable statement and one that indicates a particular philosophical view of where knowledge comes from, especially for education practitioners. Of course, education is a diverse, active field and numerous research projects are conducted involving the history, economics, politics, philosophy, psychology and sociology of education, together with comparative and international studies. There is considerable work done regarding curriculum and student testing. However, as has been argued previously, epistemological research does not feature prominently, meaning that teachers have limited access to discussion regarding the production of student knowledge as well as their own professional knowledge. In relation to identifying the actual types of action research that are possible, Carr and Kemmis drew on the theories of Habermas and his approach to three forms of knowledge: the empirical-analytic, the hermeneutic-intrepretive and the critical, each based on the a priori cognitive interest of technical, practical and emancipatory respectively. Action research that focuses on the technical and practical restricts the process of self-reflection, while emancipatory action research intends that self-reflection for all participants, including researchers, will open up questions of human meaning, justification and change. Personal investigations of this type for students and teachers alike cannot be arranged in advance, but must emerge from action and inquiry as ideas and problems are enacted and encountered in practice.

There is a constant policy battle regarding whether curriculum should be more school-based or centre-based, with neoliberal efforts to firmly institute the latter through externally imposed 'standards' (see below) and national curriculum. On the other hand, pedagogy is still generally seen as the prerogative of the teacher, of the professional, although critics are not backward in providing advice to teachers in how they should act. What this means overall is that the complicated and tense arrangements faced by teachers, while difficult, contain scope for change options and can still be redrafted for progressive epistemological intent. DuFour *et al.* (2008, pp. 14–17), for example, suggest and detail professional learning communities as:

> educators committed to working collaboratively in ongoing processes of collective inquiry and action research to achieve better results for the students they serve. Professional learning communities operate under the assumption that the key to improved learning for students is continuous, job-embedded learning for educators.

They designate six characteristics of professional learning communities as: (1) shared mission, vision, values and goals, all focused on student learning; (2) collaborative culture, also focused on learning; (3) collective inquiry into best practice and current reality; (4) action orientation and learning by doing; (5) commitment to continuous improvement; and (6) results orientation. This work demonstrates close similarities with the philosophy of democratic inquiry and action research and also the notion of 'learning organisation', as outlined by Senge (2006) and 'communities of practice' by Wenger (1998).

Professional learning and research for teachers must be in the hands of the profession. The thorny question of 'standards' comes into play here – a favourite of conservative policy makers and bureaucrats alike to be imposed on recalcitrant teachers. Formal examination of candidates for entry to the profession is increasingly suggested (Mehta and Doctor, 2013) over and above successful completion of tertiary studies. It is usual however for the philosophy of 'standards' embraced by bodies external to the profession to be a source of power, to centre on a range of hierarchical steps that can be conveniently measured, akin to checking the grease trap in the fish and chip shop. Of course it is important for the airline pilot to go through the flight plan before take-off, or for the nurse to make sure that all instruments have been sterilised and recorded before the operation, but such considerations do not constitute the 'standards' of teaching. A progressive approach to teaching standards is epistemological, experiential and emancipatory, one that is monitored collaboratively with colleagues, not by simplistic and behaviourist measurement of testing and other means. Empirical data is sometimes useful in terms of broad trends across populations, but gross trend data such as the number of students passing mathematics, or the number of students from low-income families taking senior physics, does not usually provide detail and guidance for improvement.

Over recent years, teacher and student portfolios have been developed as a progressive and professional process of monitoring teaching and learning progress. For teachers, portfolios may consist of curriculum plans, student work samples, diary entries, various assessment outcomes and analyses, cases and commentaries, photographs and video of classes and professional learning activities, including professional writing. For students, there is a range of similar materials, including work samples, extracurricular activities, teacher and parent comments, video of classes and student self-assessment. These compilations enable collegial roundtable discussions to occur with appropriate groups of principals, teachers, students and parents in relation to agreed rubrics of progress that are reviewed over time. Comparisons with external data can be made within this context, including norm-referenced material if so required, but the emphasis is on the use of data to inform local practice, rather than external data being the sole determinant of practice: practice-informed evidence rather than evidence-based practice.

Marshalling professional knowledge and meaning

Where does professional educational knowledge come from? If it is difficult to identify new knowledge that has been produced by the limited outcomes of formal educational research, then how do teachers and researchers engage and think about their experience in order to create new insights and conjectures? This goes to the nature of educational practice itself, that is, how does the experience of practice at the sociology–epistemology interface (see Figure 0.2 in the Preface) construct knowledge? This question needs to be considered epistemologically.

In his seminal work on the history of action research noted above, McTaggart (1991, pp. 33–35) pointed out that the 1980s had produced substantial theorising on the development of action research as the 'praxis of critical social science'. He listed five requirements of action research if it was to become the *only* form of inquiry of an education science. In summary, these requirements are:

1   a rejection of the positivist notions of rationality, objectivity and truth
2   an acceptance of the need to accept the interpretive categories of educators
3   provision of ways of distinguishing inadequate, internally inconsistent and ideologically distorted interpretations from those that are not and suggest ways in which undeveloped understanding can engage the three registers of language, social relationships and practice
4   identification and exposure of those aspects of the existing social order which frustrate the pursuit of rational goals and a critique of grounded theoretical ways of overcoming such obstacles
5   a commitment that the status of educational enquiry will be determined by the ways it relates to practice and the struggle for educational enquiry and improvement.

These aspirations need to be implemented in epistemological practice, but still understood in terms of general, descriptive models. When individuals say that they 'know' something, what exactly do they mean? At one moment, they have a 'feeling' of 'not knowing' the difference between heat and temperature, but then at the next moment, they have a different 'feeling' of 'knowing'. Perhaps when a neural network or circuit (scenario, schema) reaches a certain threshold of electrical current (complexity) due to the combination and relatedness of varied experience, a chemical is released into the body that imparts a new state of consciousness for the organic being. At the same time, a new scenario is created that forms a new baseline of perspective, an integrated response to the notions of 'rationality, objectivity and truth' in the first requirement above.

Humans respond to the totality of their experience not separated into the qualitative and quantitative data of researchers. The 'totality of experience' can be likened to the process of 'narrative' raised in Chapter 10 (Goodson and Gill, 2011) and the argument of what happens in practice being mirrored by what happens in the brain. For example, when considering a set of graphs, the researcher goes through a similar epistemological process of interpretation as described. When considering a set of interviews, the researcher goes through a similar epistemological process of interpretation, with new neural networks of original understanding being formed. The development of 'mixed methods' (Creswell, 2009) as a research methodology to meld qualitative and quantitative approaches does not really resolve the problem of different experience; when different data sets are available, they still have to be analysed and interpreted by humans for human meaning, as a totality. Consequently, when working at the interface of sociology and epistemology (schools, classrooms, meetings), education professionals need to ensure that they recognise their immersion in a network of practices that mirror neural networks and that an ongoing process of integrated interpretation, reflection and critique is required by teachers and students together. Learning as social practice means that knowledge is tentative, emerging from the experiential practice that is available; the Year 8 student who does not have the 'knowing feeling' of 'heat' and 'temperature' in June, may be transformed by the experience of 'humidity' in July.

There is an enormous sense of knowing, of life and continuance when coming out the front door in the morning and being met by the first, brilliantly red rose of the season, a single bloom swaying gently in the breeze, its velvet texture contrasting starkly with green leaves and grey sky. These are the learning moments of being human, of farmers observing their next harvest, of sailors feeling the movement of the ocean beneath their feet, of students heating mercuric oxide. Classroom teachers, as professionals, need to be able to create a set of teaching and learning conditions that enable learning moments such as these and the practice interface to be fully experienced. It is probable that traditional, teacher-centred classrooms will not provide the necessary conditions, where students and teachers can negotiate and decide in small groups, have resources at their fingertips that will support experiment, are encouraged to utilise new technologies for learning and to interpret and conclude in their own way. Democratic, self-directing learning circles or culture circles of Freire are more likely to proceed in this way, within broad guidelines for assistance, sometimes reaching forward into the unknown, sometimes discussing recognised knowledge and approaches with more experienced colleagues.

As Paris (2012, p. 95) has proposed, the notion of 'culturally sustaining pedagogies' may be appropriate for establishing this purpose, to 'perpetuate and foster – to sustain – linguistic, literate and cultural pluralisms of the democratic project of schooling.. He argues that a pluralist society (such as a classroom) needs within-group and across-group cultural practices to 'exist and thrive'. A progressive paradigm of the sporting team, hobby group, coffee club or social media is perhaps more appropriate for modern school organisation than the conservative classroom of submissive knowledge transmission and acceptance. If this is not the case, then teachers will struggle to be professional in their own right – spectators and not collaborative producers of knowledge, a futile relationship with students and learning.

A final point needs to be emphasised here before moving to the concluding chapter. Inquiry and experiential processes of knowledge creation do not exist in mid-air; they exist in relation to all other knowledge, capability (Bessant, 2014) and experience of humankind. When an adult or student first loads a spring and notes the extension, there will be thoughts of explanation. Initially, such thoughts will occur without reference to the experiments of the scientist Robert Hooke in Oxford some centuries ago. Making a professional judgement, the teacher will introduce a systematic way of considering the behaviour of the spring and suggest that the results obtained can now be checked with what Hooke discovered. Comparisons will depend on the equipment available, the accuracy of the readings and previous experience of the experimenter. It is not necessary for the teacher to insist that current results accord exactly with Hooke's law, but can suggest a range of further experiments to investigate.

Similarly, in the humanities, it will be possible to consider different explanations for the changing geography of a particular environment, either scientific, regarding the action of wind and water, or cultural, regarding the constant grazing and burrowing of animals, mythical or real. The argument for passing on of predetermined knowledge is usually political or sociological, not epistemological; to maintain a particular point of view, not to encourage independent learning. If knowing and learning do involve the generation of new neural networks and scenarios through experience, then, similar to the debate between quantitative and qualitative methodologies, this will be strengthened by the presence of networks and scenarios that include current, accepted knowledge. Teachers and students then need to work with a combination of current and emerging knowledge for interpretation rather than have a one-dimensional approach to the simplistic consent of what is thought to be 'known'. It is 'known' and accepted that the capital city of Italy is Rome, that World War II began in September 1939, that metals expand when heated and contract when cooled. But these are weak scenarios epistemologically. Stronger scenarios or clumps of neurons are created when personal experience and inquiry combine both what is 'known' by others and what is 'becoming known' by learners. All learning occurs in this democratic, integrated way, whether categorised as literacy, numeracy, mathematics, science or arts. This gives new professional and epistemological meaning to Newton's famous statement that 'If I have seen further than others, it is because I have stood on the shoulders of giants.'

Note

1 Case and commentary writing that includes a case conference is a professional learning strategy that you can suggest at your first school as a means of investigating classroom issues for change and improvement.

12 Towards a new reflexive sociology of knowledge

Greeted by a new red rose in the morning
velvet texture, swaying in a gentle breeze
contrasting with leaves of green and sky grey
startled by the calm of unexpected beauty
generates thoughts of life and continuance,
unfolding patterns of layered scarlet geometry
proving curious mathematics of the universe.

Bourdieu began his book *Sketch for a Self-Analysis* (Bourdieu, 2007) with the words 'I do not intend to indulge in the genre of autobiography, which I have often enough described as both conventional and illusory' (p.1) and later, 'To understand is first to understand the field with which and against which one has been formed' (p. 4). It would seem that autobiography had little significance for Bourdieu and its personal accuracy can always be doubted in relation to the field. It could also be interpreted that Bourdieu was placing emphasis on the field, or social practice and activism, as a structuralist and to ensure that the reader is clear that cognitive change occurs when the habitus-field relationship is fluid and reflexive. With these thoughts in mind, I will attempt to write this final chapter with a personal, reflexive quality (habitus-field), bringing together the main issues raised throughout the book in relation to who I am (habitus) and what has formed me to this point (fields). Could it be that writing this book has been an important aspect of reflexivity, a working example, in action? For the reader, I hope similar relations can be visualised, conscientised. Like Bourdieu, it means beginning not at my beginning, but at the period of global transition to neoliberalism.

My working life in education has straddled the neoliberal period and, consequently and overwhelmingly, has been a life of enormous frustration, the constant struggle to make progressive change to benefit the vast majority of children against the unrelenting dominance of neoliberalism. Coming into teaching from the intense anti-Vietnam War experience in Australia meant that my life of a social activist continued at school and in the cauldron of the teachers' union. With the expansion of secondary education that was occurring, teachers were involved in three big issues that they saw as holding back the learning of children: class sizes, school buildings and the need to register qualified teachers (known as 'control of entry' to the profession).

As the 1980s progressed, a further big issue became prominent, that is, the bitter conflict between the 'whole language' or experiential approach to reading and the phonics or grammar approach. Governments of different outlooks were also becoming more insistent that subject content should be of a particular type and developed the tendency of issuing 'guidelines' or 'standards' for teachers to adopt. New technologies were gradually being introduced into schools as well, but their exact benefit was unclear – a situation that remains essentially the same today. These big ideas of class size, buildings, registration, literacy and standards were matters of great debate throughout the profession and had a strong framework of student learning. Unfortunately, it is difficult to discern the big ideas of education being pursued by the profession today.

After my university studies in chemistry and working as an industrial chemist for a pharmaceutical company, I began teaching with a strong background in and respect for modern science and mathematics. I remain highly respectful of the manner in which scientists continue to explore new realms of understanding, proposing extraordinary, sometimes whimsical, ideas that stretch imagination. My support for Dewey and inquiry learning, coupled with enthusiasm for Papert and Logo, made it inevitable that artificial intelligence (AI) and its possible impact on education would grab my attention. I embarked on a personal program of study regarding AI and, although realising we were still in its initial stages of development, was totally engrossed by new areas of learning that could be opened up for all children; indeed, for all humans.

It was during this time that I came across a book by Roger Penrose (1989) called *The Emperor's New Mind*. Like Papert, Penrose was a mathematician from Oxford and was concerned with the potential of the new technology to impact on mind and our understanding of mind. His amazing book went into many of the issues I was considering at the time: AI, connections between physics, mathematics and human thinking, quantum mechanics and the problem of human consciousness. I found it fascinating that it was mathematicians who were raising issues of such philosophical importance.

Penrose has continued to publish a series of books and papers on these topics and has pushed our thinking into new areas of possibility. In *Shadows of the Mind* (2005), Penrose developed his notion of human consciousness to new levels involving a quantum process within cytoskeletons and microtubules. The cytoskeleton holds the framework of the human biological cell in shape and 'appears to play a role for the single cell rather like a combination of skeleton, muscle system, legs, blood circulatory system and nervous system all rolled into one!' (p. 358). The cytoskeleton contains microtubules, cylindrical tubes of protein polymers, also found in neurons, perhaps being responsible for the strength of synapses. We need not be concerned with the fine detail of Penrose's argument here, but he writes (p. 374):

> Let us then accept the possibility that the totality of microtubules in the cytoskeletons of the large family of neurons in our brains may well take part in global quantum coherence – or at least, that there is sufficient quantum

entanglement beween the states of different microtubules across the brain – so that an overall *classical* description of the collective action of these microtubules is *not* appropriate. We might envisage complicated 'quantum oscillations' within microtubules, where the isolation that the tubes themselves provide is sufficient to ensure that not all quantum coherence is lost.

With amazing perspicacity, Penrose theorises that human consciousness arises from quantum activity as described, involving the microtubules of cytoskeletons. What he is attempting to achieve is an explanation for mind and consciousness that does not involve classical but quantum mechanics. In this way, the mind is not a separate entity to brain, suggesting instead that consciousness is a function of organic being. Regardless of what we might think of the Penrose postulate, it is a wonderful example of how science works, taking current and incomplete knowledge and leaping the tall buildings of intellect for new explanations of humanity and universe. At the moment, such thinking within physics involves, for example, black holes, string theory, existence of multiverse and dark matter and, as mentioned, consciousness. Recently, we have witnessed the development of atomic energy, structure of the DNA molecule and research into AI.

We should expect the same of education and learning, but the challenging and exciting big ideas are simply not there. Could it be expected that a series of big questions equivalent to the magnitude of those of physics should arise from the key domains of education, that is, the domains of schooling, knowledge, curriculum, pedagogy and assessment? In the scientific tradition of Bourdieu and Penrose, I now take a professional risk in proposing a brief set of my own 'big ideas' and 'big questions' arising from the considerations of this book to establish the 'continuity' of progressive sociology and epistemology for the learning benefit of all students and of humanity. Table 12.1 should be seen as being illustrative only given the space that has been available within these pages to develop ideas succinctly.

Whether or not these statements and questions approach those of Penrose and Hawking can be debated, but they have their own educational significance. Being strongly epistemological, they tend to remove education from political polemic and refocus on the nature of learning for all children. The nature of learning is conceptualised as a starting point in pragmatic terms as the means of pursuing social justice epistemologically. This then becomes a unifying factor for researchers, philosophers and teachers around the world: can information escape from black holes? is equivalent to: how do all students grapple with the complexities of black holes? After each word in the statements and questions is defined for shared agreement, work by practitioners around the world can proceed for contestation and refinement over the years ahead. There is a strong focus on practice and investigating the conditions for practice that engages different cultures and perceptions. I suggest that the direction and intent of statements and questions such as these do not characterise education worldwide at present and do not impinge markedly on the philosophy of most schools and teachers.

Table 12.1 Education domains and big ideas/questions arising

Education domain

Schooling

That the purpose of schooling is to provide a democratic epistemological framework of continuity and pragmatic inquiry for all students, regardless of background

How can a new sociology of reflexive knowledge guide education practice at the practice interface of sociology and epistemology?

Knowledge

That knowledge is constructed by pragmatic social practice to provide meaning and to guide further experience

What are the characteristics of classroom environments such that human reflexivity, awareness and consciousness are enhanced for ongoing learning?

Curriculum

That students and teachers pursue their own negotiated learning interests within curriculum guidelines developed by the education profession

How does critical learning being pursued by students and teachers connect with generalised understandings of society?

Pedagogy

That approaches to teaching and learning must reflect inquiry processes of the brain

How do practices at the practice interface between sociology and epistemology act holistically to support learning?

Assessment

That knowledge formation by students must be supported by procedures that enhance the construction and reconstruction of experience

What epistemological features of assessment can be incorporated into classroom practice so that formal assessment is redundant and abolished?

Returning to practice: phronesis

Why have I been attracted to the notion of practice all these years, from my entry to teaching and wondering at the lack of connection between practice and theorising? Could I have been wrong? Do humans really learn by being told what is correct by others, by authority? My only reflection on this problem is that my childhood and adult life has been one of reading and inquiry and that this accords closely with the work on pragmatism by Dewey and others and the place of action in learning. My mother always said that I took after her and her father as great readers in the family. When I came across Bourdieu, it made sense to see my field experientialism as interacting and connecting with my habitus formation, creating an evolving progressive approach to knowledge, teaching and learning. I grew up in a country town close to an ocean beach where I could be found every day, winter and summer, swimming, running, exploring and thinking. I well remember my parents telling stories about growing up during the Great Depression, of men knocking on the door hoping to obtain something to eat, or an odd job around the house, of waiting for the hen to lay so that there would be one egg for the entire family to share. These stories are still very real for me, helping create a lifelong democratic habitus I'm sure, concerned with justice and liberty for all working people. It seems that the emerging habitus (or the quantum consciousness of Penrose) took this general direction – to have done otherwise is unthinkable now. For these apparent reasons, I remain comfortable in continuing to support the notions of practice, inquiry, experience, reflection and reflexivity as they apply to all learning and to continue to read critically what the education profession is saying about sociology and epistemology. In this regard, the action research story is far from complete, with its research outcomes still far from expansive and its theorising still unfolding. Stephen Kemmis (2012, p. 894), for example, continues to push forward in researching educational practice and praxis and notes that:

- an Aristotelian view of praxis holds in much Anglo-American-Australian usage today, or praxis that involves 'action that is morally committed and oriented and informed by traditions in a field', while there is
- a post-Marxist sense in much of Europe, such that 'social formations, ideas, theories and consciousness emerge from human and collective social praxis and that social action (praxis) makes history'.

In describing the double purpose of education as 'living well' and working to create a 'world worth living in' (p. 895), Kemmis argues that the practice of education is both 'praxis in the neo-Aristotelian sense' because it is concerned with good for humankind and 'praxis in the post-Hegelian, post-Marxian sense' because it orients into historic modes of social existence that are good for all. Kemmis and colleagues are also developing what they call 'practice architectures' (p. 898) involving the dimensions of 'sayings' (in the cultural-discursive dimension in semantic space), 'doings' (in the material-economic dimension in physical space) and 'relatings' (in the social-political dimension in social space). The notion of 'practice architectures', as defined, locates this work firmly in the traditions of Habermas (language), Dewey (inquiry, occupations) and Freire (culture, power). Perhaps it can also be related to MacIntyre's 'internal goods' of practice, as discussed earlier.

For teachers, the theory of practice architectures allows the projects within which they are currently involved to link with the practice traditions that inform each aspect of their work. For example, teachers involved in literacy projects can analyse their discussions (sayings) in terms of the language claims of Habermas, can contrast how they are pursuing their research and professional learning of literacy (doings) with the inquiry theories of Dewey and how they are negotiating (relatings) change of curriculum with colleagues. For this process to guide 'living well' and 'a world worth living in', there needs to be a shared understanding of how such worlds are constituted and how social and educational critique proceeds accordingly. It is possible to envisage school classrooms being organised along the lines of sayings, doings and relatings as well, as students pursue philosophical investigations into knowledge. The action research story has reached the point of laying the basis of education as a democratic social science through the practice of practice architectures, where all teachers and students construct a dignified existence of knowledge production for the public good.

In a similar approach to Kemmis, other attempts are being made to theorise the practice of progressive education within the context of social science. In Chapter 2, reference was made to Flyvbjerg (2001) and his reconceptualisation of social science itself through the notion of phronesis. According to Flyvberg, phronetic social science does not pursue abstract knowledge and generalisation as per the physical sciences, but looks to understanding and meaning of particular issues in particular contexts. Schram (2012, pp. 18–19) summarises the main features of phronetic social science in four ways: (1) as offering a critical assessment of power values and supports questions of what we ought to do; (2) social inquiry is a dialogical process of practical reason rather than theoretical reason; (3) a contextual notion of truth that is pluralistic and culture-bound guiding practice; and (4) interpretive social inquiry is a powerful practice that can challenge power and encourage social change for the better.

If phronesis is the human disposition to do good and praxis is the ethically informed action in pursuit of phronesis, then there is a clear philosophical framework for education and teachers when they walk into classrooms every day to assist all children with their learning. The five domains of education suggested above – those of schooling, knowledge, curriculum, pedagogy and assessment – can all be analysed and evaluated in relation to the disposition and action of phronesis/praxis and changed to produce greater alignment. School mathematics and science are the prime candidates for change in this regard and new appropriate integrated formations have been discussed previously (Chapters 5–8). Theorising of phronesis/praxis and practice architectures alters the balance towards habitus in our quest for understanding, but there are numerous occasions when theorising is ahead of practice, such as existence of the Higgs bosun and the nature of AI. It is up to teacher-theorists and practitioners to devise the new fields of classroom experience so foreseen.

Considerations of the practice interface

My proposal for a practice of practice interface between sociology and epistemology in schools is a big idea that challenges sociologists and epistemologists. It extends past the debate initiated by *Knowledge and Control* (Young, 1971) and attempts to break the deadlock that afflicts the conservative sociology of schooling and education. The practice interface must provide a way forward for coping with the dominant view in sociology, oft repeated, that:

> Consistently with previous research, family income and maternal educational qualifications yielded modest to moderate effects on social adjustment and moderate to strong effects on language/literacy (e.g. Yeung *et al.*, 2002; George *et al.*, 2007). Specifically, children with educated parents (degree level or vocational equivalent) were on average about six months ahead in language/literacy compared with their peers whose parents did not have any educational qualifications.
>
> (Hartas, 2011, p. 907)

If we can put aside for the moment the implication that families on low income and with low formal qualifications are deficient, we cannot ignore the conservative paradigm of knowledge adopted by schools, the traditional pedagogies favoured by teachers and the epistemological basis of assessment instruments used in mass testing programs. In an important book that followed his initial work, Young (1998, pp. 168–182) included a final chapter entitled 'From the "new sociology of education" to a critical theory of learning'. As a significant figure in the sociology of education and its history, it is important to trace Young's thinking over the years. He raised the issue of 'reflexivity' in terms of Beck's sociological 'reflexive modernisation' and related this to education through the concept of schools seeking to improve themselves within an encompassing learning society. Beck's view is somewhat truncated in that the institutions of modern life are not likely to reflexively confront their own prejudice and economic failures (as per global financial crises), rather to only improve their own narrow directions. Young discussed the distinction between sociology *for* schools that is concerned with the vibrant transformation to educational practice compared with sociology *of* education that identifies and describes the conditions that impact on schools and teaching. While he supported both, it is unfortunate that this did not happen, due mainly, I suspect, to not only the development of neoliberalism and its dominant features, but the weakness of sociology as well. In his usual comprehensive manner, Young outlined a number of factors that have impacted on sociology since 1989 – factors such as the battle for what he termed 'intellectualist' (internal debates) versus 'politicist' (external education policy) stances within sociology itself and issues that needed to be confronted within the development of mass schooling, including the public–private debate and resulting changes in teacher education. He then concludes with a brief discussion of working towards a critical theory of education and learning. Young (p. 181) notes that 'a focus on learning rather than on institutions such as schools, subjects, or curricula must be at the centre of a critical education theory of the future'. The main elements of such a theory would need to be that:

- it has a concept of the future and of education in relation to a vision of a society of the future
- it connects rather than insulates the concepts and approaches developed by the different education disciplines
- it gives primacy to the issues of learning and the production of new knowledge
- it has an educational purpose associated with realising the emancipatory potential of learning for all people throughout their lives
- it is critical in relation to the expansion of mass schooling and formal education generally as well as of the limits of learning in workplaces and communities.

It was my personal interest and reading that introduced me to the detailed work of Dewey and Freire and my own subsequent thinking about how these ideas could change teaching practice and the nature of schooling. The combination of practice and theorising always seemed logical to me. I have attempted to make up for lost ground since my transfer to the university sector, but I am somewhat professionally embarrassed, if not regretful, that for many years I did not participate in the debate regarding sociology and the sociology of education. Surprisingly, perhaps, I am thankful that I came to this dilemma with a science and mathematics experience, as it seems that many academics and teachers with a humanities and arts background have a limited understanding of the philosophy of mathematics and science and the progressive contribution that it can make to educational sociology and epistemology. For these reasons, I find the work of Young and colleagues such as Whitty (1985), who have been active during the neoliberal period, the period of my working life, not only inspirational but also extremely valuable for me in trying to undertake my own reflexive analysis and critique of education, schooling and teaching. Rightly or wrongly, I have consistently advocated a broadly comprehensive curriculum – not based on the disciplines – to benefit all children, provided that it is attended by a progressive epistemology that recognises and respects the culture and experience of local families and communities as the basis of learning. Michael Young's current position may differ from this view.

In his recent *Bringing Knowledge Back In* (2008), referenced earlier, Young mounts an extensive argument for the sociology of education moving from social constructivism to social realism. He discusses key features of the work of Dewey, Durkheim, Bernstein and others to support his case. How do we ensure as a democratic human right that all children access and do not neglect privileged knowledge at school? What distinguishes my conclusion from that of Young centres on a more detailed consideration of how human epistemology actually works and, for the purposes of this book and for teachers, how it works at the practice interface of sociology and epistemology. I have discussed a neural network of scenarios, schemata or practices that exist in the human brain, constantly interacting, changing, impacting with the continuity of experience. This overcomes the problem of taking theoretical structures of knowledge established by theorists (Bernstein's horizontal and vertical structures, for example) and imposing such structures on children in schools. The neural network model means that, rather than locking children into a particular, externally decided and imposed structure of knowledge, children are moving at the speed of light between and across networks as they experience and consider meaning. Some of these networks will involve disciplinary knowledge in a vertical or horizontal sense, but this occurs in relation to all other networks.

Bourdieu's sociology of practice

I have given a commitment to try and live a humble life, reflexively. In the current political context and from a sociological point of view, I take this to mean fearless confrontation of my views and actions with the market ideology of neoliberalism wherever I can. From an epistemological point of view, it means involvement in fields of activity that can relate to and challenge who I am for more critical understanding. From an educational point of view, it means establishing environments of learning that are democratic and experiential, respecting the culture of local families and students. Compiling the thoughts in this book has been a difficult reflexive experience on my part, the opportunity to reconsider long-held views in relation to counter-views in the recognised literature. Bourdieu had a similar approach to sociology, to adopt a rigorously reflexive stance towards the conduct of sociology itself as a field of study and research. In taking up the central questions of subjectivity and objectivity, Bourdieu (2000, p. 119) comments, 'To practise reflexivity means questioning the privilege of a knowing "subject" arbitrarily excluded from the effort of objectification.' He goes on to explain (p.120):

> How can one fail to recognise that the 'choices' of the 'free' and 'disinterested' subject glorified by tradition are never totally independent of the mechanics of the fields and therefore of the history of which it is the outcome and which remains embedded in its structures and through them, in the cognitive structures, principles of vision and division, concepts, theories and methods applied, which are never totally independent of the position occupied within the field and the associated interests?

This is Bourdieu's struggle against determinism, dogma and ignorance. He is saying that human actors cannot extract themselves from social reality and the impact that existing in the world has and continues to have on thinking. He advises practitioners to objectivise sociology and, themselves, to utilise the procedures of reflexivity to scrutinise their own perceptions and outlooks so that the structures of tradition and comprehension can be subject to scrupulous critique. Bourdieu summarised his reflexive methodology for sociology in the following terms (Grenfell, 2008, p. 222):

- Analyse the position of the field *vis-à-vis* the field of power.
- Map out the objective structure of relations between the positions occupied by agents who compete for the legitimate forms of specific authority of which the field is a site.
- Analyse the *habitus* of agents; the systems of dispositions they have acquired by internalising a deterministic type of social and economic condition.

While these points are directed at reflexive sociology, let us briefly consider how they might be applied by a classroom teacher. This could include the development of a habitus-field analysis grid (see Table 10.1). Initially, the teacher would consider the position of the classroom in relation to major issues of power and tension that are internal (e.g. teaching strategies) and external (e.g. state examinations). Second, the teacher charts the relative positioning of school authority that impact on the classroom involving, for example, the school board, principal, curriculum and parent committees and staff who also teach similar topics. Most particularly, from an epistemological point of view, the teacher will chart the habitus of students and the factors that may have contributed to the 'who I am' of students. Hopefully the teacher will have worked with students over time in compiling a habitus-field analysis chart (or an adaptation thereof) so that the information recorded is as complete and accurate as possible. When all three steps have been finalised, teachers and students can discuss their interpretation of the information and charts and identify or suggest various connections and questions arising. It will most likely be that further investigation and gathering of data will be required, probably continuously, to make sense of the settlements that are negotiated in classrooms every hour.

The significance of the neural network model of reflexivity (Figure 12.1) is that it thwarts the tendency to still see habitus as dominating field, rather than in relation to field. This brings the culture and experience of children into play as the basis of learning and cannot presuppose a deficit intellect because of family income. Development of the habitus-field analysis grid should enable students and teachers to discuss how they 'see' or think about ideas under study and not be prejudicial regarding different thoughts and viewpoints. Bourdieu states in relation to the object of research that 'What counts, in reality, is the rigour of the *construction* of the object. I think that the power of a mode of thinking never manifests itself more clearly than in its capacity to constitute socially insignificant objects into scientific objects' (Bourdieu and Wacquant, 1989, p. 51, quoted in Grenfell, 2008, p. 220). This is the challenge for all teachers of all subjects – to involve children in experience that enables them to construct their own 'objects to think with' in relation to the preferred 'objects' that are suggested by the teacher and curriculum. It may be that appropriate objects are difficult to provide for all ideas all the time in every school subject, but it is entirely possible to fashion a learning situation that is primarily experiential and reflexive for the construction of epistemological objects for some topics and for some of the time. The construction of neural objects in the minds of children cannot be predetermined and will have infinite variation in classrooms, but they will become apparent through continuing discourse and experiment.

The nomenclature used by Bourdieu in relation to his theorising is descriptive, meaning that his model and criticisms of it must remain at the level of words, for the time being. However this is not unusual, given that there are many areas of research and human endeavour that have not been fully validated as attempts at explaining observation are made. Black holes, a world of ideal mathematical forms, dark matter and human consciousness, come to mind, let alone religious metaphysics. The concept of learning 'structure', for example, remains obscure, with Piaget's comment that structure as an idea central to his epistemological theories is located halfway between the psychological and the physiological. Bourdieu's translated sentences are often long and convoluted for the reader, sometimes making it difficult to keep track of the number of ideas contained therein. For example, in his important early work that defined habitus, he makes the following statement (Bourdieu, 1977/2003, p. 78):

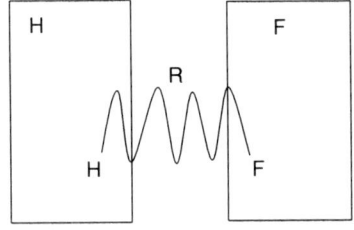 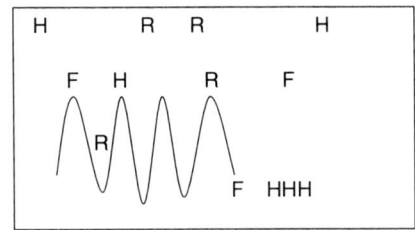

Figure 12.1 Reflexivity as separate and networked neural processes

The habitus, the durably installed generative principle of regulated improvisations, produces practices which tend to reproduce the regularities immanent in the objective conditions of the production of their generative principle, while adjusting to the demands inscribed as potentialities in the situation, as defined by the cognitive and motivating structures making up the habitus.

I take this to mean that the habitus responds and relates to the particular field of activity being experienced, tending to reproduce current responses of the habitus, at the same time as being impacted by the field. Bourdieu's use of the word 'practices' seems to refer to the overall response of the human organism to the experience, but he also introduces the notion of 'the cognitive and motivating structures making up the habitus'. The adjectives 'cognitive' and 'motivating' add a layer of compexity to the concept of 'structure' and may be there to indicate that the properties of some structures cause a particular response in relation to the properties of other structures; sometimes the response is 'fear', sometimes the response is 'knowing'. Bourdieu provides added detail when he continues (p. 78):

> These practices can be accounted for only by relating the objective *structure* defining the social conditions of the production of the habitus which engendered them to the conditions in which this habitus is operating that is to the *conjuncture* which, short of a radical transformation, represents a particular state of this structure.

Where I have used the word 'property' above, Bourdieu now comments on a 'particular state' of structure. Perhaps at this stage the model of habitus-field-reflexivity needs to be extended to allow for greater definition. If the theory of habitus-field-reflexivity is considered as an integrated totality similar to that depicted in Figure 12.1, then the existence of neural networks can help explain how human 'structures' actually work. Existing structures of the brain such as neural networks (states) have been created through experience (known as habitus), with other new neural network structures (known as field) impacting on and interacting with habitus as they are formed (known as reflexivity). Which neural network takes precedence at a particular time, or prevails unchanged for a long time, depends on its electrical strength and the range of networks that are generated and interact.

Bringing divergent ideas together in what Einstein described as the 'creative leap', or perhaps the 'paradigm shift' of Kuhn, is easily explained by the neural network model: for the child writing a poem, likening the starlit sky to the artist's canvas requires experience and networks of both. Exactly why one network relates to another is not known, although it is possible that all networks are relating to all other networks all the time, at the speed of light. I am reminded of the debate regarding AI and criticism, not only that nothing will be achieved to benefit humankind, but that it is a murky area of research that should not be pursued: we don't want the robots to take over, after all.

Marvin Minsky, as one of the original and continuing thinkers regarding AI, has grappled with these issues over a lifetime. His book, *The Emotion Machine* (Minsky, 2006), previously referenced, gives much more detail than what can be summarised here. A diagram (p. 293) that suggests how knowledge might be organised in the brain is provocative, drawing on his 'society of mind' model (Minsky, 1986), with 'societies' or 'scenarios' being large neuronal assemblies.

It is precisely for these reasons that it is important for progressive educators to not only be aware of the latest research regarding neuroscience, but to participate in ethical research projects that are seeking to support and not discredit human capability. I am suggesting that progressive neuroscience can make a major contribution to epistemological practice and theory.

Towards a new reflexive sociology of knowledge

A number of new ideas and perceptions have been proposed in these chapters that can excite and formulate a new reflexive sociology of knowledge for teachers. The direction is new because of new epistemological concepts such as the practice of interface between sociology and epistemology that breaks the cul-de-sac that the sociology of education has reached on social justice questions. The direction is reflexive because this is the major concept that enables the relation between thought and action to constitute learning and to frame learning environments in schools. The direction is sociology *of* knowledge to indicate the task of learning continuity, of relating the socio-economic conditions that exist outside school to knowledge production for all students in school. Finally, the overall direction is epistemological because, although setting out to bridge sociology and epistemology and perhaps to change both, it is teacher-theorists as epistemologists that will resolve the difficult issues of learning encountered. Kincheloe (2003, p. 54) put it well when he stated:

> In what might be described as the tacit ontology of Cartesianism, students and teachers are not encouraged to confront why they tend to think as they do about themselves, the world around them and their relationship to that world. In other words, students and teachers gain little insight into the

forces that shape them – that is, that construct their consciousness, produce their subjectivity. In addition, this uncritical articulation of curriculum and pedagogy is virtually unconcerned with the consequences of thinking, as it viewed cognition as a process that takes place in a vacuum. Thinking in a new way always necessitates personal transformation; indeed if enough people think in new ways, social transformation is inevitable.

With these commitments, challenges and practices in mind, the main features of a reflexive sociology of knowledge related to the five domains of education above (Table 12.1) can be outlined as follows in eight statements.

That a reflexive sociology of knowledge:

- Schooling:
    - envisages democratic society and schooling for all citizens regardless of economic and cultural background
    - investigates and critiques political and educational systems regarding social justice and equity
    - adheres to a reflexive sociology of knowledge that systematically challenges assumptions, processes and outcomes in relation to contrasting lifeworlds

- Knowledge:
    - adopts pragmatic approaches to knowledge that conceptualises teaching and learning as social practice, enabling continuity of culture, experience, inquiry and reflexivity
    - ensures respectful connections between social and community knowledge and conditions and school knowledge and conditions

- Curriculum:
    - designs curriculum practices that relates disciplinary knowledge to local knowledge and practices

- Pedagogy:
    - sustains phronetic teaching practices of practice, partnership and praxis that immerse teachers and students in philosophical knowledge regarding the public good

- Assessment:
    - integrates assessment of learning into curriculum practices in accord with non-judgemental and non-competitive support for the production of pragmatic knowledge.

I hope this draft program remains true to the principles of major theorists we have discussed, those of Dewey, Freire, Bourdieu, Bernstein, Young, Kincheloe and Stenhouse, along with others who work within the same tradition of practice. Two obvious questions arise from this proposal: will it make any substantial difference to the lives of all children in schools, particularly for those from low-income families and how will it be put into best effect by teachers? The features bear little resemblance to sociology that concentrates on the characteristics of society that are external to schools, but takes such issues and links them epistemologically with school programs; this applies to the nature of knowledge itself with the inclusion of non-dominant disciplinary knowledge. The effective abolition of formal assessment as it is now known is a revolutionary step, directly challenging the accountability measures of neo-liberalism. Whether or not teachers will be attracted to the proposal and investigate how their current programs can be adapted is, of course, up to them.

Reflexively and honestly considering our own views can happen at any time, in conversation with students, at a research meeting, or at the game. Should these results really be published if we haven't used more than one methodology to produce them? How does our imagination put 'tree' and 'flower' together in our minds, if 'wattle' has never been experienced? This makes it difficult and unfair for the child in the creative writing class. Bourdieu's suggestion above regarding reflexive sociology involved analysis of our position in social space, our position in the field and position in the scholastic universe. A group of teachers could ask these sorts of questions in relation to the features of reflexive sociology of knowledge and regarding their work of reviewing a curriculum guide. Similar to application of the habitus-field analysis grid discussed earlier, the teachers could briefly outline their own social backgrounds and viewpoints, then their work and connections in their particular educational fields, including their academic locations and networks, and finally their particular interests and aspirations within the general field of scholarship and power. In this way, all participants begin to draw links between their social, research and educational experience and begin to unravel the positions they now adopt. In open and honest conversation with the group of colleagues, they begin to exercise self-critique and engage different viewpoints to both challenge and strengthen current understandings.

This type of process is also possible with students, adapted for different age levels, so that connections between the different fields experienced by students will emerge, prompting new programs of teaching to meet specific need. Reflexive relationships require respectful and democratic conditions and civic courage to confront personal and professional issues that are usually excluded from all aspects of knowledge production. Their exclusion of course may help to explain why progress with ideas that are original and challenging is slow, particularly when fields of activity have strong boundaries and are privileged.

Thus, we have the perceived conflict between reason and imagination, the a priori and transcendent on the one hand and the supposedly unreliable, spontaneous and creative on the other – conceptual ideas that are the preserve of the sophisticated elite on the one hand and perceptions and practices that are 'rough and ready' for the majority on the other. Freire (1998, p. 54) has a word of encouragement however when he comments: 'I like to be human because in my unfinishedness I know that I am conditioned. Yet conscious of such conditioning, I know that I can go beyond it, which is the essential difference between conditioned and determined existence.'

What this book has traversed is exactly this territory – a critical, self-reflexive process of reviewing the world as the reasoned and imaginative property of all citizens regardless of background. A reflexive journey for myself as well. As best I understand it, Bourdieu proposes that it is not so much the objectivation of the experience of the subject that is crucial for reflexivity, but objectivation of the constraints of experience and the conditions of possibility that takes our learning and understanding forward. To achieve this status, objectivation must bring the practices of a reflexive sociology of education and epistemology together if a comprehensive analysis, critique and subsequent practice are to be made. To remain at the level of describing social circumstances without taking the next step of drawing consequences and continuing action for epistemological experience denies the culture, knowledge and dignity of working people everywhere. This is at the centre of social justice and deficit learning questions in schools and the assumed sovereignty of conservative orthodoxies. Respecting and progressively integrating reason, inquiry and critical reflexivity in all education projects and research is the arch enemy of ideologies that take immiseration by the hand.

References

Appadurai, A. (2006). The Right to Research, *Globalisation, Societies and Education*, 4(2), 167–177.

Arnold, J., Edwards, T., Hooley, N. and Williams, J. (2012). Conceptualising Teacher Education and Research as 'Critical Praxis,' *Critical Studies in Education*, 53(3), 281–295.

Ball, A. F. (2012). Presidential Address. To Know is Not Enough: Knowledge, Power and the Zone of Generativity, *Educational Researcher*, 41(8), 283–293.

Ball, S. J. (2010). New Voices, New Knowledges and the New Politics of Education Research: The Gathering of a Perfect Storm? *European Educational Research Journal*, 9(2), 124–137.

Ball, S. J. (2012). *Global Education Inc. New Policy Networks and the Neoliberal Imaginary*, London: Routledge.

Battiste, M. (2008). The Struggle and Renaissance of Indigenous Knowledge in Eurocentric Education, in Villegas, M., Neugebauer, S. R. and Venegas, K. R. (Eds) *Indigenous Knowledge and Education: Sites of Struggle, Strength and Survivance*, Cambridge: Harvard Education Review Reprint Series No. 44, 85–91.

Beattie, M. (2009). *The Quest for Meaning: Narratives of Teaching, Learning and the Arts*, Rotterdam: Sense Publishers.

Bellos, A. (2010). *Alex's Adventures in Numberland: Dispatches from the Wonderful World of Mathematics*, London: Bloomsbury.

Bernstein, B. (1971). On the Classification and Framing of Educational Knowledge, in Young, M. F. D. (Ed) *Knowledge and Control: New Directions for the Sociology of Education*, London: Collier Macmillan, 47–69.

Bernstein, B. (2010). Vertical and Horizontal Discourse: An Essay, *British Journal of Sociology of Education*, 20(2), 157–173.

Bessant, J. (2014). A Dangerous Idea? Freedom, Children and the Capability Approach to Education, *Critical Studies in Education*, 55(2), 138–153.

Birmingham, C. (2004). Phronesis: A Model for Pedagogical Reflection, *Journal of Teacher Education*, 55(4), 313–324.

Boleyn-Fitzgerald, M. (2010). *Pictures of the Mind: What the New Neuroscience Tells us About who we are*, New Jersey: Pearson Education.

Bourdieu, P. (1971). Intellectual Field and Creative Project, in Young, M. F. D. (Ed) *Knowledge and Control: New Directions for the Sociology of Education*, London: Collier Macmillan, 161–188.

Bourdieu, P. (1977/2003). *Outline of a Theory of Practice*, Cambridge, UK: Cambridge University Press.

Bourdieu, P. (1990a). *The Logic of Practice*, Stanford, California: Stanford University Press.

Bourdieu, P. (1990b). *In Other Words: Essays Towards a Reflexive Sociology*, Stanford, California: Stanford University Press.

Bourdieu, P. (2000). *Pascalian Meditations*, Cambridge, UK: Polity Press.

Bourdieu, P. (2007). *Sketch for a Self-Analysis*, Cambridge, UK: Polity.

Bourdieu, P. and Passeron, J-C. (1997). *Reproduction in Education, Society and Culture*, London: SAGE Publications.

Bourdieu, P. and Wacquant, L. (1989). Towards a Reflexive Sociology: A Workshop with Pierre Bourdieu, *Sociological Theory*, 7(1), 26–63.

Bourdieu, P. and Wacquant, L. J. D. (1992). *An Invitation to Reflexive Sociology*, Chicago: University of Chicago Press.

Bourdieu, P. *et al.* (2002). *The Weight of the World: Social Suffering in Contemporary Society*, Cambridge, UK: Polity.

Bowles, S. and Gintis, H. (1976). *Schooling in Capitalist America: Educational Reform and the Contradictions of Economic Life*, London: Routledge and Kegan Paul.

Boydston, J. A. (Ed) (1989/2008). *John Dewey: The Later Works, 1925–1953, Volume 16, 1949–1952*, Carbondale: Southern Illinois University Press.

Bridges, D. (2003). *Fiction Written under Oath? Essays in Philosophy and Educational Research*, Dordrecht: Kluwer Academic Publishers.

Bruce, B. C. and Bloch, N. (2013). Pragmatism and Community Inquiry: A Case Study of Community-Based Learning, *Education and Culture*, 29(1), 27–45.

Bruner, J. (1979). *On Knowing: Essays for the Left Hand*, Cambridge, USA: Harvard University Press.

Cajete, G. A. (2012). Decolonising Indigenous Education in a Twenty-First Century World, in Waziyatawin and Yellow Bird, M. (Eds) *For Indigenous Minds Only: A Decolonization Handbook*, Sante Fe: SAR Press, 145–156.

Carr, W. and Kemmis, S. (1986). *Becoming Critical: Education, Knowledge and Action Research*, Geelong: Deakin University.

Carr, W. and Kemmis, S. (2005). Staying Critical, *Educational Action Research*, 13(3), 347–357.

Chomsky, N. (2004). *The Generative Enterprise Revisited*, Berlin: Mouton de Gruyter.

Christie, M. (2005). Aboriginal Knowledge Traditions in Digital Environments, *Australian Journal of Indigenous Education*, 34, 61–66.

Clandinin, D. J. and Connelly, F. M. (1994). Personal Experience Methods, in Denzin, N. K. and Lincoln, Y. S. (Eds) *Handbook of Qualitative Research*, Thousand Oaks California: SAGE Publications, 413–427.

Clandinin, D. J. and Connelly, F. M. (2000). *Narrative Inquiry: Experience and Story in Qualitative Research*, San Francisco: Jossey-Bass Publishers

Cochran-Smith, M. and Lytle, S. L. (2009). *Inquiry as Stance: Practitioner Research for the Next Generation*, New York: Teachers College, Colombia University.

Connell, R. (2009). Good Teachers on Dangerous Ground: Towards a New View of Teacher Quality and Professionalism, *Critical Studies in Education*, 50(3), 213–229.

Cozolino, L. (2013). *The Social Neuroscience of Education: Optimising Attachment and Learning in the Classroom*, New York: W. W. Nortonand.

Creswell, J. W. (2009). *Research Design: Qualitative, Quantitative and Mixed Methods Approaches*, 3rd edition, Los Angelesand: Sage Publications.

Darling-Hammond, L. (2010). *The Flat World and Education: How America's Commitment to Equity will Determine our Future*, New York: Teachers College, Columbia University.

Darling-Hammond, L. (2012). The Right Start: Creating a Strong Foundation for the Teaching Career, *Phi Delta Kappan*, 94(3), 8–13.

Delpit, L. (2006). Lessons from Teachers, *Journal of Teacher Education*, 57(3), 220.

Denzin, N. K. and Lincoln, Y. S. (2000). *SAGE Handbook of Qualitative Research*, 2nd edition, Thousand Oaks, California: SAGE Publications.

Denzin, N. K. and Lincoln, Y. S. (2003). Introduction: Revolutions, Ruptures and Rifts in Interpretive Inquiry, in Denzin, N. K. and Lincoln, Y.S. (Eds) *Turning Points in Qualitative Research: Tying Knots in a Handkerchief*, Walnut Creek: AltaMira Press, 1–15.

Dewey, J. (1958). *Experience and Nature*, New York: Dover Publications.

Dewey, J. (1966). *Democracy and Education*, New York: Macmillan.

Dewey, J. (2012). *Unmodern Philosophy and Modern Philosophy*, Edited and with an introduction by Deen, P., Carbondale: Southern Illinois University Press.

Dodson, M. (2003). The end in the beginning: re(de)finding Aboriginality, in Grossman, M. (Ed) *Blacklines: Contemporary Critical Writing by Indigenous Australians*, Melbourne: Melbourne University Press, 25–42.

DuFour, R., DuFour, R. and Eaker, R. (2008). *Revisiting Professional Learning Communities at Work: New Insights for Improving Schools*, Bloomington: Solution Tree Press.

Durst, A. (2010). *Women Educators in the Progressive Era: The Women behind Dewey's Laboratory School*, New York: Palgrave Macmillan.

Ernst, P. (1998). *Social Constructivism as a Philosophy of Mathematics*, Albany: State University of New York Press.

Esquith, R. (2009). *Lighting Their Fires: Raising Extraordinary Children in a Mixed-Up, Muddled-Up, Shook-Up World*, New York: Viking.

Evans, G. (2006). *Educational Failure and Working Class White Children in Britain*, New York: Palgrave Macmillan.

Fals-Borda, O. (1991). Some Basic Ingredients, in Fals-Borda, O. and Rahman, M. A. (Eds) *Action and Knowledge: Breaking the Monopoly with Participatory Action Research*, London: Intermediate Technology Publications, 3–12.

Feinberg, W. (2012). The Idea of a Public Education, in Borman, M., Danzig, A. B. and Garcia, D. R. (Eds) *Review of Research in Education: Education, Democracy and the Public Good*, 36, AERA, 1–22.

Fischman, G. E. and McLaren, P. (2005). Rethinking Critical Pedagogy and the Gramscian and Freirean Legacies: From Organic to Committed Intellectuals or Critical Pedagogy, Commitment and Praxis, *Cultural Studies-Critical Methodologies*, 5(4), 425–447.

Flyvbjerg, B. (2001). *Making Social Science Matter: Why Social Inquiry Fails and How it can Succeed Again*, Cambridge, UK: Cambridge University Press.

Freire, P. (1972a). *Cultural Action for Freedom*, Harmondsworth: Penguin.

Freire, P. (1972b). *Pedagogy of the Oppressed*, Harmondsworth: Penguin.

Freire, P. (1998). *Pedagogy of Freedom: Ethics, Democracy and Civic Courage*, Lanham: Rowman and Littlefield.

Gardner, H. (1995). *Leading Minds: An Anatomy of Leadership*, in collaboration with Laskin, E., New York: Basic Books.

Gardner, H. (1999). *Multiple Intelligences: New Horizons*, New York: Basic Books.

Gee, J. P. (2012). *Social Linguistics and Literacies: Ideology in Discourses*, London: Routledge.

Gee, J. P. and Hayes, E. R. (2011). *Language and Learning in the Digital Age*, London: Routledge.

George, A., Hansen, K. and Schoon, I. (2007). Child Behaviour and Cognitive Development, in Hansen, K. and Joshi, H. (Eds) *Millennium Cohort Study Second Survey: A User's Guide to Initial Findings*, London: Institute of Education, 6–35.

Glass, R. D. (2001). On Paulo Freire's Philosophy of Praxis and the Foundations of Liberation Education, *Educational Researcher*, 30(2), 15–25.

Gonzalez, N., Moll, L. and Amanti, C. (Eds) (2009). *Funds of Knowledge: Theorising Practices in Households, Communities and Classrooms*, New York: Routledge.

Goodson, I. F. and Gill, S. R. (2011). *Narrative Pedagogy: Life History and Learning*, NewYork: Peter Lang.

Goodson, I. F., Biesta, G. J. J., Tedder, M. and Adair, N. (2010). *Narrative Learning*, London: Routledge.

Grenfell, M. (2004). *Pierre Bourdieu: Agent Provocateur*, London: Continuum.

Grenfell, M. (Ed) (2008). *Pierre Bourdieu: Key Concepts*, Durham: Acumen.

Gurung, R. A. R., Chick, N. L. and Haynie, A. (2009). *Exploring Signature Pedagogies: Approaches to Teaching Disciplinary Habits of Mind*, Sterling Virginia: Stylus.

Habermas, J. (1984). *Theory of Communicative Action*, Volumes I and II, Boston: Beacon Press.

Habermas, J. (1992). *The Structural Transformation of the Public Sphere: An Enquiry into a Category of Bourgeois Society*, Cambridge: Polity Press.

Harris, S. (1990). *Two-Way Aboriginal Schooling: Education and Cultural Survival*, Canberra: Aboriginal Studies Press.

Hartas, D. (2011). Families' Social Backgrounds Matter: Socio-economic Factors, Home Learning and Young Children's Language, Literacy and Social Outcomes, *British Educational Research Journal*, 37(6), 893–914.

Harvey, D. (2005). *A Brief History of Neoliberalism*, Oxford: Oxford University Press.

Hawking, S. (2001). *The Universe in a Nutshell*, London: Bantam Press.

Hickman, L. A. (1990). *John Dewey's Pragmatic Technology*, Bloomington, Indianapolis: Indiana University Press.

Hickman, L. A. (2007). *Pragmatism as Post-Postmodernism: Lessons from John Dewey*, New York: Fordham University Press.

Hooley, N. (2009). *Narrative Life: Democratic Curriculum and Indigenous Learning*, Dordrecht: Springer.

Hooley, N. (2013). Exposing the Intricacies of Pre-service Teacher Education: Incorporating the Insights of Freire and Bourdieu, *Review of Education*, 1(2), 125–158.

Hooley, N., Watt, T. and Dakich, E. (2013). *Learning in Motion: Connecting Schools and Knowledge for Aboriginal and Torres Strait Islander Children: Investigating iPads for Learning and Literacy*, Research Report, Melbourne: Victoria University.

Hughes, P. (2000). *Research, Outcomes and Action in Primary Aboriginal Literacy*, paper presented at the Aboriginal Education Literacy Conference, Adelaide.

Hughes, P., More, A. J. and Williams, M. (2004). *Aboriginal Ways of Knowing*, Adelaide: Paul Hughes.

Jackson, P. W. (1998). *John Dewey and the Lessons of Art*, Newhaven: Yale University Press.

Kalantzis, M. and Cope, B. (2008). *New Learning: Elements of a Science of Education*, Melbourne: Cambridge University Press.

Kalantzis, M. *et al.* (1996). A Pedagogy of Multiliteracies: Designing Social Futures, *Harvard Educational Review*, 66(1).

Karmel Report. (1973). *Schools in Australia: Report of the Interim Committee for the Australian Schools Commission*, Canberra: Australian Government Publishing Service.

Kemmis, S. (2009). Understanding Professional Practice: A Synoptic Framework, in Green, B. (Ed) *Understanding and Researching Professional Practice*, Rotterdam: Sense Publishers, 19–38.

Kemmis, S. (2012). Researching Educational Praxis: Spectator and Participant Perspectives, *British Educational Research Journal*, 38(6), 885–905.

Kemmis, S. and McTaggart, R. (1986). *The Action Research Planner*, Geelong: Deakin University.

Kilpatrick, W. H. (1918). The Project Method, *Teachers College Record*, 19, 319–334.

Kincheloe, J. L. (2001). Describing the Bricolage: Conceptualising a New Rigor in Qualitative Research, *Qualitative Inquiry*, 7(6), 679–692.

Kincheloe, J. L. (2003). Critical Ontology: Visions of Selfhood and Curriculum, *Journal of Curriculum Theorising*, 19, 47–64.

Kincheloe, J. L. (2004). Refining Rigour and Complexity in Research, in Kincheloe, J. L. and Berry, K. S. (Eds) *Rigour and Complexity in Educational Research: Conceptualising the Bricolage*, New York: Open University Press, 23–49.

Kincheloe, J. L. (2009). No Short Cuts in Urban Education: Metropedagogy and Diversity, in Steinberg, S. R. and Kincheloe, J. L. (Eds) *Diversity and Multiculturalism: A Reader*, New York: Peter Lang, 379–410.

Kincheloe, J. L. (2011a). Describing the Bricolage: Conceptualising New Rigour in Qualitative Research, in Hayes, K., Steinberg, S. R. and Tobin, K. (Eds) *Key Works in Critical Pedagogy: Joe L. Kincheloe,* Rotterdam: Sense Publishers, 177–190.

Kincheloe, J. L. (2011b). On to the Next Level: Continuing the Conceptualisation of the Bricolage, in Hayes, K., Steinberg, S. R. and Tobin, K. (Eds) *Key Works in Critical Pedagogy: Joe L. Kincheloe,* Rotterdam: Sense Publishers, 253–277.

Lakatos, I. (1976). *Proofs and Refutations: The Logic of Mathematical Discovery*, Cambridge, UK: Cambridge University Press.

Langton, M. (2013). *Boyer Lectures 2012. The Quiet Revolution: Indigenous People and the Resources Boom*, Sydney: Harper Collins Publishers.

Leslie, D. and Mendick, H. (Eds) (2014). *Debates in Mathematics Education*, London: Routledge.

Lévi-Strauss, C. (1966). *The Savage Mind*, Chicago: Chicago University Press.

Levinson, M. and Hooley, N. (2012). *Investigating Networks of Culture and Knowledge: A Critical Discourse between UK Roma Gypsies, Indigenous Australians and Education*, paper presented at Annual Conference of British Educational Research Association, Manchester, September.

Lomawaima, K. T. (2008). Tribal Soverigns: Reframing Research in American Indian Education, in Villegas, M., Neugebauer, S. R. and Venegas, K. R. (Eds) *Indigenous Knowledge and Education: Sites of Struggle, Strength and Survivance*, Cambridge: Harvard Educational Review Reprint Series No. 44, 183–203.

Luna, J. M. (2010). The Fourth Principle, in Meyer, L and Alvarado, B. M. (Eds) *New World of Indigenous Resistance: Noam Chomsky and Voices from North, South and Central America*, San Francisco: City Lights Books, 85–99.

Macfarlane, A. H., Glynn, T., Grace, W., Penetito, W. and Bateman, S. (2008). Indigenous Epistemology in a National Curriculum Framework? *Ethnicities*, 8(1): 102–127.

MacIntyre, A. (1983). *After Virtue: A Study in Moral Theory*, London: Duckworth.

Mao Tse-Tung. (1968). On Practice, in *Four Essays On Philosophy*, Peking: Foreign Languages Press, 1–22.

Margolis, J. (1999). Pierre Bourdieu: Habitus and the Logic of Practice, in Shusterman, R. (Ed) *Bourdieu: A Critical Reader*, Oxford: Blackwell Publishers.

Marks, G. N. (2010). What Aspects of Schooling are Important? School Effects on Tertiary Entrance Performance, *School Effectiveness and School Improvement*, 21(3), 267–287.

Martin, K. (2009). Aboriginal Worldview, Knowledge and Relatedness: Re-conceptualising Aboriginal Schooling as a Teaching–learning and Research Interface, *Journal of Australian Indigenous Issues*, 12, 66–78.

Maton, K. (2003). Reflexivity, Relationism and Research: Pierre Bourdieu and the Epistemic Conditions of Social Scientific Knowledge, *Space and Culture*, 6(1), 52–65.

McDermott, J. L. (1981). *The Philosophy of John Dewey,* Vol. I and Vol. II, Chicago: The University of Chicago Press.

McLaren, P. (1999). A Pedagogy of Possibility: Reflecting Upon Paulo Freire's Education: In Memory of Paulo Freire, *Educational Researcher*, 28, 49–56.

McLaren, P. and Jaramillo, N. (2007). *Pedagogy and Praxis in the Age of Empire: Towards a New Humanism*, Rotterdam: Sense Publishers.

McTaggart, R. (1991). *Action Research: A Short Modern History*, Geelong: Deakin University.

Mehta, J. and Doctor, J. (2013). Raising the Bar for Teaching, *Phi Delta Kappan*, 94(7), 8–13.

Meier, D. (2002). *The Power of Their Ideas: Lessons from America from a Small School in Harlem*, Boston: Beacon Press.

Meyer, L. (2010). Introduction: A Hemispheric Conversation Among Equals, in Meyer, L and Alvarado, B. M. (Eds) *New World of Indigenous Resistance: Noam Chomsky and Voices from North, South and Central America*, San Francisco: City Lights Books, 7–37.

Minsky, M. (1986). *The Society of Mind*, New York: Simon and Schuster.

Minsky, M. (2006). *The Emotion Machine: Commonsense Thinking, Artificial Intelligence and the Future of the Human Mind*, New York: Simon and Schuster.

Moll, L. C. (2014). *L. S. Vygotsky and Education*, New York: Routledge.

Moll, L., Amanti, C., Neff, D. and Gonzalez, N. (2009). Funds of Knowledge for Teaching: Using a Qualitative Approach to Connect Homes and Classrooms, in Gonzalez, N., Moll, L. and Amanti, C. (Eds) *Funds of Knowledge: Theorising Practices in Households, Communities and Classrooms*, New York: Routledge, 71–87.

Moore, R. and Muller, J. (1999). The Discourse of 'Voice' and the Problem of Knowledge and Identity in the Sociology of Education, *British Journal of Sociology of Education*, 20(2), 189–206.

Nakata, M. (2007). The Cultural Interface, *The Australian Journal of Indigenous Education*, 36, Supplement, 7–14.

NAPLAN. (2015). *National Assessment Program – Literacy and Numeracy*, Canberra: Australian Curriculum, Assessment and Reporting Authority, accessed at http://www.nap.edu.au/naplan/naplan.html, January 2015.

NCTM. (2013). National Council of Teachers of Mathematics, accessed at http://www.nctm.org, April 2014.

NSTA. (2013). National Science Teachers Association, accessed at http://www.nextgen science.org, April 2014.

Papert, S. (1980). *Mindstorms: Children, Computers and Powerful Ideas*, Sussex, UK: Basic Books.

Papert, S. (1992). *The Children's Machine: Rethinking School in the Age of the Computer*, New York: Basic Books.

Paris, D. (2012). Culturally Sustaining Pedagogy: A Needed Change in Stance, Terminology and Practice, *Educational Researcher*, 41(3), 93–97.

Pearl, A. and Knight, T. (1999). *The Democratic Classroom: Theory to Inform Practice*, Cresskill, New Jersey: Hampton Press.

Penrose, R. (1989). *The Emperor's New Mind: Concerning Computers, Minds and the Laws of Physics*, London: Oxford University Press.

Penrose, R. (2004). *The Road to Reality: A Complete Guide to the Laws of the Universe*, London: Jonathan Cape.

Penrose, R. (2005). *Shadows of the Mind: A Search for the Missing Science of Consciousness*, London: Vintage.

Plowden Report. (1967). *Children and Their Primary Schools: A Report of the Central Advisory Council for Education (England)*, London: HMSO.

Prendergast, C. (2003). *Literacy and Racial Justice: The Politics of Learning after Brown vs Board of Education*, Carbondale: Southern Illinois University Press.

Pring, R. (2004). *Philosophy of Education: Aims, Theory, Common Sense and Research*, London: Continuum.

Pring, R. (2007). *John Dewey: A Philosopher of Education for our Time?* London: Continuum.

Ravitch, D. (2010). *The Death and Life of the Great American School System: How Testing and Choice are Undermining Education*, New York: Basic Books.

Reyhner, J. (2008). American Indian/Alaska Native Education: An Overview, Northern Arizona University, accessed at http://jan.ucc.nau.edu/~jar/AIE/Ind_Ed.html, November 2012.

Rodriguez, G. M. (2013). Power and Agency in Education: Exploring the Pedagogical Dimensions of Funds of Knowledge, in Faltis, C. and Abedi, J. (Eds) *Review of Research in Education: Extraordinary Pedagogies for Working Within School Settings Serving Nondominant Students*, 37, AERA, 87–120.

Rowe, K. (2005). *Teaching Reading: Report and Recommendations, National Inquiry into the Teaching of Reading*, Canberra: Department of Education, Science and Training.

Sahlberg, P. (2011). *Finnish Lessons: What can the World Learn from Educational Change in Finland?* New York: Teachers College, Columbia University.

Salazar, M. del C. (2013). A Humanising Pedagogy: Reinventing the Principles and Practice of Education as a Journey Toward Liberation, in Faltis, C. and Abedi, J. (Eds) *Review of Research in Education: Extraordinary Pedagogies for Working Within School Settings Serving Nondominant Students*, 37, AERA, 121–148.

Saunders, L. (2007). Professional Values and Research Values: From Dilemmas to Diversity, in Campbell, A. and Groundwater-Smith, S. (Eds) *An Ethical Approach to Practitioner Research: Dealing with Issues and Dilemmas in Action Research*, London: Routledge, 62–74.

Schatzki, T. R., Cetina, K. N. and Savigny, E. V. (2001). *The Practice Turn in Contemporary Theory*, London: Routledge.

Schram, S. (2012). Phronetic Social Science: An Idea Whose Time has Come, in Flyvbjerg, B., Landman, T. and Schram, S. (Eds) *Real Social Science: Applied Phronesis*, Cambridge UK: Cambridge University Press, 15–26.

Schwab, J. (1978). The Practical: A Language for Curriculum, in Westbury, I. and Wilkof, N. J. (Eds) *Science, Curriculum and Liberal Education*, Chicago: The University of Chicago Press, 287–321.

Semali, L. M. and Kincheloe, J. L. (1999). Introduction: What is Indigenous Knowledge and Why Should we Study it? In Semali, L. M. and Kincheloe, J. L. (Eds) *What is Indigenous Knowledge? Voices from the Academy*, New York: Falmer Press, 3–57.

Senge, P. M. (2006). *The Fifth Discipline: The Art and Practice of the Learning Organization*, London: Random House.

Shulman, L. S. (2005). Signature Pedagogies in the Professions, *Daedalus*, Summer, 52–59.

Smith, L. T. (1999). *Decolonising Methodologies: Research and Indigenous Peoples*, Dunedin: University of Otago Press.

Snyder, I. (2008). *The Literacy Wars: Why Teaching Children to Read and Write is a Battleground in Australia*, Crows Nest, NSW: Allen and Unwin.

Stark, J. L. (2014). The Potential of Deweyan-Inspired Action Research, *Education and Culture*, 30(2), 87–101.

Steinberg, S. R. and Kincheloe, J. L. (2009). Smoke and Mirrors: More than One Way to be Diverse and Multicultural, in Steinberg, S. R. and Kincheloe, J. L. (Eds) *Diversity and Multiculturalism: A Reader*, New York: Peter Lang, 3–22.

Stenhouse, L. (2012). Research as a Basis for Teaching, in Elliott, J. and Norris, N. (Eds) *Curriculum, Pedagogy and Educational Research: The Work of Lawrence Stenhouse*, London: Routledge, 122–136.

Tryggvason, M-T. (2009). Why is Finnish Teacher Education Successful? Some Goals Finnish Teacher Educators have for their Teaching, *European Journal of Teacher Education*, 32(4), 369–382.

Turkle, S. and Papert, S. (1992). Epistemological Pluralism and the Revaluation of the Concrete, *Journal of Mathematical Behaviour*, 11(1), 3–33.

Turner, V. (1967). *The Forest of Symbols: Aspects of Ndembu Ritual*, Ithaca: Cornell University Press.

UN. (2013). *Who are Indigenous Peoples?* Fact Sheet, Indigenous Peoples, Indigenous Voices, United Nations, accessed at http://www.un.org/esa/socdev/unpfii/documents/5session_factsheet1.pdf, January 2014.

United States. (2008). *Reading First*, Washington: US Department of Education.

US Department of Education. (2013). *No Child Left Behind*, accessed at http://www.ed.gov/nclb/landing.jhtml, January 2014.

Victoria University. (1997). *Teachers Write: A Handbook for Teachers Writing About Changing Classrooms for a Changing World, The Western Melbourne Roundtable Innovative Links Project, 1994–1996*, Ryde, NSW: National Schools Network.

Victoria University. (2011). *Vision Unlimited: Inspiring Participant Knowledge in Schools. Researching Site-Based Pre-service Teacher Education*, Melbourne: College of Education, Victoria University.

Vygotsky, L. S. (1978). *Mind in Society: The Development of Higher Psychological Processes*, Cole, M., John-Steiner, V., Scribner, S. and Souberman, E. (Eds) Cambridge, MA: Cambridge University Press.

Wenger, E. (1998). *Communities of Practice: Learning, Meaning and Identity*, Cambridge: Cambridge University Press.

Whitty, G. (1985). *Sociology and School Knowledge: Curriculum Theory, Research and Politics*, London: Methuen.

Wilkinson, R. and Pickett, K. (2010). *The Spirit Level: Why Greater Equality Makes Societies Stronger*, New York: Bloomsbury Press.

Williams, R. (1989). *Resources of Hope: Culture, Democracy, Socialism*, London: Verso.

Willis, P. E. (1977). *Learning to Labour: How Working Class Kids Get Working Class Jobs*, England: Gower.

Wilson, E. O. (1998). *Consilience: The Unity Of Knowledge*, London: Little, Brown.

Wilson, S. (2008). *Research is Ceremony: Indigenous Research Methods*, Halifaxand: Fernwood Publishing.

8Ways. (2012*). 8 Aboriginal Ways of Learning Factsheet*. Accessed at https://intranet.ecu.edu.au/__data/assets/pdf_file/0008/364877/Indigenous-CC-Factsheet-8-Ways-120518.pdf, December, 2012.

Yeung, W., Linver, N. and Brooks-Gunn, J. (2002). How Money Matters for Young Children's Development: Parental Investment and Family Processes, *Child Development*, 73(6), 1861–1879.

Young, M. F. D. (Ed) (1971). *Knowledge and Control: New Directions for the Sociology of Education*, London: Collier Macmillan.

Young, M. F. D. (1998). *The Curriculum of the Future: From the 'New Sociology of Education' to a Critical Theory of Learning*, London: Falmer Press.

Young, M. F. D. (2008). *Bringing Knowledge Back in: From Social Constructivism to Social Realism in the Sociology of Education*, Oxford: Routledge.

Zipin, L. (2009). Dark Funds of Knowledge, Deep Funds of Pedagogy: Exploring Boundaries Between Lifeworlds and Schools, *Discourse: Studies in the Cultural Politics of Education*, 30, 317–331.

Index

High Plains Passion